The Dawning of America: 1492-1789

John A. Schutz

University of
Southern California

Vincent P. DeSantis,
General Editor

FORUM PRESS

Library of Congress Catalog Number:
80-68812

ISBN: 0-88273-109-2

Maps by Dan Irwin

Contents

Preface

The origins of the nation and its early development cover about three hundred years if we date our beginnings with the great exploit of Christopher Columbus in 1492. But who can say when our national history began? A look at Washington, D.C., gives us a view of ancient Greece and Rome, or the cathedrals of the Middle Ages. A pause in the Capitol will draw us back into the centuries of legislative experience in England and the colonies.

History is very much a pattern of thought and development, adding color, fiber, and size to the fabric. Early American history is very much the origins of our modern nation. It gave us the people, institutions, traditions, and most of all the independence and Constitution that we cherish. It gave us that host of leaders of which our history would be poorer if it were not for their wisdom, sacrifices, and dedication to the ideals that have become part of our daily lives.

This book is the first in a series of six covering the history of the American people. Most are already published, or will be by the time this book is printed, and together the six survey the major currents of American development.

My experience in writing these essays has reminded me again of the great variety of national figures and episodes which could be part of the story. A few hundred pages seems to be a mound of paper at page one, but hardly sufficient when one turns to the millions of good men and women whose pens or deeds are worthy of remembrance in history. But selection is necessary, and many notable people will be forgotten.

My appreciation must be given to Frank J. Klingberg and Louis Knott Koontz who introduced me to early American history, and to my friends of student days, Wilbur Jacobs and Samuel C. McCulloch who shared then their enthusiasm of Indians or Anglicans. Those days, alas, are distant, and many students have now joined me in their love for early American history—Ralph Crandall, Michael Gorn, Eric Christianson, Oliver Rink, Steve Sale, Robert Oaks, and Bruce Henry. I appreciate the editorial help of William Fowler, Jr., and my acquaintances at the Forum Press, particularly Erby Young. Lastly, may I thank Lynn O'Leary-Archer and JoAnne Grose for their editorial help in typing the manuscript.

John A. Schutz

1

In the Beginning

In the 1490s Englishmen received the news of Christopher Columbus' voyages to the Western Hemisphere as exciting adventures that could increase trade and wealth. For years to come, rumors of his daring exploits for Spain were the gossip of merchants and seamen, and they pressed their monarch Henry VII to support like voyages. Though Henry was always willing to encourage trade, he had only cautious appreciation for backing expensive voyages into distant lands and for challenging Spain as a rival. His people were exhausted from the Hundred Years' War and the economic disintegration that had occurred, and time was needed, he believed, to heal political ills. Though England and Wales were making progress toward overcoming their problems, Henry had plans for an alliance with Spain and refused to give any more than token support for overseas expeditions which might arouse the Spanish monarchs.

The King was willing, notwithstanding, to test the possibility of profitable expeditions into North America, and he sponsored the voyages of the Cabots, Venetian seamen then in England, who sought royal favor. In 1497, John Cabot sailed into the harbors of Nova Scotia, sighted Newfoundland and, in 1598, visited the Chesapeake Bay. Nearly a decade later Sebastian Cabot, his son, sailed into what may be the Hudson Strait, but a claim of finding a northwest passage to the Orient, like similar claims of his father, interested few of their supporters when the unfavorable reports of the northern lands and seas became known to them.

Contrariwise, the exploits of Portuguese and Spanish explorers in the fifty years after Columbus' discoveries won home support and attracted European envy. The Portuguese continued their successful explorations of the African coast, entered the Indian Ocean, and established bases in India and on islands in the East Indies. The Spanish, with expeditions by Hernando Cortes, Francisco Pizarro, and Vasco Núñez de Balboa explored the West Indies, Mexico, and Peru. Ferdinand Magellan in 1519 gave dimension to the knowledge of the hemisphere by sailing into the Pacific Ocean and then across the Pacific to the Philippine Islands. His surviving officers and men on the *Vittoria* would circumnavigate the globe and return to Spain in 1522, making their exploit one of the most heroic and magnificent of the age. Spain's power was impressive not only generally for Europe but specifically for England, whose Queen Catherine was aunt of Spain's reigning monarch Charles I.

Spain and Portugal gave Europe more than a vision of a wide, new world of magnificent distances; they opened up trade in the Orient, developed products in America, and discovered vast riches in minerals. Spanish conquerors in Mexico and Peru found quantities of gold and silver that dazzled the mind, and heard rumors of immense riches in cities that were made of gold. The apocryphal tales had the value of keeping excitement intense, but accidental finds of gold and silver were frequent enough to give credence to most wild stories. These conquests were followed by the exploitation of highly intelligent native peoples who may have numbered into the millions (modern historians estimate fifteen million), and by the building of imperial centers, trading posts, and supply parts for shipping. Plantations spread across the fertile lands of Puerto Rico, Cuba, and Hispañola, developing quantities of exportable sugar, cacao, cochineal, and tobacco which were soon to be in great demand throughout Europe. Mines in Mexico and Peru seemed to give out an inexhaustible quantity of gold and silver.

No other European conquests of such grandeur and importance like those in America and the Orient had ever occurred. The wealth in the hands of Spain and Portugal was inestimable. Spain's gross tonnage from Seville, for example, increased five times in the sixty years before 1600. The naval forces of both countries thus protected this commerce from European rivals, but its value aroused the greed of pirates, smugglers, and adventurers who wanted to share it. So long as England and Spain were allies, Englishmen refrained from piracy, but the traders of other countries, though weaker than Spain, supported their seamen secretly and enlarged by various methods public ways of topping the lucrative trade.

Expansion of English Trade

English expansion of trade in the sixteenth century grew rapidly. It was the result of internal peace, a strong monarchy, and the sale of monastic lands which enlarged agricultural acreage and production. English vessels plied the seas from Scandinavia to the Mediterranean, touching at ports in the North and Baltic Seas and as far away as the Levant. The trade was profitable and encouraged caravans in Russia and the Levant to contact distant merchants in India and the Far East. In time, merchants sailed into the Indian Ocean by way of South Africa and laid the foundation of a commercial group known as the East India Company.

The enticement of these opportunities brought a response in England for additional products to trade. Farmers increased their production of wheat and opened large areas to sheep for the production of meat and wool. While most Englishmen lived on farms, there was much home industry, much skilled labor, and many small factories here and there. The "putting out system" was used extensively, in which wool was distributed to spinners or thread to weavers, and the labor was done in the home. Many artisans, scattered through the small towns that dotted the countryside, divided their time between farm and spinning wheel. Though they were extraordinarily restless as artisans, they were intensely loyal to the government and very industrious. The center of energy for the nation was London. Even in the sixteenth century it dominated the economic and political life of the nation.

In London lived many wealthy people of the nation—men like Sir Thomas Smith, who helped found the East India Company and the future companies that settled Virginia and Bermuda. Smith and other merchants like him put their wealth into stock and invited tradespeople (who were larger in numbers than the merchants) and often wage earners to join them. The companies permitted capital to be accumulated, opportunities to be enlarged, and ownership to be easily transferred by the sale of stock. Smith and his friends stood at the top of the economic ladder as directors of these companies. They were becoming entrepreneurs who examined daily projects that required financing or offered to others possibilities for profit. They had at their disposal for investment much capital from thrifty artisans, and a labor market that was replenished by the migration of country people to the city.

Though this activity was encouraged by Henry VII and his Tudor successors, their interest in colonization was always limited. The voyages of the Cabots stand out as exceptional occurrences. Under Henry VIII (1509-1547) the nation became involved in religious reform, European wars, and family alliances; Henry never was interested in explorations. Under his son Edward VI and daughter Mary I, England opened a northern trade route to Russia and sent Sir Hugh Willoughby to seek a northeast passage to China, but Willoughby's death in Icelandic waters discouraged his backers. His chief pilot, Richard Chancellor, salvaged the voyage by taking another ship to the mouth of the Dvina and leading a trading group to Moscow. Others looked for a northeast passage which would reduce the dangers of attack from Spain or Portugal during the voyage to the Orient. Relations with the Catholic powers were strained, and traders feared being seized if they went into southern waters. Colonization, however, was not a driving motive of any voyage.

English efforts until 1558 were incidental to economic development at home or in nearby European waters. During the reign of Elizabeth I (1558-1601), however, many in the court encouraged expeditions to distant lands, and a new mood of investigation and enterprise arose. Such people as Sir Humphrey Gilbert, Sir Walter Raleigh, and the Earl of Leicester were enthusiasts. Their interest took several forms: fishing, colonization, and exploration for a northwest passage. Nonetheless, each had a quickening influence upon the other, and together would inspire plans for England's first colonies in America.

Under Elizabeth the traditional Tudor relations with Spain weakened and eventually were broken by years of war. English merchants resumed trade along the African coast and challenged the monopoly of Spain and Portugal in America. They not only sailed throughout the North Atlantic area, but men like John Hawkins also engaged in the slave trade which sold blacks at good profits to Spanish colonists. He traded, too, with the Canary Islands and examined the possibilities of smuggling in Brazil and along the coasts of the Spanish colonies. Slave trading for him was profitable, but the challenge to Spanish authorities who suffered commercial losses brought retaliations. An unfortunate Spanish assault upon Hawkins at Vera Cruz in 1569 set off a series of bloody attacks that gave Hawkins, Francis Drake, and Thomas Cavendish license to waylay Spanish galleons. Drake's sack of Venta de las Cruces in 1572 brought £40,000 in stolen loot, but his later voyages from port to port in the Spanish empire not only ransacked them but frightened the inhabitants. His much publicized capture of the Cacafuego off Panama added magnificent wealth to his collection of loot.

English Search for Markets

In the meantime, knowledge of America multiplied greatly and

Sir Walter Raleigh ordering the standard of Queen Elizabeth to be erected on the coast of Virginia. *(Library of Congress)*

inspired other English adventurers to seek colonies where they could develop their own supply of gold, silver, or plantation products; Englishmen were already present as fishermen in Newfoundland waters. Along with the Basques and Bretons the English often manned as many as fifty ships, and the English promoters, concerned about the rivalry, wanted bases along the shores to protect their fisheries. They mixed these interests with the desire to seek a northwest passage to Cathay, and a group led by Humphrey Gilbert gained royal permission to find the passage. In 1576 Martin Frobisher, with these plans in mind, sailed into Baffin Bay and picked up some black ore along the way. This possible evidence of wealth led to a second voyage, and merchants and noblemen of London in great excitement came forth with money to finance an intensive search of the region. In 1578 fifteen ships sailed to those northern waters, where samples of the black ore were gathered in various places, but, unfortunately, they proved to have no value. The grand design of the voyage thus failed to meet the expectations of its backers. However, Gilbert had not awaited the results of this search, but about the same time headed an expedition to Newfoundland where he planned to establish a colony. His ships carried tens of carpenters, masons, metalworkers, and settlers, who would be the vanguard for other Englishmen. Trinkets were also put aboard for Indian trade. Unfortunately, misfortunes crowded upon the four ships, and two of them sank en route, drowning most of the artisans and Gilbert himself. Possibly the only practical accomplishment of the voyages was the founding in 1583 of St. Johns, Newfoundland, as a fishing port.

Promptly Gilbert's charters were assumed by Sir Walter Raleigh in 1584, and he petitioned successfully for their confirmation and enlargement by Elizabeth. Raleigh, a favorite of the Queen and a gentleman of action, was an enthusiast for the empire. Forthwith he organized expeditions to the Chesapeake and the South. In making these plans, Raleigh fell under the influence of the Richard Hakluyts, uncle and nephew, who were related to the Gilberts. The younger Hakluyt had studied at Christ Church, Oxford, and was working then in the Paris embassy. In both places he had collected information on navigation and Spanish colonization, and surrounded himself with mathematicians and geographers. While in Paris he issued tracts on "western planting," and in his *Divers Voyages Touching the Discoverie of America and the Islands Adjacent,* he asked English authorities to reverse a ninety-year policy of neglect by supporting the establishment of colonies.

Voyages of Discovery

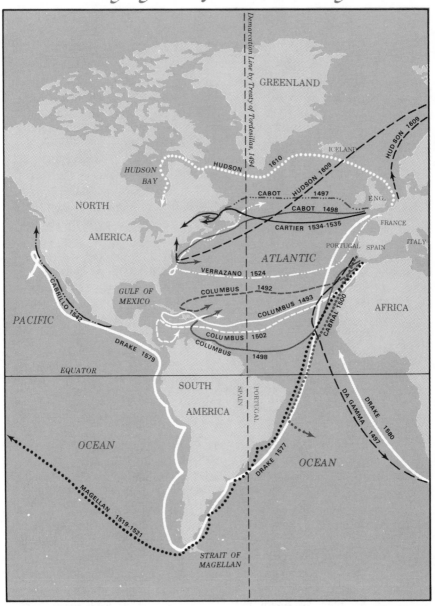

Colonies in Virginia

Soon after Raleigh received his charter, he sent a scouting expedition in 1584 to the Virginia coast. His seamen reported back almost in the words of Richard Hakluyt's *Discourse Concerning Western Planting* that there was good soil, plenty of land, and friendly Indians. Excited by this report, Raleigh sent Sir Richard Grenville, his cousin, to plant the first English colony. With ten ships and much equipment, Grenville easily put his passengers on Roanoke Island in Pimlico Sound where they scattered in parties to explore the strange countryside. John White, a skillful painter as well as cartographer, sketched the Indians, landscape, and flowers, and noted Indian customs which seemed quaint to him. Thomas Hariot, the future distinguished scientist, collected important data on the area in preparation for his *Brief and True Report of the New Found Land of Virginia* which was published in 1588. Both men found few Indians in the Virginia area—certainly not enough to interfere with plans for colonization.

With Ralph Lane in charge of the colony, the 107 settlers built houses, sought sources of food, and conducted extensive observations of the rivers and bays. They contacted the Indians who were at first friendly; then misunderstandings over customs led to an English raid, in which an Indian village was burned. The settlers had little respect for the Indians and almost no feeling for Indian rights of prior settlement. Since the Indians had little of value in Europe, Grenville left for a raiding voyage on Spanish trade. Near the Bermudas he captured the *Santa Maria* which was laden with gold, sugar, ivory, and hides. Its capture made possible Raleigh's reinforcement of the colony the next year. The raiding expedition, however, delayed Grenville's return voyage to Virginia for some weeks.

In the meantime, Ralph Lane explored the Chesapeake area and looked for a better site on which to plant the colony. His men encountered serious conflict with the Indians during their searches and a clash or two occurred. The Indian presence was admittedly a difficulty, but Lane had no hesitation about taking their lands, even though it might bring violence and war. However, he liked what he saw of the region, the fertile soil, the favorable climate, and the strategic position near the Spanish empire (he urged attacks upon Puerto Rico and Hispañola).

The land was nonetheless distant from England. Governor Lane and the colonists, lacking supplies and fearful of a Spanish attack upon their base, accepted an opportunity to break camp when Francis Drake, homeward bound from a raiding trip in the West Indies, visited them in the late spring of 1586. Hardly had they abandoned the area when Grenville arrived with ample supplies and men. Thus disappointed at the hasty departure of the settlers, he tarried only long enough to leave more men to hold the area and sailed for home in search of adventure.

In early 1587 a new expedition, with 117 men and women, gathered at Plymouth, England, and sailed finally by way of the West Indies for Roanoke Island. The squadron, consisting of three small ships under the command of John White as governor of the colony, was bound by specific instructions from Raleigh to select a good site in the Chesapeake Bay area and call it Raleigh. When the expedition reached Roanoke in July they could find no survivors of the earlier party, and only a few abandoned buildings. White unloaded provisions from the ship, but realized that he must return home for additional provisions if they were to survive. In the meantime his daughter, Eleanor Dare, gave birth to a daughter who was christened "Virginia." Morale was good as plans were made to move the colony into Chesapeake Bay or Albemarle Sound. For this purpose, White left a ship and then hurried off to England for the supplies.

His return was unexpectedly delayed several times—until 1590— because England was engaged in the famous battle of the Armada with Spain. Though Raleigh and Grenville had provisioned ships waiting to sail for Virginia, they were ordered to fight the Armada, and Raleigh was soon occupied with many other duties. When White finally reached Roanoke in 1590, he found only the heavy cannon, the palisade, some chests with papers, and a carving or two on trees, with the word *Croatoan*. Extensive investigation was cut short by a violent storm and by the reluctance of the captains to tarry longer. So into mystery fell this colony, "the lost colony of Virginia." Raleigh, to his credit, never gave up the hope of locating these colonists. The last attempt he made was in 1602. Probably the Indians held the answer, and their tales in 1607 described a few survivors at some distant clearing: men, boys, a young girl, and a few tame turkeys.

Raleigh's interest in Virginia lingered for years, but he was engaged in many things, not the least of which were the preparations in England to hold off attacks by Spain. In the battle of the Armada his part is unknown, though biographers have him rushing to sea and serving aboard a ship in the English fleet. Whatever his service, Raleigh involved himself in the fighting, sought heroic action, and battled for political favor; the colony in Virginia faded for a time from his mind. Hostilities with Spain, however, continued until 1604, and Raleigh joined an expedition to Guiana in hope of finding gold and breaking Spain's monopoly, took part in an attack upon Cadiz in 1596, and fought with the Earl of Essex in Ireland. War for him, as for Drake and Hawkins, brought moments of glory, but it retarded the colonization movement.

Northern Colonies

In the 1590s, the Queen's influential minister, Lord Burghley, pondered the possibility of establishing American colonies when shortages of supplies threatened the economy. He preferred colonies in the northern regions, possibly because his attention was drawn to the St. Lawrence Gulf by the recent capture of two privateers. The *Bonaventure* of St. Malo had a cargo of walrus oil which could be used as a substitute for olive oil. The *Catherine* of St. Jean de Luz was full of furs from Canada. Somehow Burghley contacted merchants in Bristol and London and put them in touch with some friendly Basque fishermen; their plans developed into a mixture of piracy and fishing, with the objective of finding cargoes of walrus oil, whalebone, and cod. Efforts to fill their ships in 1592 and 1593 were disappointing but also enticing. The problem, the promoters discovered, was the ability of their Basque competition to reach the fishing banks before they could. If they had a base in America, then they could have also the advantage of an early departure for the fishing areas.

Wild plans soon followed. Someone suggested that religious followers from Francis Johnson's community of Brownists be invited to join the project. Many were either in jail or forced to live in exile because they refused to worship according to the ritual of the state church. In exchange for release from prison and liberty in America to worship as they pleased, they would become colonists. Lord Burghley was undoubtedly active behind the scenes, and a group of London merchants were the promoters. They arranged shipping, gathered Johnson's flock, and completed the financing. To be specific, they created an informal business venture, using these religious people as workers, and secured governmental approval for the colonists to leave England. The Privy Council, however, wanted proof of their loyalty by requiring an oath of allegiance. Both colonists and promoters knew this enterprise was a marriage of convenience and hoped for the best.

In 1597 the promoters planned a two-ship, preliminary investigation of a site on the Magdalen Islands in the St. Lawrence Gulf. They urged the selection of four Brownists to make the voyage and recommended that leaders of the congregation choose people who had skills as craftsmen, artisans, and farmers. Those selected were Francis and George Johnson, Daniel Studley, and John Clerke, whose conduct during the voyage can best be described as "enthusiastic." These men had suffered prison terms for their religious beliefs and were deeply committed to their faith. Nonetheless, they were a rigid, tenacious, talkative, and unrealistic lot who tried to evangelize the crew during the voyage and passed out printed sermons to seamen in port. The crew reacted sharply by threatening violence as a protest against preaching.

Besides this agitation, the captains lost each other in the dense fog and rough seas of the St. Lawrence Gulf, and the *Chancewell* could not find the Magdalen Islands. It found Basques and Bretons instead, and the skirmishes left the English seamen with not much more than their ship and clothes. The *Hopewell* at first did better than its sister ship. It located the Magdalens, only to be involved in a fight with the encamped Basques. Finally it had to retreat, but when there was no place to settle on the islands the captain sailed the *Hopewell* to Cape Breton, where by chance it met its sister ship. Sizing up the situation, Francis Johnson and his colleagues agreed with the captains to return home. The tough Basque whalers were too much for them; there was a spirit of piracy in the air, and the English crews looked for prizes as they tried to imitate Hawkins and Drake in bringing home great wealth.

The unfavorable reports of the captains, however, forced the promoters in England to ponder their plans for a colony. But three ships were launched in 1598, and perhaps others in 1599. The promoters encountered opposition from English ministers who were reluctant to make attacks on the Basques and Bretons and to alienate King Henry IV of France. The ministers may have discouraged additional voyages. The Brownists, having exiled themselves in Holland, disputed from there the reasons for the failure of the colony. Francis Johnson kept alive his contacts with the London business community, and he may have journeyed to England in an effort to negotiate another proposal. Other religious groups criticized Johnson and his associates for their conduct as they heard reports of the 1597 voyage. Between 1610-1620 while Johnson served as pastor of the Brownist church in Amsterdam, his experiences and ideas become known to the larger community of Englishmen in Holland. Many may have received inspiration, however, from Johnson for wanting to plant a colony in America.

Over these decades, English ardor was twice cooled by the failures of colonial ventures. These failures were accepted as a matter of course by Richard Hakluyt, the most confirmed imperialist of the day, but Hakluyt never gave up the idea that colonies would add to English wealth. He and his London merchant friends sponsored voyages and talked up the idea of further investigations; they often found support from West Country men who looked for new fisheries and fur trading areas. Two of the important men of the day were Sir Thomas Smith and Sir Ferdinando Gorges, both wealthy, adventurous, confirmed imperialists. In the years after 1600 they became more and more interested in the coast of Maine, Cape Cod, and Martha's Vineyard, and also in the areas of Chesapeake Bay and Virginia.

The End of an Era

Despite these efforts, colonization until 1600 had a minor impact upon England. While some merchants pondered the value of colonies for increasing trade, commerce was flourishing. Merchantmen were everywhere in European waters: they sailed regularly around Africa to India and the East Indies, and acted as pirates and smugglers in Latin American waters. London, the nation's center, had grown to a population of nearly 225,000, but some interior towns like York, Salisbury, and Norwich were approaching 15,000. The nation's total population was also growing and rose from three to four million in the sixteenth century. Most of these urban areas of the interior depended upon trade for their existence, while many port cities looked outwardly for foreign commerce.

The prosperity brought rewards to these cities, and venture capital was available for sound, even speculative enterprises. People seemed to be busy, but there were many looking for jobs and opportunities, some experiencing unemployment and some complaining over their lot. Changes in land ownership and use, called enclosure, were forcing thousands into the towns and cities, creating disruption of life, unrest, and overcrowding as they sought new opportunities.

England in 1600 was admittedly nearing the end of an era. Elizabeth I had ruled for forty-two years, and with a well-selected, vigorous group of advisers, had governed wisely. Her reign compared favorably with her predecessors, Henry VII and Henry VIII, and in many ways was even more lustrous. National peace, contentment, and prosperity had been spread to a large area, and the people were proud of their nation. Wealth was entering the country from India, Europe, and Africa, and improved methods of farming were also increasing prosperity. The spirit of the nation was reflected in its poetry, its theater, and its prose, or in short, in the growth of a sophisticated culture that made people proud to be Englishmen. No age could be more aware of itself than to have a Shakespeare, Bacon, and Spenser, a Drake, Burghley, and Raleigh, and an Elizabeth.

But there were strains, too, in these last years of the reign. Some people were weary of the continued hostilities with Spain, others desired changes in religious policy, and still others worried about the rise in prices that were causing hardships for all classes. A few people criticized the crime, the immorality, the display of wealth, the poverty and the unemployment. Swearing, bearbaiting, cockfighting, and betting upset other sensitive people. In anguish they called for reform of society. Only a few people, however, were ready to abandon England for the wilds of America or to seek exile in a foreign country. Some Brownists were in Holland;

other Englishmen were living in France and Spain; but none of these would assert that he lived in a reformed land.

If restlessness disturbed England in the 1600s, it had not yet aroused enough people to create a pool of potential colonists.

Plymouth Rock, 1620. Engraving by J. Andrews, 1860. *(Library of Congress)*

2

The Founding of Colonies:
Virginia, Bermuda, and Maryland

When Elizabeth I died in 1603, bringing a colorful reign of forty-five years
to a quiet end, she was succeeded by her nephew, King James VI of
Scotland, who was warmly welcomed to England. His reign opened with
much popular acclaim and the expectations of a new dawn. James I of
England (1603-1625) was a talented, godly man whose stubborn habits of
mind irritated even his friends. One historian has described him as a
"sublime mediocrity" who distrusted original ideas of every kind. That
was a major weakness, but in 1603 he succeeded to many problems caused
by inflation, depressed conditions, and poverty that were aggravated by his
desire to make peace with Spain. Though that peace of 1604 was generally
popular with the masses, some merchants and courtiers missed the
opportunity to engage in raiding expeditions, piracy, and looting of
Spanish ships. After the peace, their commerce suffered much from
Spanish trade regulations which denied them direct contacts with the
empire. Many of their ships, moreover, were delayed in passage when
Spain suspected trade with the Dutch, who were revolting against the
empire and adhering to the Calvinist religion, but were still nominally
Spanish nationals. English voyages also suffered from the uncertainty of
ocean passage and from some severe losses while held in Spanish ports.

Over the long period of James' reign conditions at home remained
difficult for the merchants. A depression-like economy, disturbed by war
and increased taxes, upset them, and they looked outside of England for
relief. Joining the merchants were poorer Englishmen who were ready to
risk life and limb for a chance to find new opportunities. Some of these

people were without employment; more were troubled by low wages; even more were affected by other kinds of worries. A few were unhappy over the king's religious policies, feeling that he was not purifying the Church of England according to Calvinist ideas. Others wanted changes in society: fewer plays, cockfights, and gambling. Unrest was then increasing for various reasons, and for many people the merchants' desire for new markets was a way of escaping England.

The search for trading opportunities more than anything else led to the formation in 1606 of two Virginia companies, one for the London merchants and another for the Plymouth merchants. The companies were permitted to occupy the North American mainland between latitudes 30 degrees north and 45 degrees north, roughly from the Cape Fear River to Passamaquoddy Bay. No settlements, however, were to be permitted one hundred miles between company settlements, but each company was limited to definite areas as an additional precaution against rivalry. The London promoters, succeeding to Sir Walter Raleigh's interests, recruited Sir Thomas Smith, Sir Thomas Gates, Richard Hakluyt, George Somers, and George Popham to serve as advisers and investors. The experiences of the Plymouth Company will be described in the next chapter.

Under Smith's leadership, merchants bought shares and planned for a plantation in present-day Virginia, which would develop a trade base for the shareholders through commerce with the Indians. Preparations were readied in 1606 and a small fleet was assembled. Captain Christopher Newport, an experienced merchant seaman, was placed in charge of the three-ship fleet, the *Susan Constant,* the *Goodspeed,* and the *Discovery.* On them were put approximately 141 workers, artisans, adventurers, and farmers especially recruited for company service. Though Newport followed a familiar route via Nevis in the West Indies to the Chesapeake Bay, the voyage was unusually long, from December 20, 1606 to April 26, 1607, and full of bitter moments in wintry seas. The passengers, however, arrived in fair shape. Upon reaching the Chesapeake, they sailed upstream on the James River about thirty miles, and their leaders then selected a low-lying, marshy location for this outpost of empire.

The party was instructed when it reached Virginia to open a sealed box which would give them the names of the councillors, and the council would then choose its president. Named were such men as Newport, Edward Wingfield, John Smith, John Ratcliffe, and George Kendall. As their first executive act, they chose Wingfield as their president and then divided the party into three parts: one to fortify the post, another to plant vegetables, and another to explore the river and countryside for items of trade. Some of the men obviously looked for precious minerals and, in

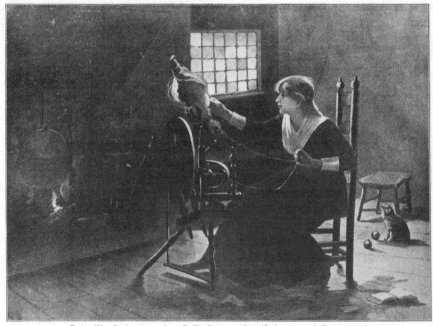

Priscilla Spinning, by G.R. Barse, Jr. *(Library of Congress)*

1608, even for gold, which was the great prize of Spain in Mexico and Peru. Ship stores were also in great demand, particularly timber for masts, yards, and bowsprits. Supplies of pitch and tar were valuable as well as turpentine and resin.

In the quiet of this wilderness outpost there was soon ill feeling and discord. The strain of unfamiliar surroundings, hard work, and hunger ruffled tempers, and men turned on each other especially when deaths from illnesses depleted their ranks. Kendall was accused of conspiracy and ordered shot; Wingfield, charged with many contradictory and petty things, was sent home when Newport left for provisions and additional workers. Others, like Robert Hunt, the first minister of the post, tried to calm tempers and John Smith, the twenty-eight-year veteran of wars in Transylvania and Hungary, offered his services as leader. Smith made practical use of his contacts with the neighboring Indians to buy provisions. He imposed discipline by keeping the men busy, maintaining sanitary conditions, and diversifying the food supply. While he was leader in 1608, the death rate dropped and conditions seemed stabilized.

Due primarily to Smith's energetic leadership, the colony survived the winter of 1608-1609. Conditions remained critical, however, because there was illness, poor morale, laziness, and a weak governing structure. The promoters in England also realized this deficiency and, in procuring a charter revision in 1609, enlarged the number of stockholders, amassed many settlers, and tightened control of the colony in America. Sir Thomas Smith took over supervision of financial operations for the company in England, and Thomas West, Lord De La Warr, agreed to rule as resident governor or through deputies. More than 659 persons and 56 firms now joined the enterprise, giving it the appearance of a united London effort to make colonization successful. Both Smith and De La Warr, men of prominence and wealth, gave the company unusual presence in London by their willingness to support its operations. In 1612 stockholders gained not only the right to vote but also one hundred acres of land. Bermuda was added as an asset. When colonists were sent to develop plantations, the company was granted the privilege of staging lotteries throughout England, and these raised considerable amounts of necessary capital to pay expenses.

With the reorganization in 1609 the company sent nine ships and over 500 men, women, and children as colonists. Unfortunately, a severe hurricane scattered the ships and wrecked the vessel carrying the new company leadership, Sir Thomas Gates and Sir Thomas Dale. The delay was serious because John Smith, still acting as governor, was wounded by an accidental discharge of gunpowder and was forced to leave the colony's direction to George Percy who had to face, in addition to the usual problems, Indian attacks and growing illness among the workers. The winter of 1609-1610, known as the "Starving Time," was so bitter that many people died of malaria and dysentery; one man was convicted of cannibalism and executed. By the time Gates arrived in May 1610, the population of 490 had been reduced to 60. Gates's first impressions depressed him and he decided to abandon the colony. On his way down the James River he met Governor De La Warr, who quickly reversed Gates's decision. A renewed effort by them was then made to salvage the colony. With about 500 new settlers the men took stern measures to clean up the post, plant crops, and erect housing. Discipline was made strict by imposing hours of labor, hours for religious worship, and hours for relaxation. But there were some advantages too. The new leadership spread the settlers into communities—Henrico, Point Comfort, and Kecoughan—where there were some pleasures of town life. Jamestown had by 1611 one hundred wooden houses and Henrico had at least one brick building.

Life still remained hazardous both within and outside these villages. People died in large numbers (and some returned home when their period of service was completed), but in spite of a continuous flow of people to Virginia there were only 351 people alive in 1616. To entice settlers the company permitted a few Virginia settlers to lease or own land and to

The first day at Jamestown. *(Library of Congress)*

engage in agriculture. They experimented with various kinds of crops and found that tobacco was the most lucrative. It was relatively easy to grow, yet sometimes the quality of the leaf was poor. But production grew rapidly from 2,300 pounds in 1616 to 49,500 in 1618. The planters soon discovered, however, that shippers and dealers had taken advantage of them, and that the return was frequently too small to justify their exertions. Angry and bitter, the planters filed their protests with company officials who, in turn, recalled the deputy governor and forced a company reorganization. In spite of some disillusion the colony grew by several hundred people in 1617 and 1618.

New Men Take the Helm

In 1618 a group of English merchants, including Sir Edwin Sandys, Sir Nathaniel Rich, and John and Nicholas Ferrar, took over the company's leadership and recommended a series of reforms, a new administration and a set of measures to pump new life into the colony. Sir George Yeardly, a retired soldier and former deputy governor, was named governor. He was known to be fair-minded and decisive and quickly became well liked by his fellow associates.

Arriving in Virginia early in 1619, Yeardly brought instructions for the establishment of a new government, which included a body of laws, plans for a legislature, and a design for representative government. The franchise was extended to all males who would live in one of four counties and who could vote for officials on all levels of government including burgesses to the assembly. The counties, James City, Charles City, Henrico, and Kecoughan (Elizabeth City), were not really counties in the later sense, but more like centers of population than administrative units. The legislature met on July 30, 1619, the first to convene in British North America, and consisted of six councillors and twenty-two burgesses who sat in a single room. During its six-day session the legislators passed laws to regulate Indian trading relations, set prices and quality for tobacco exports, regulated conduct on the Sabbath, and outlawed swearing, idleness, drunkenness, and similar kinds of wickedness. Yeardly was instructed by the merchants to make plans for a university and college for Indians, a glass factory, shipyard, ironworks, and other enterprises. Finally, the company advised Yeardly to encourage the development of a balanced economy, with trade and crafts and crops equally promoted. Self-sufficiency in food stuffs was urged, but tobacco and other money crops would be welcomed. The company promised, moreover, vast numbers of new colonists who were ready to come because of the continued dissatisfaction with politics in England.

Meanwhile, in London, Sir Edwin Sandys, in place of Sir Thomas Smith, urged people to settle in Virginia. A prominent politician, son of the Archbishop of York, and a member of Parliament, Sandys was widely known, and known, too, as deeply interested in Virginia. The colony was most popular in the public consciousness and an amazing number of people from the trades and merchant community decided to make their homes in America. In a short time perhaps as many as three thousand people arrived in the colony, giving the towns a boom-like appearance as well as the noise and press of crowds that excited colonists and old-time adventurers alike. However, most realized quickly that there were too many people for these outposts and too little housing, food, sufficient preparation, and financial backing from London.

In the early spring of 1622 the first blow occurred. A surprise Indian attack devastated Jamestown and the surrounding countryside. Over 350 people lost their lives within a few hours. The colonists hit back at the Indians, burned their fields and villages, scattered them into the forests, and took as many lives as possible. But Virginia towns were now vulnerable to attack, and in taking precautions the people crowded into the villages and were ravaged themselves by disease from congestion and unsanitary conditions.

Deaths from hunger, disease, and Indian raids marked life in the Virginia towns. The disaster brought a sharp reaction which took the form of bitter protests to the stockholders and the English government. In the meantime, company leadership in London was severely divided over the company's consumption of and part in the English market shared with Spanish Venezuela. Opposition over the market got sufficiently heated for the leadership to split and turn upon itself—upon Sandys and his clique. Additional problems occurred when the English government cancelled the company privilege to hold lotteries in order to raise money for the enterprise.

With crises in leadership and finance pressing upon it, the company was also embarrassed by being taken over temporarily by the Privy Council and forced to stand investigation. Council committees quickly recommended direct government rule of the colony. While the company protested, the government brought legal action to dissolve it. To gather additional supporting evidence, council agents were dispatched to Virginia to look into company affairs. Conditions were undoubtedly poor, but the agents were not well received at Jamestown because the settlers feared for their representative institutions if the company was dissolved. Whether their fears were fully justified is a matter of debate, but the opposition to the agents served notice on the English government that some local government was justified. The opposition, however, did not delay legal proceedings against the company. In May 1624 the court of King's Bench declared the company's charter vacated, and Virginia became thus England's first royal colony. A commission was then appointed to study local government, and it recommended the rule of a governor and a council of twelve.

The Royal Colony

Before plans could be finalized for Virginia's new government, the old king died. His son, Charles I (1625-1649), delayed action on any reorganization until he had an opportunity to review the political and economic conditions in the colony. The king's advisers convinced him that he should leave the day-to-day rule of the colony to Governor Sir Francis Wyatt and the council, who would consult informally with the assembly from time to time. Between 1625 and 1639 the government depended primarily upon the interaction of the governor and council. Although these relations were often strained by arguments, much happened that was positive in the colony. In 1639 Charles regularized the practice of consultation with the assembly and consented to annual meetings.

Virginia developed slowly but surely. The serious crises of the early 1620s passed easily, with the possible effect of putting Virginia into a

First meeting of the assembly in Virginia. *(Library of Congress)*

secondary role as people chose new homes elsewhere in America. Colonies were planted in the West Indies, in New England, and in the northern Chesapeake Bay (Maryland). Three to four times more people went to colonies other than Virginia, which listed only fifteen hundred people in its census of 1625. Among these were 269 women and 23 blacks. Ten years later the population reached five thousand; by 1642 it had reached eight thousand. Families came; homes were established; gardens and vegetable patches were planted. Virginia's villages, though small, took on the appearance of communities. The quality of people remained about the same—the leaders were college graduates or sons of wealthy families, while the planters and laborers were drawn from the artisan and farming classes of England. Perhaps a shift occurred in the 1630s, with fewer college graduates in the leadership group and more restless, ambitious merchants and speculators predominating. In the migration there were undoubtedly some people who were unhappy with English politics and took the opportunity to settle in the colony.

During these years after 1625 Virginia grew more and more tobacco, and lands were being cleared with more plantings in mind. Planters worried about the oversupply of tobacco as prices fell, and urged upon the governor controls of price and quality. The assembly codified the regulations in 1633, but then added legislation that restricted acreage, defined grades, and required all tobacco to be sent to Jamestown for transshipping. Regulations such as these were often grouped with others requiring plantings of grain crops. There was danger that food would be in short supply as planters tried to get their share of the tobacco market. Still, the Virginia climate was temperate, animals quickly multiplied, crops were abundant, and people were healthy as long as they did not crowd into the towns.

People tended to cluster in this type of society where there was concentration upon a plantation crop. The labor force consisted mostly of indentured servants—English people who worked for some years to cover the costs of their passage to Virginia. Freedom then followed with continued service on the farm or with an independent existence elsewhere in the colony. Settlers lived along the many rivers, which became highways of trade, and tended to associate with neighboring farming groups. Their churches were erected at a crossroads where they gathered once or twice a week. The Anglican priest and his family often lived at a nearby plantation and rode over to the church to conduct Sunday morning services. Protestant Christianity had an impact upon the lives of inhabitants who were readers of the Bible, defenders of the reformed faith, and sermon tasters. Occasionally, ministers who were Puritans entered the colony and stirred up religious controversy because they challenged Catholic practices in the Anglican church and urged changes.

While Virginians were God-fearing people, they spent most of their time facing the hardships of survival. Breaking the soil was hard work, and living in frontier conditions presented them with daily health problems. Life was often made harder by the hundreds of Indians who lived near their farms and communities. Life was precarious wherever one ventured, and between Englishmen and Indians a general hostility persisted that threatened to break into war at any time. This condition, however, did not prevent trade in skins and friendly exchanges on an individual basis. A few marriages occurred between the races, and some missionary work by Anglican priests was often attempted. But general hostility prevailed and tended to destroy most positive effects of conciliation.

As Virginia grew in the numbers of Englishmen, the population spread from the original bases on the James River to plantation settlements along the rivers to the north. Virginia has fortunately many rivers draining into the Chesapeake Bay, and these rivers provide the basis of penetration for many miles into the interior.

The soil was good along these rivers, and the tobacco culture flourished over the years. It depended, too, upon the labor of many people working in the fields, and most of them in these years were English

The great Powhatan. *(Library of Congress)*

indentured servants who secured their westward passage in exchange for their labor while their master was given fifty acres of land by the colony for transporting each of them. These twin agents of expansion thus spread Virginia north and west along the Chesapeake Bay and distant from the capital at Jamestown.

These developments required changes in Virginia government, and in the early 1630s eight new counties were erected. Other counties followed in the 1640s and 1650s. Local government took form and roughly resembled shire government in England. Justices of the peace became the primary judicial officers in hearing petty cases, and they joined with other justices to form session courts to hear serious issues. Jury trials were provided for defendants, and appeals to the governor and council were available. Punishment for the convicted was generally milder than in England, but in ordinary cases of lawbreaking the whipping post, ducking stool, and pillory were regularly used; in very serious cases the hangman's rope often was stretched. The justices had many duties, administrative as well as judicial. For many years of the century, one served also as the sheriff; some served as coroners, probate justices, and collectors of fees; and occasionally justices served as surveyors of land. As population grew these duties were separated from the justice's office.

Local government involved many of the same people. Those representatives of the people who were called to the legislature were frequently the justices of the peace, the captains of the militia forces, and members of the vestry which supervised religious affairs. They had either the leisure or the interest, and as a group they kept local government responsive to popular needs. Important in this process of responding to government needs was their use of English institutions. This group had to modify and shape these institutions, however, to frontier and primitive conditions so that the names of old offices did not always mean that the official's duties were similar to those in England. The vestrymen, for example, in Virginia managed church affairs and contracted with the minister, while in England the minister owed his selection to the bishop and enjoyed some independence in his relation with parish authorities.

Maryland

As Virginia developed in population and spread along the rivers emptying into the Chesapeake Bay, the colony faced competition from other English settlements. In 1634 a group of colonists under the leadership of Leonard Calvert sailed up the Chesapeake Bay into the Potomac River and selected a fine site near the banks of St. Mary's River, probably as beautiful and healthful a place as one could find. The nearly 300 settlers were religious refugees—Catholics and others—and people in search of a better life than the one they were experiencing in England.

The Calvert family had for some years been looking for a place to settle Roman Catholics. George Calvert, a convert to the faith while he served in Ireland, had held high posts under James I and associated with important leaders of the Virginia company. His son Cecilius married into the Catholic Arundel family, also interested in American affairs, and the joint families were supporters of the king. Calvert became Lord Baltimore because of his service as member of the Privy Council.

Although Calvert first wanted to establish a colony in Newfoundland, the cold winters and limited opportunities of the north country forced him to look elsewhere. With the aid of Charles I, in 1632 he secured a title to land on the eastern side of the Potomac River, thence from the Chesapeake to the Atlantic Ocean. Boundaries remained an issue for the family with Virginia and later with English colonies to the north.

When Lord Baltimore died in 1632, his son Cecilius Calvert became head of the colonization project, and he actively promoted the migration from England of anyone interested in Maryland. His brother Leonard Calvert went out in his place to America and served as governor until his death in 1647. For those many years that Cecilius lived he never came to the colony because he was pressed by problems of politics and finance and had to remain in England. He ruled through governors and officials and modified local policies by sending directions from London.

To the initial settlement of Maryland at St. Mary's, almost three hundred people came on the *Ark* and *Dove* in 1634. The group was composed of sixteen gentlemen and their families, plus artisans, farmers, and servants. Two Jesuit priests and members of religious communities accompanied the party, and they offered mass on arrival in thanksgiving for the safe voyage. Probably more of the original settlers were members of the Church of England than the Roman Catholic church, but at first distinctions in religious ceremonies may not have troubled the Protestants as they faced the trials of the frontier existence with their Catholic associates.

Lord Baltimore and his sons wanted a colony that was patterned upon feudal and manorial traditions. As the lands were laid out below the Patapsco River, on the north bank of the Potomac River, on both shores of the Patuxent, and on Kent Island, about sixty manors were created. Their size varied from a few acres to thousands, and certain landholders were designated lords of the manor, with rights to hold court and collect fees for services. Men would be tied to the land like the serfs of old and hold land in common ownership. Not too much should be made of these feudal trappings, except to describe the early spirit of Baltimore's plans. The feudal forms faded gradually, and in their place were the forms of traditional English government: men were free to move around the colony and own land. The community around St. Mary's fell under the authority of the governor and council and, as the colony grew, small administrative units called hundreds were created which provided the offices of coroner, constable, conservators of the peace, and their services. However, the hundred itself faded as counties developed and with them the coming of the offices of sheriff, justices of the peace, coroners, and constables. Since population grew slowly, counties multiplied slowly too. Maryland had about 2,000 people in 1640. Thus central government was also modest, primarily in the hands of the governor, a small council, and an assembly. The first assembly met in 1635 and modeled itself quickly after Parliament. Its arguments with the governor over demands to pass laws, participate in policymaking, and share in the judicial process often reflected those of Parliament and the king at home. The assembly was at first composed of free men and delegates, and their expertise was amateurish, but the growth of population forced the restructuring of membership and the emergence of a two-house legislature with elected or appointed members. The position of proprietor evolved, too, and his powers generally were shared with the elected assembly. The proprietor's relations with the home government also changed because of deteriorating relations with Parliament which was critical of his Catholic beliefs. Lord Calvert thus remained in London ever ready to counter the threats of his enemies.

As institutional development in the colony roughly resembled Virginia's, so also was there a similar social and economic life. Maryland and Virginia were esssentially parts of a single community. Tobacco was the principal crop, but not the only crop, since Maryland's communities were nearly self-sufficient in food stuffs. Tobacco was the money crop in that its sales paid taxes, duties, tithes, and debts. But there were also grains to sell, cattle, fruits, and vegetables to use. Farms often were large in acreage, but they were only partly cultivated because of the scarcity of laborers. Manpower was obtained by importing English indentured servants, who were expensive and never available in the numbers required to bring more land under cultivation. In addition to the white indentured laborers, Marylanders bought the services of blacks, who quickly became slaves. By mid-century perhaps a few hundred blacks were living in Maryland as slaves. Virginia, at the same time, with the larger population, had about 1500.

The causes of the existence of slavery in the English empire has aroused much discussion among scholars. But the fact is that the numbers of slaves were small. The question of why blacks should be enslaved is perplexing, and why their number relative to indentured servants remained small in the seventeenth century is likewise puzzling. An examination of Virginia laws indicates that blacks were generally treated differently than white servants. Color, language, education, and customs obviously played their part in creating a low status for blacks. Since blacks were thus handicapped, they did not have the usual advantages of the law that protected white servants. It is possible, too, that slavery for blacks in other countries became an example for Virginia and Maryland to follow. Land policy may have been an important consideration in retarding slavery. For most of the seventeenth century, farms were small and scattered, and servants, though important, were limited in number on any farm. White artisan laborers seemed to offer better service than blacks when small numbers were used.

The Rule of William Berkeley

After 1640 both Virginia and Maryland grew well in population and food production, along patterns set in the 1630s. Both colonies were troubled, however, by the revolution against Charles I in England and the outbreak of religious differences. The provinces often were touched by the revolutionary politics, but escaped serious involvement in the war. Virginia was, moreover, fortunate to secure in 1642 the services of Sir William Berkeley, who brought assurances that there would be no return to the rule of the Virginia Company. Virginians worried about this possibility into the 1650s—perhaps their fears were greater than the reality, but the governor benefited as a symbol of royal power in gaining support. Berkeley, then thirty-four years of age, was a graduate of Merton College, Oxford, and was well-connected in English politics. He possessed a winning personality and an ability to mollify politicians in the legislature. His philosophy was conservative enough also to please those who backed the king in the civil war at home where issues of royal power to tax, imprison, and call Parliament into session irritated many people. Berkeley favored regular meetings of the legislature, the right to petition, and the right of a jury trial. One suspects that the basis of Berkeley's popularity was his known concern for the interests of farmers and land speculators and the good sense that he displayed in helping them solve their problems. In time he became a planter, the owner of a fine house and prosperous estate reputed to be among the best in Virginia.

During the early years of his governorship Berkeley inspired or approved much legislation which beneficially affected many people. He agreed to repeal poll taxes and modify certain land taxes which were assessed on land value and the ability to pay. He freed some debtors from prison. Representation was changed for membership in the legislature, limiting the number of burgesses to four for each county and five for Jamestown. Berkeley was a strong supporter of the Church of England, and in disputes with Puritans he backed the Church even as the English government was being dominated by Puritan leaders. His firm policies probably reduced religious tension and factionalism in Virginia.

The most serious crisis of the decade occurred in 1644 when Indian parties moved upon farmers living south of the James River. The attacks took the lives of five hundred people and spread terror through the settlements lying along the river. The Indian chief, Opechancanough, whose warriors had wreaked such havoc on the colony in 1622, hit again in 1644 with even greater vigor. He heard rumors that the colony was weak because of the civil war in England, and he wanted to turn back the waves of settlers who were harming the tribe's hunting grounds.

Berkeley and his lieutenants counterattacked with little sympathy. They used Virginia's large population and food resources to take the offensive. In a year of bloody fighting and bitterness, they surprised Opechancanough and captured him, but the chief was soon murdered in prison. Atrocities on both sides brutalized the battles, and hundreds of Indians lost their lives. In the end a peace treaty divided frontier lands between white and red men, assuring the Indians of hunting land and regulating trading practices. Berkeley's government quickly erected a few forts and passed laws to supervise migration into frontier areas. The peace of 1646 proved that Virginia's population of 8,000 was too large and too scattered for the Indians to deal a single death blow to the colony's existence, but not strong enough to force the Indians from all their hunting areas.

The Puritan Revolution

Threats to the colony's home rule also arose from the revolutionary government in England. For years arguments between Puritans, parliamentarians, and others with Charles I and his friends had created much bitterness. In disgust large numbers of people migrated to the colonies instead of living under these conditions, but most stayed in England and, in 1640, began a struggle that drifted into violence and excess. Most Virginians, like their governor, Sir William Berkeley, were royalists and

Anglicans at heart because that relationship seemed to guarantee the colony of home rule instead of company rule. Their rights and privileges, moreover, were derived from the royal connection since the dissolution of the company in 1624, and they would face under any other authority the problem of dealing with people who might want to restore company rule.

When the revolutionaries rashly executed Charles I in 1649, royal officials in Virginia reacted against this violence by branding the action as treason. Legislators passed a bill threatening severe punishment for anyone conspiring to overthrow the colony's government. Their objective was not to set up another royal government but to hold down the bitterness and tension of the English civil war. The legislators tried to avoid internal dissension and applied pressure successfully to the small Puritan community, many of whom responded by drifting into Maryland. Legislators also had trouble with the Society of Friends, or Quakers, who held radical views on the Bible and the Trinity as well as on the relationship of persons to government. The sect aroused much emotion, but Virginians again maintained internal peace. The colony suffered also from irregular trade with England and the uncertainties of revolutionary politics. The new government touched Virginia in various ways. Trade (navigation) laws were passed in 1651 prohibiting commerce with foreign nations, and commissions were sent to investigate Virginia politics. Berkeley responded by raising a militia force, but good sense prevailed, probably in the face of certain punishment from England, and he resigned his position. The arrangements with the English government appeared reasonable and mild, and one of the commissioners, Richard Bennett, became governor and served until 1655. Berkeley removed himself quietly to his estates and awaited hopefully the return of the monarchy.

In the late 1650s Samuel Mathews, Jr., served as governor. Young, impulsive, and forceful, he upset some Virginians by taking too much government into his own hands. Too much may be made of Mathews' independent spirit because Virginia grew greatly in population during this time, perhaps to 30,000, and much progress was evident in the spread of people and the success of agriculture. Indian relations were occasionally threatening, but no serious war broke out. There was, however, some restlessness, reflective of this growth, but Virginia was well established as a colony in 1660.

Maryland and the Puritans

The uneasiness Virginians felt in the late 1650s was a typical feeling for Marylanders, because throughout their history they had much to worry about. The colony from the beginning maintained a precarious balance between Catholics and Protestants which was frequently disturbed when troublemakers from Virginia and elsewhere migrated into the colony. Tensions were so great in 1645 and 1646 that Governor Calvert took refuge in Virginia to escape Protestant abuse.

Baltimore responded to this uprising by issuing instructions to guarantee tolerance. Realizing that his Roman Catholic subjects were in the minority, he sought to protect them by encouraging fair treatment for all who believed in the divinity of Christ. He urged the settlers to live in peace, to love one another, and to refrain from slander and threats in daily relations.

His gentle reminder, of course, had some influence, but men remained suspicious, fearful of each other, and edgy. Other problems, too, disturbed the colony. Boundary relations with Virginia were personified by a rivalry between William Claiborne and the Calverts. It originated over Maryland's charter that took Virginia territory away from the colony, but spread to trade, land claims, Indian trade, and suspicion over religion. Claiborne stood often in the wings, awaiting an outbreak of trouble in the colony, and then moved to attack Calvert.

His opportunity came in 1649 when Charles I was executed by the English revolutionary government and when the acting governor of Maryland proclaimed Charles II as king. The governor's contempt for the prerogatives of the English government rightly angered many in England. They reacted by ordering the same commissioners who were then investigating Virginian loyalty to look also into the loyalty of Marylanders. Their findings were predictable and led to the removal from office of Governor William Stone, a Puritan, the dismissal of his council, and the appointment of new officials. Popular reaction to this intrusion into colonial politics, however, was equally hostile, forcing the commissioners themselves to retreat a bit and restore Stone and his secretary to office. In the end the people were compelled, nevertheless, to recognize the revolutionary authority of the English government in Maryland.

Swift changes in home politics, meanwhile, favored Lord Baltimore who took the offensive. He ordered Stone to restore the proprietorship and require of everyone an oath of fidelity. Opposition from the Puritans quickly arose; they recruited Claiborne and the governor of Virginia who managed to unseat Stone and elect an assembly, primarily Puritan in numbers, which passed laws against the Catholic minority. Emotion ran high, and each of the factions raised armed forces and met finally on the Severn River. The resulting clash was victorious for the antiproprietary group, who scattered or captured the opposition. At least four were hanged or shot. For the survivors who were not captured, their lands were either seized outright or subjected to severe penalties. The Jesuit priests fled and their religious facilities were plundered.

Since Baltimore had not formally lost his proprietorship, the Virginia and Maryland Puritans took their assault upon him directly to the English government. Petitions to Oliver Cromwell, the Lord Protector of England, denounced Baltimore and urged dissolution of the proprietorship. The heat was too great for Cromwell, who referred the petitions to his committee on foreign affairs, where they cooled off for two years while each side became restless over the delay and sought help.

Acting as a mediator, Governor Edward Digges of Virginia proposed a peace without victory in 1657. The plan was welcomed by the disputants who accepted its terms readily. Baltimore's rights as proprietor were recognized, while the Puritans were assured of protection against retaliation. The peace normalized conditions; Marylanders argued again with their governor and he argued with the proprietor! By 1660 bitterness among most leaders had turned the colony into warring factions, and the future again looked bleak. Fortunately Charles II, the son of the slain Charles, had just ascended the throne, and he urged Marylanders as a gesture of loyalty to cooperate with Lord Baltimore, his good friend, in finding a solution to their problems.

By 1660 the Chesapeake colonies had a sound population base. People were flocking into the settlements and the foundations for English communities were well laid. The colonies were agricultural, primarily composed of small farms that grew tobacco as a principal crop. There was an abundance of food, good land, a magnificent highway system of navigable rivers, and a favorable climate. The Indians, though ever present, were pacified by force that permitted the English population to grow in numbers and prosper.

In the meantime, the English empire had expanded in size. Colonies were founded on Caribbean isles and into the area of present-day New England. An empire had taken form while Virginia and Maryland were developing, and to New England's colonization we now turn.

3

The New England Colonies

Cod, herring, and mackerel were the symbols of early New England in the years before 1620 when wilderness conditions were breached occasionally by fishing villages. The Bible, church, and minister shared honors with the fish after 1620 when thousands of godly men and women sought refuge on those northern shores. The fishing banks extended from Cape Cod to Newfoundland and were valuable assets for merchant companies whose ships regularly plied those waters. Fishing stations for many years were maintained along the coast to salt and dry fish in preparation for the long voyage to markets in Europe. Since the work was seasonal, only a few men stayed through the winter, and little food was grown in the villages.

Fishing took many men annually to New England, but land promoters occasionally wanted to combine fishing and colonization. About the same time as the expedition to Virginia in 1606, the Plymouth Company sent out an expedition to the Sagadahoc River in Maine. The specific promoters, George Popham and Raleigh Gilbert, collected colonists for a settlement which would combine fishing and agriculture to support it. Poor management, the death of Popham, and bad weather led to the failure of the enterprise. Sir Ferdinando Gorges, however, in association with merchants from Bristol and Plymouth, tried to develop fishing stations and spent a fortune between 1608 and 1620 in exploration and colonization, which brought him little or no return in spite of great efforts. He then reorganized the Plymouth Company, calling it the Council of New England, and made its principal business the selling of land grants. His plans were spacious and feudal, with vast baronies and manors for sale and designs for towns and cities. His need for money, however, limited his promotion, and suspicion and distrust ruined the project.

Through the years stations, or outposts, dotted the rocky coast, sometimes without Gorges' knowledge. These were primarily inhabited by fishermen or by English gentlemen with servants. Those at Hull, Lynn, Cape Ann, and Piscataqua were fishing posts which had some permanent buildings, but the one at Wessagussett (Weymouth) was founded unsuccessfully many times. The village at Mount Wollaston, established by Thomas Morton to trade with the Indians, gained notoriety in Puritan histories. Apparently the inhabitants tolerated loose living and pagan customs such as dancing around a maypole and renaming the village Merry Mount.

Plymouth Colony

The most enduring of all these early villages was Plymouth, which has come down in American tradition as the township that inspired Thanksgiving Day, the family holiday of reverence to God for the gifts of the harvest and abundant life. Plymouth hoped to support itself by fishing and the fur trade, and the venture was financed in part by the Plymouth Company. The English backers of the colony were led by Thomas Weston, merchant and ironmonger, and a group of London merchants who included John and Abraham Peirce. They planned a plantation within the territory of the Virginia Company, and upon the advice of a religious group in London called Separatists who wanted to leave the state church, they contacted in Leiden similar religious folk who were restless under Dutch rule.

These Separatists in Holland had originally gathered at the manor house of Scrooby on the road between London and Edinburgh. Pressure to conform under pain of arrest, however, forced these farmers to leave England in 1608. In Leiden they gathered in the congregation of John Robinson and attracted such practical men as William Bradford to be their leaders. As craftsmen and petty merchants they found places to work in the city, but for all sorts of reasons including cultural differences they became dissatisfied. The overtures of the London merchants, therefore, were timely and attractive. The negotiations brought the formation of a joint stock company in which they promised their labor as partners in the enterprise. The London merchants provided the group with transportation, laws of their own, freedom to worship, and the promise of a godly life, in exchange for their work as farmers, fur trappers, and fishermen.

Preparations were completed for the use of two ships, but the

The *Mayflower*. Engraving published 1905 by John Lowell and Co. *(Library of Congress)*

Speedwell was unseaworthy and the *Mayflower* was small. The party trimmed its size and 149 passengers and crew packed into the *Mayflower* for a voyage that took sixty-five storm-tossed days. Only four passengers died at sea, but many were weakened in health and once ashore fell victims to scurvy and winter cold.

The landfall at Cape Cod in November 1620 presented problems of charter rights. The winter was already too bitter, and the passengers decided to ask their merchant associates in London to secure permission from the Council of New England to settle there. For the present, the passengers pledged themselves in the now-famous Mayflower Compact to live in an orderly fashion under God and the king—to "Covenant and Combine ourselves into a Civil Body Politic." After choosing John Carver as their governor, they left the ship in parties to explore the surrounding country and selected in time a site for their village. Along a road running up from the sea, they allotted spaces for houses and gardens and built a warehouse. But not much could be done because the weather turned cold and sickness carried off almost half the settlers in the coming winter months. For the survivors hard work in 1621 followed. Houses were built, fields were planted, and the area was explored. With the help of a few Indians, they obtained a good harvest and welcomed a few more settlers.

Plymouth folk were humble people, lacking in education and capital, and the colony reflected this inheritance in its institutions, its poor harbors and land. Population thus grew slowly because the colony was off the beaten path of American migration and offered less than Massachusetts Bay and Connecticut. Townships developed, a representative assembly evolved, and a small colony of sturdy families took root. Its population stood at 300 in 1630, 3000 in 1660, and 13,000 in 1691. Through its years as an independent colony, Plymouth offered almost no formal education to its children, and none of its youth enrolled at Harvard College in nearby Massachusetts Bay Colony. Few people had university education, and in its leading township, Plymouth, there was no resident minister for many years before 1669.

Plymouth's relations with the London merchants soon proved to be unprofitable for both. Fishing and fur trapping were unsuccessful pursuits as moneymaking ventures. In breaking with their merchant supporters, the colonists were left on their own resources which, for most, meant lives as farmers. As their numbers grew, the people accepted the challenge and spread across Plymouth north from Barnstable to Scituate and westward to Taunton and Swansea. Founding small towns through the colony, they searched for the good land, exchanged it frequently for other land, and moved to neighboring towns. A restlessness was ever present among the people, but many collected pieces of land and found places to settle which apparently brought them satisfaction. They usually married in their mid-twenties, gave birth to large numbers of children, and lived rather long lives themselves. For males who survived childhood the mortality figures compare favorably with present figures in the United States. Complica-

Pilgrims signing compact on board the *Mayflower*. Engraving by Gauthier, 1857. *(Library of Congress)*

tions of childbirth reduced life expectancy for women below that of men, but women surviving into their sixties lived longer than men.

With families of seven and eight children surviving past their twenties, one wonders why the population did not grow faster than it did. But the population remained small and institutions were also simple. Self-government rested upon the *Mayflower Compact* and upon the merchant patent of 1630 which was obtained from the Council of New England. Actually government had no legal basis, but rested upon traditions and upon the implied consent of the kings. The freemen of the colony thus gained the privilege of electing the governor and other officials, and of making laws in the General Court. Two representatives from each town, sitting with the governor and assistants, debated the needs of the colony and put their agreements into the form of laws.

The governor for most of the years between 1621 and 1655 was William Bradford, who was only thirty-one when he succeeded John Carver. With men of noble stamp like William Brewster, Myles Standish, and Edward Winslow at his side, he made the important decisions for thirty-three years and kept the colony on its course. Bradford described these early years of Plymouth life in his *Of Plymouth Plantation*,

1620-1647, a remarkably beautiful, yet simple story of a brave people who ventured into the dangers of the western seas to find homes in a distant, isolated land. Bradford was a poet, too, and these few lines give a bit of the man's spirit:

> In wilderness he [God] did me guide,
> And in strange lands for me provide.
> In fears and wants, through weal and woe,
> A Pilgrim passed I to and fro.

The Massachusetts Bay Colonies

Unlike the Plymouth epic, the fishing station of Cape Ann and the village at Naumkeag (Salem) seem obscure today in telling the story of early New England. These posts, nonetheless, were the acorns of the movement that brought Puritans by the thousands to Massachusetts Bay. The founders of the Massachusetts Bay Company modeled their organization on the Virginia charter of 1612 and formed a corporation similar to a trading company. The governing body of the company (the General Court) consisted of a governor, his deputy, and eighteen assistants. The investors of the company were motivated by a mix of religion and commerce. Enough felt, however, that its charter should be taken to America so that the colony could be free from hostile influences in England.

Formation of the company took place in March 1629. Plans were then made for the migration of many people, for supplies, arms, manpower, books, and the distribution of lands for settlement. In the meantime, John Endicott had arrived at Salem with forty settlers and prepared for the coming of ships. The *George* was the first to arrive, bringing cattle; the *Talbot* and the *Lyon's Whelp* arrived a week or two later with their "cargo" of settlers. The newcomers immediately lent their help to building houses, tilling the soil, and planting crops. Morale was high and one minister declared New England to be "a more healthful place" than any other in the world.

In forming their church at Salem, the settlers gave thanks to God for the remarkably easy voyage to America. Almost no one fell seriously ill, and the seas were reasonably calm. Samuel Skelton and Francis Higginson became ministers of the church in Salem, and they and the congregation covenanted themselves to "walk together." Unlike the Pilgrims, these people were congregationalists, believers in the autonomy of the congregation and in a membership of God's elect. They wanted to create a holy society, a model of reform for decadent England—"a city upon a hill."

The Reformation had left a legacy of debate in England regarding the extent of reform that should be accepted by the Church of England. Elizabeth I had tried to find a compromise that kept most essentials of Catholicism—the mass, the sacraments, church organization, and tradition. It emphasized ritual, pageantry, and the church membership of all Englishmen. On these points Pilgrims and Puritans disagreed with the Church of England: both rejected the Book of Common Prayer, most sacraments, and the mass. The Pilgrims felt the Church of England was beyond reform, while the Puritans had hope, maybe only a forlorn hope, of changing the church. Both were Calvinists, believers in predestination and primitive Christianity, and advocates of a pure form of worship. Their interpretation of purity included emphasis upon the Bible, preaching, and a simple church interior and form of worship. Some hoped to change society, remove competition, and reduce the impact of a commercial society. Most were not united on these ideas of reform and faced a new problem in America of putting theory into practice.

The church in Salem was moderately separatist at its foundation. Congregation and ministers united to worship God, and their decisions set the pattern for the New England way. Their independence of the Church of England in worship, their emphasis upon the Bible as the rule of discipline, and their reliance upon preaching were certainly remarkably different from the mother church.

While these changes in the rule of worship may have disturbed the London company directors, the people who prepared for the voyage in England expected something like these practices when they came to America. In 1630, the first great wave of migration hit American shores. Under the leadership of John Winthrop of Groton, in Suffolk, a thousand passengers headed for Massachusetts Bay. The fleet, consisting of seven ships, left on March 29, 1630, with the Reverend John Cotton preaching the farewell sermon near the docks and John Winthrop carrying the charter to the American colony.

Winthrop, destined to be governor of Massachusetts Bay for many years, had attended Cambridge University, practiced law, held judicial offices, and managed estates. He was mild-mannered, deeply committed to Puritanism, and felt that there was danger for humankind in staying in England. He suffered much personal agony as he looked away from England's shores and to the promised land. He assured his wife, who remained behind, that he would think of her on "Mondays and Fridays at 5 of the clocke at night, . . . till we meet in person."

Meanwhile, Endicott and other Puritan leaders had explored the coast and decided upon a capital farther south than Salem. The peninsula of Charlestown seemed appropriate to some leaders, but Winthrop in 1630 first thought Newton would be better and then chose Shawmut (or Boston). Sickness was great in 1630 and 1631 when hundreds of people died from scurvy and other illnesses. The threat of famine, too, frightened many, and a few people returned to England instead of facing the peril. But relief ships brought lemon juice and supplies, and many people were heartened by the hand of God.

The need for a strong leader was apparent to Winthrop and the company assistants, and they enforced rules of behavior and put the people to work. Their problems were complicated by many things, not the least of which was the unfamiliarity of the landscape and the raw conditions of life. Most people did not know each other and were confronted with problems that were unusual and threatening to their lives. They built their homes poorly and their temporary houses often burned, sometimes destroying all their precious belongings. Other, wild-spirited folk molested the Indians, violated standards of decency, or broke regulations. Some of these people had to be whipped; one or two were banished. Winthrop ruled by divine inspiration in these emergencies and expected respect and obedience from the people as one's obligation to God. Since most settlers were Puritans or religious reformers, they accepted willingly the divine obligation. They pressed Winthrop, nevertheless, to transform company rule into representative institutions as quickly as possible. This pressure was such that he and the assistants moved to qualify males as freemen, to provide representatives in the General Court, to offer themselves for election, and to accept the necessity for laws passed by the freemen. This process was evolutionary, but the people were insistent upon a voice in their government. As regular meetings of the General Court (the legislature) were held, the problems that Winthrop and the assistants had to settle personally were now collectively discussed and given legislated solutions.

The Haven Ports

Charlestown and Boston were haven ports for the hundreds of people arriving each year. They tarried awhile in the ports until their leaders found a suitable place to migrate. With the help of the governor and assistants, town sites were selected, groups formed, and exploratory parties sent forth. One after another of the townships were founded, and people moved out to them. The process of selecting a hospitable place to live was often not easy, and families moved about until they discovered a congenial group. For most of the settlers life in the new townships frequently brought their first taste of harsh reality—if the ocean voyage had not done it previously—because they were now forced to cut trees, remove stones, and break the ground. For many this experience was a change of occupation from artisan or merchant to farmer. For all the frontier was a lesson in solitude and privation that surely must have tested the fiber of every person's character. Governor Bradford of Plymouth probably reported the complaints of many people when he found the mosquitos unbearable, the land barren, the water poor, and the country full of wolves and foxes.

The people organized themselves thus into communities in order to avoid the hardships of the frontier. They lived in clusters and went outside town centers to work on their farms. In the centers they had lots for gardens and minor pasturage, and built their homes along a street or two on which there was a meeting house and common conveniences such as a well, mill, and a blacksmith. Most villages were organized around the church, which some people joined while most at least attended services. The tone of church life varied from village to village, but depended upon the minister who had often accompanied townsmen from England. (In later years young men were drawn from Harvard or Yale colleges to be the ministers.) The minister and an elected group of advisers got religious and cultural activities underway in the new town as soon as possible.

Interpretation of the Bible was so important to these people that they sought ministers who provided satisfactory discipline and observance. For some settlers the need of special interpretations took them into the Connecticut Valley, to Rhode Island, or New Hampshire, or to town after town in Massachusetts Bay. What seems to be a small matter of interpretation to the modern mind was crucial to these early settlers. The result was, therefore, that most townsmen varied slightly in religious observance, and the variations often made the difference in their relations with the minister. Indeed, it determined even their willingness to formally join the church as members.

Most churches in New England in this settling time were Congregational and Puritan in form. The churches were literally meeting houses, and absent were those things traditionally associated with a church: the pulpit, special windows, instrumental music, particular furniture. Church services included hymns, but without accompaniment. The sermon was the major event of a Sunday morning, and it was generally directed to the understanding of a complicated biblical passage or to some observed weakness in community relations. There was much self-examination in the privacy of one's home, but frequently the careless were called forth before the congregation to repent of their sins.

The church service was indeed simple, though personal and communal in a soft blend of village piety. The only other part of the church was the school. It provided reading, thinking, and writing, and all young persons were given knowledge of the biblical story as soon as they were able to understand. Congregationalism emphasized the Bible as a key to one's heavenly future. The personal responsibility to study its meaning was ever present in the home and meetinghouse.

Congregationalism even in these remote villages had an imperative in its observance that determined the character of the people. Salvation was selective for everyone, and no one was ever certain if God had chosen him or her. A good life, hard work, successful pursuits, and insightful reading of the Bible may have been signs of God's working in humankind, but there was always a doubt. Life became a struggle for grace, perhaps for that chance to save one's soul. Salvation was not a matter of good works, but of grace that was not a reward for anything the human being could do.

Villagers were obviously God-driven persons. They gauged their successes and failures by the flow of grace. God was ever present in their lives to reward and punish, to approve and disapprove. Each day was a divine experience for which they thus kept diaries or notes on how they fared in their relations with God. The villagers offered prayers of thanksgiving, of humiliation, and of fasting and searched the heavens for signs of the divinity.

The villagers, too, thought of the material life and their relations with other human beings. Each of the tens of little townships quickly set up local government. Usually the people met a few times each year to handle problems, and one meeting in late March was selected for the election of town officials—selectmen, constables, tithing men, assessors, a clerk, and a treasurer—who carried on the formal affairs of the community. Another meeting in May sent a representative to their respective legislature in the capital at Boston, Hartford, or Providence. But life tended to be local in interests and problems so that the March elections for selectmen were often the most important events of the year. They set policy for the school, planned improvements on town buildings, or determined the tax rate. Sometimes nothing could be done to satisfy anyone, and they sent the issue to the legislature for mediation.

For many towns there was a second civil organization, the land proprietors, who distributed unused land. In the original settlement individuals often had shares of the landed area of the township. Since there was more land than anyone could use, the land was held in trust and distributed according to need and demand. Meetings of the proprietors occurred from time to time, and their decisions to offer land could add desirable people to the town and keep young people at home as residents. As the land was distributed, towns split into small parts, or people lacking new land went to nearby areas and began new towns.

The lands of New England differed greatly in fertility and utility. Farms along the Connecticut River were generally excellent, sometimes even in the meadows or between hills. Everywhere farming was hard work, however, because of rocks and brush, and clearing the land took years. After a few years of exertion with little improvement, the sons found work as fishermen or seamen, and the fathers searched their minds for something to diversify their labor. Many offered their labor as blacksmiths, tavern- or innkeepers, coopers, distillers of molasses, housewrights, and teachers.

The Early Years

During these hard years before 1660 population grew rapidly. The rush of people continued into the 1640s, bringing probably twenty thousand settlers. Then the Puritan Revolution in England reduced to a mere trickle the former flow of immigrants. The New England people were preoccupied themselves with their own doctrinal controversies and with problems of survival. In search of good land they spread through the coastal areas and along the rivers. The isolation apparently was extraordinarily beneficial, and few diseases reached epidemic levels. People lived longer than those packed into European cities, and the healthy diet and work were equally good. Families multiplied and enlarged. Even so, the early settlers were generally people in their thirties, a husband and wife, two children, and maybe a servant. In the first generation the multiplication of people would be limited by age and circumstances of settlement, but in generations to come the natural increase of families would be reflected in population growth.

Life in Boston had at first the sober quality of these Puritan immigrants. It was full of people waiting to leave for townships in rural and coastal sites. It was full of ships and their seamen along wharves, of ministers and merchants, and of some adventurous folk and misfits. Boston never developed into a holy city, a new Jerusalem, or a mecca because Puritanism failed to develop a new kind of society. Also Congregationalists looked to their local communities and suspected any other focus of religious inspiration. Nonetheless, Boston as the capital, then as the mart of New England, had great influence, and the leaders of some congregations like John Cotton and Richard Mather had a prominence among ministers that was well recognized.

Boston was frequently the hotbed of antagonisms. As center of the colony's government, the town witnessed the evolution of the legislature from the corporate body that had arranged the passage of people to New England to a primitive legislative body. Decisions by the assistants were made in 1630 that freemen should elect the officials and assistants of the colony, and in 1631 that all freemen must qualify as church members. Other decisions followed providing for the election of the governor by the representatives in the assembly, the full participation of the representatives in legislating taxes, and the separation of the upper and lower houses of the assembly in 1644. In the meantime, debate over what constituted the colony's laws brought forth a commission that studied the Bible, the Common Law, and English statutory law, and finally it came forth in 1648 with "The Book of Laws and Liberties Concerning the Inhabitants of Massachusetts." It modified English practice by limiting the number of death penalties and simplifying judicial procedures.

In the evolution of a civil commonwealth, the clergy had an important part, but they refrained from holding offices. They offered advice when asked (and often when not asked) and in general they insisted upon being supported in their endeavors to assure a reformed religious order in the colony. Civil authority made inquiry into the qualifications of the clergy, legislated against breaking the Sabbath, and passed laws from time to time declaring fast days and thanksgiving days. The line between the civil and religious authority was blurred; perhaps one could describe the line as one of cooperation in the general task of building a moral society.

Roger Williams

By the early 1640s Massachusetts had nearly forty churches and a large number of well-educated, outspoken ministers who were debating the nature of the "New England Way." All sorts of issues arose, but probably a most interesting situation occurred when clergy turned upon each other as they struggled to test the true meaning of the Bible. Roger Williams' ideas caused the first great dispute. Beginning in 1631 when he arrived in the colony, Williams attracted people to him because of his personality and intellect. He was first invited to be a teacher in the Boston congregation of John Wilson who was returning to England for his family. Williams put conditions on his acceptance: the congregation had to break ties with the Church of England and declare itself a Separatist church. Philosophically it was a large matter for both parties, but when the congregation refused, Williams journeyed to Salem to fill a vacancy in that church, then to

Plymouth, and finally back to Salem where he served for a short time again as an occasional preacher.

When the minister of the Salem church died, the members called Williams as their pastor. His possible succession attracted the attention of the clergy and members of the General Court because he was constantly raising issues that were irritating and inflammatory. He had questioned the legal basis of the charter by asserting that title to land originally belonged to the Indians. He also questioned fundamental biblical concepts about the power of the civil magistrate to become involved in religious matters. And he asserted that the magistrate must not tender oaths to those not members of the church. But more extreme, he questioned whether God's elect should pray with those not yet members of a church.

Williams' habit of drawing interpretations to their ultimate meaning excited many people, but none more than the members of the legislature, who now summoned him to make personal explanations. Threats by members and stubbornness on the part of Williams resulted in the withdrawal of the pastorate in Salem and Williams' banishment to England. Illness and fear of politics at home forced him in 1636 to escape southward to Rhode Island.

Anne Hutchinson and Robert Child

In the meantime, the colony was aroused by Anne Hutchinson, who arrived in 1634 with her husband William and some members of her large family. Like Williams, Anne was an attractive, inquiring person. As a midwife she gave resumés of the Sunday sermons to other women, particularly of those sermons given by her friend John Cotton. On difficult points, she added her own explanations, sometimes insights that were more exciting religiously than the original. Soon she drew men as well as women to her meetings, which were so popular that the room was often packed.

These sessions may have wrinkled a forehead or two and shook a head, but they were generally inoffensive to most people since lay leaders were welcomed in the church. Unfortunately, Anne's ideas clashed with those of the crusty and dogmatic John Wilson, an old-fashioned hell-raiser who had recently returned from England. She sensed error in his sermons when he urged public morality and repentance, practices that seemed like a covenant of works. The sermons raised the question of preparation to gain God's grace. Was it permissible, and how much was effective?

Anne Hutchinson in time became a critic of other ministers. Her audience broadened when important leaders joined her discussions and when she visited some of the neighboring churches. Rumor spread, too, that she was voicing the opinions of John Cotton, the colony's distinguished cleric. Her position hardened to include an attack upon all the clergy save Cotton and John Wheelwright (her brother-in-law). They were guilty, she said, of preaching a covenant of works, not of grace, and falling into the error of popery. Her emphasis was upon salvation as a mystical experience, as an inward dwelling of the Holy Spirit that bypassed the institutions of church and state. She grew more outrageous to the clergy, moreover, as she developed her thoughts, particularly when she cast doubts on their own justification and when her followers refused to listen to pastor John Wilson's sermons.

The inflammation spread widely, touched Cotton and Wheelwright, and the legislature felt the need of a day of fast and prayer. The elections of 1637 brought orthodox John Winthrop back into office and unseated many officials as well as the governor. Immediately steps were taken by the victors to stamp out what they considered a great contagion. A synod was called at Newtown in August, and clergy even from Connecticut attended. The clergy collected some eighty-two errors and refuted them. The legislature then brought judicial proceedings against many of Anne Hutchinson's followers and sentences of banishment were passed. Mrs. Hutchinson was charged, questioned, and also banished. Most of her followers within the year left for Rhode Island or New Hampshire.

These serious attacks on orthodoxy were soon followed by others. Dr. Robert Child, a Presbyterian, urged the colony to adopt the rules and practices of his faith in England. As victors in the English political struggle with King Charles I, the Presbyterians had abolished the episcopacy and set up a parish concept of church membership which seemed appropriate for New England. Child and his friends then drew up a Remonstrance in which they complained about the limited church membership of Congregationalism, the narrow franchise, and the lack of a printed body of laws, and urged reform. They planned, if remedy was not forthcoming, to take their grievances to Parliament.

The legislature quickly reacted and called Child and others before it. Bonds to guarantee good conduct were required, but when two of the accused refused, they were jailed, and court action was taken to fine all of the remonstrants. Some escaped, but Child was severely fined and his papers seized. But his appeal in England was ignored as the nation was threatened by another civil war, as the English army, under the command of Oliver Cromwell, moved to unseat the Presbyterians.

The unrest in Massachusetts continued, nonetheless. Those of a Baptist mind drifted with Williams to Rhode Island where a church was founded in 1639. Those remaining at home were required to attend

Sunday sermons, but many people declined to seek church membership. Orthodoxy was not defined, except as John Cotton, Richard Mather, and others described the New England way in their writings or sermons. The General Court in 1646 decided, therefore, to assemble the ministers and ask them to issue a document on worship and discipline. For Congregationalists this invitation seemed contrary to the spirit of their church. But for harmony's sake they outlined the current system of church government and suggested ways by which church members and civil magistrates could work for consensus. Two years would pass before the document was drawn, but they were unable to handle the problems of baptism for children of members and other pressing issues of membership. The Cambridge Platform of 1648, which was the formal name of the document, became a statement of faith for the people and formalized relationships between church and state.

During these years of settlement crisis after crisis was met by John Winthrop and his colleagues. Winthrop showed a remarkable ability to weather attacks and keep the colony directed toward his goal of a stable society. His was a commitment to government that was not accountable to anyone but God; with much discretionary power from the legislature, he had to battle constantly ministers and deputies who wanted to share his rule. They forced his hand occasionally, and Winthrop modified his tactics, too, when pressure was great. To his credit, nonetheless, in a period of transition and development he gave the colony firm leadership. His government was simple, practical, and responsive, but it was a despotism "with all the efficiency of a despotism."

Before Winthrop died in 1649, the colony had made remarkable progress toward understanding the relation of Puritanism to law and of Puritanism to commerce. Puritan theories of a new kind of society were modified gradually. Law was resembling England's; commerce included competition and a search for profits. Boston was taking on the form of a trading city and her people were becoming shopkeepers. New leaders were taking over, and they wanted to increase church membership and widen the franchise.

Some elements of stability were obvious to everyone. The original population was multiplying at a good rate in spite of Indian troubles and frontier hardships. Probably 15,000 people were living in New England by 1641, perhaps 40,000 by 1665. Towns were developing rapidly, with more than thirty of them fully established in 1645. The population was well-educated by the standards of the day; one in every forty had a university degree and half the men had some form of apprenticeship. In maintaining this expertise, the colony quickly reacted to the threat of its isolation and in the late 1630s planned the college at Cambridge, which was named Harvard in honor of its first donor. In 1647 the legislature required the towns to provide some basic education for all children. Most families, moreover, had by that time taken steps to educate the youth and to ensure that the cultural memory of England remained alive in their households.

Under Henry Dunster the college developed a curriculum that resembled those of Oxford and Cambridge in England. Entrance requirements included the translation of Cicero at sight and a knowledge of Greek grammar. A memorized piece from a Latin poet or prose writer was also expected. In the first year students spent their time on logic and the classics; the second year, on Aristotle; and the third, on mathematics and astronomy. Some history, physics, and other subjects were available, depending upon the talents of the teachers. Dunster added a fourth year of study in 1653 so that one or two oriental languages, among other subjects, could be offered.

Harvard students then as now were a lively group, but Dunster had the whip to curb mischief and other forms of punishments to dampen the spirit. From his popularity one suspects that Dunster tolerated much and that the poets, teachers, ministers, and public leaders who graduated from Harvard during his fourteen years as president were a tribute to his guidance. Students entered college at the age of sixteen and a half years, lived at or near the college during their time at school, and were warmly welcomed into the community four years later at a spring commencement. The ceremony, feast, and joys of that day brought teachers, ministers, and colony officials together in a unique event of pageantry and color.

Five of the nine students who were graduated in 1642 became clergymen, but only a few remained in Massachusetts to establish a career. George Downing—famed in history for the street named after him—rose to be influential in English politics, but his choice of causes earned him the title years later of "Scoundrel" by John Adams. Both Henry Saltonstall and Tobias Barnard died in obscurity. Only William Hubbard won a reputation that reflected the effort of a college degree. His history of New England and narrative of Indian relations were certainly not brilliant pieces, but he served as an influential minister at Ipswich for over forty years.

The replenishing of the scholarly community depended upon Harvard College in the second and third generations. Classes grew slightly in size, students diversified their choices of careers, and a few went to England for additional study. Books flowed into the colony in good numbers, and Harvard's library, for example, increased its holdings by the hundreds. Since Puritans apparently enjoyed sermons, that form of literature multiplied in bulk over the years. The college received a printing press in the 1640s, and the Harvard press on demand put out almanacs, psalm books, and other legal and biblical publications. The now-famous *Bay Psalm Book* of 1640 was its first publication.

Intellectual activity in New England was limited, however, to a very small group of people. Most people were trying to combat the wilderness and survive. The ministers as a group were unique in this society because they accepted the task of making Puritanism rational to the frontier society. They met the daily problems, offered rational explanations, debated theological positions, and interpreted history in light of present-day circumstances. As religious leaders they worried about secularism, sin, a lack of fervor, and God's relations with the colony. Their explanations provided a literature for colleagues to study and debate. Such questions as infant baptism, the enlargement of church membership, and toleration of sects were issues that occupied clerical time and energy.

The Colonies in Connecticut

During these years of discussion Puritan divines and their congregations spread through New England and established colonies and towns. Sometimes settlers left Massachusetts in search of good land; at other times they sought a haven to worship as they wished. Connecticut was a popular area, but title to the land was unclear until the General Court made a formal grant of authority to prospective settlers in 1636. About that time John Winthrop, Jr., laid out a town at the mouth of the Connecticut River at what is now Saybrook. He declared himself governor of the territory as representative of a group of English promoters. Also Thomas Hooker, John Haynes, and Samuel Stone accepted Winthrop's claim and were readying themselves for the move to the Connecticut valley. The grant by the General Court recognized, it seems, a reality. The move to the forested valley quickened until towns at Windsor, Wethersfield, Hartford, and Springfield were founded. A legislature was soon convened to make the preliminary rules for the territory. In May Thomas Hooker and one hundred members of his congregation in Cambridge moved across Massachusetts toward Hartford, their cattle before them and wagons filled with possessions at their side.

For these settlers in the valley, daily life was immediately complicated by threats of a bloody Indian war. The Pequots assaulting Wethersfield and Saybrook killed nearly thirty people in 1636 and 1637. Though Puritan volunteers under John Endicott tried to mediate, their efforts were futile as the Pequots continued to raid settlements along the coast. Attacks, counterattacks, and retaliatory attacks with unusual harshness pitted Indian against Indian and Indian against white man. In one village about five hundred Indians were burned to death.

The settlers were frightened, but not shaken, by the Pequot War and its horrible end. The Pequots, in moving down the Connecticut Valley, had alienated other Indian tribes and were themselves aggressive and hard to live with. Once the Pequots were obliterated as a power, white relations with the other Indians were calm for forty years, allowing the English townships to develop in population and prosperity.

The township leaders met in 1639 (with Springfield absent because of a disagreement) to form a stable government. Much discussion had occurred about their relations with other governments in New England, but at the insistence of Thomas Hooker the delegates drew up in a few weeks a constitution which became known as the Fundamental Orders. Like the other New England governments, it provided for a legislature, governor, and popular franchise, with the stipulation that only men who were "godly" could participate in the government. The General Court had more power than its counterparts elsewhere, and had the right to dissolve or prorogue itself. The colony, in a practical sense, was republican in institutions and free from English supervision.

Under the Fundamental Orders settlers probably enjoyed a bit more liberty than those living in Massachusetts Bay. The franchise was broader, the General Assembly had more authority, and governors had less power because they could not succeed themselves. The towns of Connecticut remained isolated by forests, but the population moved into the unsettled areas along the river and absorbed Saybrook and English towns on Long Island. New Haven, however, stayed out of the union until 1664.

While the river communities grew, John Davenport and Theophilus Eaton gathered people for a town. Both had experience escaping punishment for nonconformity in England, and both were anxious for a haven that would reflect their religious views. On the Quinnipiac River in 1638 they found such a place. Buying the land from the Indians, they distributed town lots and dug cellars as their first residences. In time one hundred or more people moved to New Haven, formed a government, and invited neighboring communities to join them. Their association was relatively loose, but held together by a code of laws and a desire for trade. Merchants promoted trade with New York and sent an expedition to the Delaware River, where its efforts enjoyed limited successes. The colony had no hinterland, little industry and manufacturing, and no capital. Unlike Boston its merchants were unable to lay the basis for any extensive trade.

New Haven lingered into the 1660s as a colony. Its people prospered in agriculture, but there was discontent over the political order. Some townspeople denounced their government as tyrannical and suffered repression for their efforts. Heavy fines, oaths of loyalty, and bonds for good conduct were annoying, and in the end the inhabitants permitted Connecticut to absorb them.

During these years Connecticut owed much to the younger Winthrop, who went to England in 1660 when Charles II ascended the throne. He labored for several years to gain recognition for Connecticut as an independent colony under its constitution of 1639. He succeeded finally in getting all the essentials of home rule in a charter in exchange for a recognition by Connecticut of royal sovereignty. That success in 1662 led to the annexation of New Haven, because Connecticut was then in a legal position to take over the tiny colony without much opposition from England.

Rhode Island

Threatened, too, in 1660 was Rhode Island's charter. The colony had much internal dissension since its founding and lacked the strength and vitality of Massachusetts. Too many separate factions drifted south from Massachusetts, and none was willing to honor very long the other's ideas or the good of the whole.

Roger Williams reached the Narragansett in the cold of winter in 1636 and stayed with the friendly Indians until the spring thaw, when he completed the purchase of Indian land on the Sekonk River. With six companions he investigated an excellent site, but was warned off by agents of Plymouth colony. Moving then to the Great Salt River, he found a good place on the eastern shore which he called Providence. Soon Williams and his companions were joined by families and sympathizers from Massachusetts, and a town took form.

Providence had the advantage of an outlet to the Atlantic, but the early settlers turned to agriculture instead of commerce. Some grew tobacco and raised sheep, while subsistence agriculture was the pursuit of most. People were poor so that there were few tools and little household furnishings available, and families were so busy taking care of their needs that few community improvements were completed. Government, therefore, was meager, with Williams insisting that people live by majority rule in civil matters and refrain from interfering in religious matters. He insisted, too, that the colony's doors be always open to the oppressed, and in that spirit he welcomed the Hutchinsons in 1638.

Just after Anne Hutchinson and her husband arrived at Providence, William Coddington, one of the Hutchinsons' friends, accompanied a group of settlers by boat to the town. Inviting the Hutchinsons to join them, Coddington and the other settlers moved almost immediately to Aquidneck Island lying between Narragansett Bay and the Sakonnet River. On the north end of the island they established what became Portsmouth. Others joined them in seeking a haven from persecution. Not the least was Samuel Gorton, who was crusty, hardheaded, and difficult to manage. At first Coddington and the Hutchinsons shared in the direction of their settlement, but neither could long tolerate the views of the others, and Coddington and his friends then moved to the southern part of Aquidneck where they laid out the plantation of Newport in 1639.

Coddington urged a union of the two towns and succeeded until 1680 in maintaining a loose association. Unfortunately, in Portsmouth the Hutchinsons and Gorton quarreled, and both groups eventually had to leave the town. Gorton, in fact, was banished for his turbulent conduct, and he joined friends in Pawtuxet where he ran into more controversy. The Arnolds, Benedict and William, were not happy about having Gorton in Pawtuxet as their leader, and they secured help from Massachusetts authorities and the Indians to apply sufficient pressure. Forced to travel further south, Gorton founded a town at Shawomet (Warwick) where he was the center of bitterness for years. The Hutchinsons in the search for peace would travel finally to an isolated part of Long Island Sound, in Pelham Bay, where she and five of her children were tomahawked to death by Indians in 1643.

So Rhode Island and the plantations were founded by people with strong personalities, at least by people who valued home rule in opposition to a larger colonial base. The problems of local rule grew more serious each year. Both Massachusetts and Plymouth claimed parts of the colony. Williams in Providence apparently understood the problem sufficiently to make a trip to England in 1640 and apply for a patent. His relations with the religious independents were congenial, and he returned quickly to New England with a patent that protected Providence, Newport, and Portsmouth. Warwick was later construed to be included in the patent.

Though the settlers did not act immediately to put their new authority into practical use, in 1647 they called a general assembly to meet at Providence, and four towns sent delegates. After much discussion they adopted a constitution that provided for a popular, if impotent, assembly. Because the delegates feared strong government like that of Massachusetts, they vested the towns with power to initiate bills and power to ratify them. In short, the colony became a loose confederation that created a debating society of sixteen representatives at its head. The constitution, representing Roger Williams' cherished ideas, made certain that the civil government was based upon consent and the assembly concerned itself with civil matters. The code of laws ended with this ringing declaration: "lett the Saints of the Most High walk in this Colonie without Molestation in the name of Jehovah, their God forever and ever."

The colony had good principles, but they were not molded into a structure. Coddington immediately opposed the union and eventually succeeded in getting an English charter for Aquidneck that set it up as a separate township. The threat of disintegration of the colony was great enough for Williams and John Clarke to return to London in 1651. Their voyage was unbelievably rough and it foreshadowed, if that is possible, the debates for a cancellation of Coddington's charter. In the end, hearings before the Council of State, publications, and the help of their friends brought success and the opportunity for Williams to leave for Providence. Clarke would continue to fight in London for ten more years until Rhode Island received a new charter. Still the victory against Coddington did not bring unity to the colony. Years of argument would be waged over title to lands, boundaries, and the claims of petty men. Fortunately, in 1663 Clarke won the help of John Winthrop, Jr., who secured a new charter from Charles II. The charter did not quiet all the discordant voices of Rhode Island Puritans, but some peace at least did come to the land.

Since 1620 New England had developed into a land of small townships, relying upon small-farm agriculture, fishing, and trade by sea. Population reached approximately 40,000 by 1660 and was destined to increase substantially because of large families, a low death rate, healthful conditions, and a good diet. It was a homogeneous population made up of nearly all Protestants and Englishmen. They were Puritans, too, believing in the simplicity of church institutions, in individual responsibility, and in hard work. They were a people with families, homes, and property, and an abiding faith in God. Finally, they were developing civil institutions that provided for self-government, in that legislatures made the laws, officials administered them, and courts enforced them. England seemed far away as these colonies developed their institutions and governed themselves.

4

England's Neighbors in America

About three decades before Englishmen planted their settlements in present-day Connecticut, Dutchmen had entered the Hudson River. Under the captaincy of Henry Hudson, an adventurous Englishman in the Dutch service, these seamen sailed the *Half Moon* first into the Delaware Bay and New York Bay, then up the great river. Some exploration was completed of the mouth of the Hudson River and of Manhattan Island, but little more was done before the group returned to England as the storms of fall broke in late 1609. Hudson remembered particularly the river that bears his name as the finest to "be found, wide and deep, with good anchoring ground on both sides."

The Dutch merchants were interested in finding a northwest passage to the Pacific Ocean and to the trade of China. Their plans for Hudson would have taken him into Arctic waters, but the frozen entrances to straits and rough water encouraged him to shift his plans for exploration to the south. These activities eventually aroused some business people in Amsterdam and Hoorn, and they organized the United Netherlands Company in 1614. Their objective in sponsoring voyages was to collect information, but trade, furring, and anything else that would bring profits would also be entertained. Only four voyages were financed before a change in home government brought cancellation of the charter. Into power came the promoter, William Usselinx, who urged the settlement of Dutchmen in America for reasons of trade, riches, and new products. Enough information was available concerning New Netherland to encourage Usselinx and his friends to back further exploration. In place of the old company they chartered in 1621 a most powerful mercantile group, which was given a wide expanse of territory to exploit. That new association of merchants, the Dutch West India Company, had the authority to exploit any area from Newfoundland to the tip of South America, plus the coastal waters of southwest Africa. A group of nineteen merchants, mostly drawn from the Amsterdam Chamber of Commerce, directed company affairs. Their focus in 1624 was upon the conquest of Brazil, but they shipped a few Walloon families and other settlers to Fort Orange (Albany) and Fort Nassau (near Philadelphia). Colonists before 1628 scattered to various places, but their major settlement became New Amsterdam when company orders drew many people into that area.

Probably 270 people were settled in New Amsterdam by 1628 and a few more were residents of the forts. Population remained precariously small, nonetheless, because harsh Indian relations and company policy limited migration. Around New Amsterdam there was an appearance of prosperity. Wheat, corn, and rye flourished, and fairly large shipments of grain were exported by 1626. Exports increased yearly, perhaps to as much as 125,000 guilders of grain in 1632. Cattle breeding also flourished. Still, profits for the company were reduced by the expenses of garrisons and supplies and by the inexperience of officials who often were responsible for poor trading policies with the Indians. Losses mounted and threatened the company's existence.

A crisis in 1628 finally forced the company to open up the territory to the enterprise of individuals. Large acreage was offered to anyone who would settle sixty people. These patrons would have feudal rights on their property and trading privileges along the Atlantic coast. Five patroonships were eventually established, with kingly estates and much encouragement from the company, but only the one owned by Kiliaen Van Rensselaer was modestly successful. His success was undoubtedly the result of his continued residence in Amsterdam. Both ingenious and energetic in his plans, Van Rensselaer supplied his patroonship and maintained a small flow of settlers to the area, but like his fellow patroons he could neither keep the workers tilling the farm nor the poachers off his property.

The colony languished because of restrictions on trade and heavy overhead costs. But individuals seemed to have done very well trading in the tobacco market of Virginia or peddling products to settlers along the coasts of New England. Voyages by private merchants were not regular, but chartered ventures. Risks for them were great, with insurance rates eating into profits. Sometimes smuggled furs and tobacco helped to defray costs of the voyage and guaranteed the venture some success. Over the years good tobacco and furs found markets in northern Europe and invited merchants to make additional voyages.

To encourage commerce the company abandoned its fur trade monopoly in 1639 and put William Kieft in office as the director. While Kieft proved to be a disaster as director because of his personal habits, the end of the monopoly encouraged some Dutch merchants to compete for colony trade. In a short time they turned the fur trade into a profitable one and sought cargoes of tobacco from Virginia. Both the Gillis family enterprise and the Van Rensselaers used wealth, shipping, and influence to their advantage and made profits from low margins. Their successes probably delayed the demise of the West Indian Company and encouraged its directors to find a stronger leader than Kieft to handle business in New Amsterdam.

Peter Stuyvesant

In selecting Peter Stuyvesant in 1647, who was then governor of Curacao, the directors chose a most successful and able leader to govern the New Netherland and emphasized to the merchant community at the same time the seriousness of colony affairs. Stuyvesant, known in history for his one leg and bittersweet disposition, turned his attention quickly to reform, and he arranged for the election of an advisory council. Over the years he took their advice when it agreed with his own opinions; otherwise he rejected it, sometimes in the form of violent outbursts of temper. The colonists ultimately wanted the elimination of company rule and control over local affairs, but they had little hope of such institutions under Dutch colonialism. For many the taxes seemed unfair, the governor outrageous, and the company backward. They looked, perhaps, for an English takeover of the territory.

As bad as conditions were in New Netherland, conditions were even worse along the Delaware Bay where Sweden had planted a colony in 1638. Her West India Company sent two ships to the bay, the *Key of Calmar* and the *Griffin*, plus Peter Minuit. This former director of New Netherland, an energetic man with considerable ability, found a good site for Fort Christina and the beginning of a fur trade. He also tried to remove the Dutch from Fort Nassau, but neither he nor the Dutch had sufficient power to hurt the other. Minuit was unable to remain long in the Delaware if he were going to purchase a cargo of Virginia tobacco and avoid the storms of the Atlantic passage. He left twenty-three settlers at the new fort and the promise of early reinforcements.

The second expedition of the *Key of Calmar* entered the Delaware River in 1640 under the command of Peter Ridder, who brought additional settlers and plans for an enlarged colony. He was also interested in the fur trade and loaded a cargo of furs by the time the ship returned to

Europe in May 1641. Swedish desire for furs dominated activity as additional posts were established at the falls of the Delaware and in the interior. Some farming, however, was encouraged to provide food for the growing population that reached 400 in the mid-1640s. Under Governor John Prinz, a man of great physical strength, the colony was given energetic leadership. The Lutheran Church became the official religion of the colony, and much was done to bring in supplies and create conditions that would lift the spirits of the settlers. The Swedish government took direct control of the colony and for some years, in the late 1640s, tried to mollify the Dutch. The population, instead of growing, decreased sharply and was not more than one hundred in the early 1650s. The risk of attack from the Dutch became a possibility.

Under Stuyvesant the Dutch again became aggressive. More settlers arrived at Fort Nassau, and in 1651 the governor founded Fort Casimir down the bay from Fort Christina and brought some cannon for its defense. These threats from the Dutch were doubly serious when Sweden failed to reinforce the area from 1647 to 1653 and Prinz in disgust left for home. In absolute desolation the colony was suddenly revived by new colonists in 1653 and by the leadership of a new governor, Johann Rising. Instead of being a blessing, however, the pressure upon supplies was too great and the colony faced acute starvation.

In this crisis Rising did the unexpected by attacking Fort Casimir and inviting retaliation from the angry Dutch. The Dutch had long awaited an opportunity to remove this impediment to their occupation of the whole Delaware region, and hit back quickly with a superior force. They then incorporated the Swedes into their own struggling venture.

Bringing additional Swedes into the motley collection of peoples that lived in the New Netherland was no great issue, and Stuyvesant urged these Swedes to remain in their homes and live under Dutch rule. The colony had always had much trouble attracting settlers and had received almost anyone who would take up land. Their need was great because raids had decimated the population in the 1640s, when nearly a dozen Algonquin tribes swept down upon settlements on the Raitan River and in the New Haven Colony, perhaps killing as many as two thousand people. Villages had been reduced to ashes, and Indians, too, were set upon and slain by the hundreds until in some places their blood reddened the snow.

Such carnage slowed the development of the colony and dealt a near-fatal blow. The population was reduced by half, but also villages were burned, cattle was destroyed, and trade was disrupted. In the next decade the population again advanced, reaching nearly 5,000 people; in New England the number of settlers was now five times greater, and a thousand or more were settling in Long Island and entering New Amsterdam as traders.

Reaction of the newcomers to Dutch rule was often hostile, and they joined discontented Dutch settlers who had also urged greater participation in their government than Stuyvesant was willing to give. Some spoke openly of England's taking over the colony and although they found much support, no one raised a hand. The opportunity came, however, in 1663 when ministers of Charles II, with the help of his brother James, the Duke of York, persuaded the king to seize the territory, and members of Parliament joined in the plan by pledging even their own resources.

All considered this enterprise to be a retaking of English land and congratulated themselves on the brilliancy of the idea. The expedition was thus easily financed, and the Duke of York was awarded the territory as a proprietorship even before the completion of the conquest. Four frigates entered the harbor in August 1664, and the sight of such an awesome force compelled submission. By September a treaty was signed, a new administration took over, and New Amsterdam became New York City. The Dutch colonists went back to their country houses and trading was resumed, now within the English empire. During this crisis Connecticut had claimed Long Island, where John Winthrop led two hundred men against the islanders; but Winthrop was not willing to press the colony's aspirations when he learned of the king's plans for New Amsterdam.

French Canada

While the Dutch were developing their colony along the Hudson River, the French had a river of their own to explore and on July 3, 1608 had planted a tiny settlement at Quebec. The leader of this expedition was Samuel de Champlain, a man of inordinate curiosity who was patriotic, daring, and talented. Though Quebec struggled for survival that first winter, Champlain established it as a base for Indian trade and moved deep on both sides of the river in search of trade alliances. Quebec in Champlain's eyes was a wonderful place for a base, not only for the heights of Cape Diamond that provided control of the St. Lawrence River, but for the depth of a great river that provided easy communication with the distant Atlantic.

Even so, Frenchmen were not interested in Canada for settlement, and furring did not offer enough return to make substantial investment advisable. Quebec was left to struggle in search of economic support, and from 1629 to 1632 it actually fell into the conquering hands of Englishmen. Restored to France by the Treaty of St. Germain, Quebec lingered without much character or purpose in spite of Champlain's efforts to publicize its importance. By 1632, he counted only thirty people who were permanent residents.

To save the struggling colony the French government gave the Hundred Associates a monopoly of trade in America and a free hand in developing Canada, save that they were to bring out annually a few hundred people and to have within fifteen years 4000 permanent residents living in the territory. With help from the aged Champlain and rich merchants and financiers, the Associates tried to get their enterprise going, but the lack of government support and willing settlers and Champlain's death left the colony in crisis. In 1640, there were no more than 200 settlers living in the territory, and the Associates in France were unwilling to risk any more money. Happily, in this time of desperation, French religious groups were attracted to the area as a mission field. The challenge was even more than they could anticipate because of a rising Indian peril which threatened bodily harm, perhaps presented a martyr's death. With great zeal many Jesuits and other religious persons left for Quebec.

Undoubtedly both the prayers and sacrifices of these persons and a change of direction in French policy brought the reexamination of colonial affairs that occurred in 1660. In despair the Hundred Associates freely relinquished their charter to the government which, in turn, accepted responsibility for ruling the area. The minister of finance, Jean Baptiste Colbert, felt that the future greatness of France depended upon overseas expansion and empire and that Quebec should be part of those plans.

Though Colbert would experiment for a time by using a chartered company, which proved also to be unsuccessful, he eventually brought into Quebec experienced soldiers who built forts and checked Indian raids. Breaking up the immediate resistance of the Indians, the troops ranged widely in putting the country into civilian hands and leaving a series of alliances which assured peace for a few decades. In the 1670s the government established a royal colony which vested all authority in a Sovereign Council of five officials—religious, civilian, and military. No popular participation was recognized by the government as advisable or necessary. Indeed, the first governor general was plainly told not to call an estates-general because it was against royal policy at home. For all practical purposes, daily government was in the hands of the governor, bishop, and intendant, and the Supreme Council held all administrative, judicial, and legislative power when decisions of policy were required. The king, however, made it plain that he held the ultimate authority.

Too much can be made of this concentration of power because

Quebec was plainly struggling to survive. Officials optimistically searched for ways to entice people to live in Canada, and achieved some remarkable success. Between 1660 and 1775 approximately four thousand people arrived in Quebec; most were subsidized with transportation and land and then encouraged to marry and have large families. Population rose quickly and more than doubled by 1675, when it reached seven thousand people. By the end of the century the population had not only maintained itself, but had risen to 15,255, which was a good increase considering wars with the Iroquois and the privations of the frontier.

During these years Montreal, Three Rivers, and Quebec developed as thriving centers of trade and settlement. They were tiny islands, nonetheless, of civilization on the banks of the St. Lawrence River, which expanded inward and along the river as settlers broke the land and built their homes. A flourishing family life developed, influenced by Catholic and French traditions and surrounding a parish church which encouraged music, pageantry, and piety. Outside these tiny towns the government had awarded much land to seigniors, who were intended to develop as landed aristocrats and who would bring in colonists as their tenants. The system did not produce a feudal system nor did it attract to the colony the wealthy of France. But it gave a character and style to colonization. Those seigniors living close to the centers of commerce were able in time to prosper from their privileges, and the system did provide social distinction between seignior and tenant. The church, too, held lands as a seignior and tried to put settlers upon them, but its success was relatively modest considering the extent of its holdings. Both the Jesuits and Sulpicians were active in promoting colonization and, compared with private individuals, they were much more successful than any single rival.

The church was also important in other ways in the life of Quebec. Its influence permeated every part of the colony because missionary activity was accepted by all as a major objective of the presence of church and state in Canada. In this undertaking the Jesuits enjoyed a virtual monopoly until 1669, and their mission bands spread far and wide. The Jesuits' reports of their work spread to France and kept alive the urgency of supporting the distant colony. They were responsible in 1659 for securing the appointment of François de Montmorency-Laval, who had most powers of bishop immediately, but did not enjoy the distinction of holding the title until 1674. His eventual elevation to the bishopric was a triumph for the Jesuits not only because the bishop, like them, acted directly under the pope (unlike most French bishops who were supervised by the government), but also because he was a man of great piety.

Laval was also a powerful person with a tenacious will, great energy, and a profound sense of his religious mission. His rule from 1659 to 1684 laid a good foundation for the church, with plans for a native priesthood, an independent-minded clergy, and seminaries for training them. His successor was less judicious than he was, but Laval gave the church momentum in the form of providing church buildings, schools, and seminaries. He and his successors also sent forth missionaries into the West to visit the country of the Hurons, the Great Lakes, the Mississippi Valley, and Louisiana. Much missionary blood would be shed, but thousands of Indians heard the word of God, were baptized, and received Catholic instruction.

The governor of New France during these years was Louis Joseph, the Marquis of Montcalm, who served two terms before his death in 1698. A courageous soldier, Montcalm gave the colony a strong military policy which emphasized the fur trade and the expansion of commerce with the Indians. Posts were set up on the St. Lawrence River and Lake Ontario, and treaties of peace were negotiated with the Iroquois. Relations with these Indians always were uneasy, and in the late 1680s the French and Iroquois assaulted each other's posts. The Iroquois asked the English at Albany (Fort Orange) for help, but Montcalm was able to withstand the attack of English and Iroquois, holding off the English before Quebec and Montreal in 1690 and defeating the Iroquois in Onondaga country of New York in 1696. The luster of Montcalm's accomplishments was tarnished because he was a difficult person, often tactless and outrageous in his behavior; but he gave the colony many years of able rule. He inflicted heavy losses on the Iroquois who were pressing Canadian tribes, and he sponsored trading expeditions as well as missionary bands that took Frenchmen deep into the interior.

The most famous of the French explorers was Robert Cavelier de La Salle, whose exploits were wide-ranging, exciting, and daring, revealing an unbelievably restless temperament. He had great plans for the fur trade, and ventured down the Mississippi River to form a grand scheme to open up the west. Somehow La Salle's ambitions always turned unlucky, and he was murdered by a companion in 1687. Yet he and the other French of his day were an adventurous people, with more heroes, martyrs, soldiers, and saints than any of the other colonists.

The Nations of Iroquois

The powerful Iroquois of New York challenged both the French and English armies and held their own in the struggle to control New York by acting as a balance of power. They could not face the fighting ability of

European soldiers head-on, but depended for survival upon a good military force for protection, diplomacy, and their ability to trade. Some observers of early Iroquois habits mentioned their ferocity as a strength in their dealings with potential enemies. Only estimates are available on the Iroquois population, but in 1660 it was over 5,500 and still rising. Disease and warfare kept the number flexible, and the nations regularly adopted new members. Their fighting force was never more than 2,500, and not all of them could be used at the same time. In 1660 the Mohawk warriors were estimated at 500, the Oneida at 100, the Onondaga at 300, the Cayuga at 300, and the Seneca at 1,000—a total of approximately 2,200 men.

The first trading contact with the Dutch occurred in 1609 when Henry Hudson came up the river that now bears his name. His Dutch successors established Fort Orange (Albany) in 1624 as a trading post and a settlement also grew up around the fort. Trade developed slowly, but by 1635 as many as 16,304 skins were reported from the whole colony; a major portion of them were undoubtedly from Fort Orange. In 1657 over 46,000 beaver and otter skins were shipped to New Amsterdam from Fort Orange. The Iroquois responded to this demand by ranging into distant lands for beaver and other skins, and they expected, in turn, a widening range of consumer goods. Firearms, powder, and maintenance of the muskets were most important. Brandy, too, was a major item of trade, even though the Iroquois protested its sale and predicted that it would harm them physically. Clothes, tools, medicines, and sweets had some popularity. Trade was brisk and, in time, Iroquois and Dutch became dependent upon each other's products.

This interdependence forced the Iroquois to extend their own trading and hunting far into the west. They moved their hunting activities to the lands of the Ottawas who had become their rivals in the 1650s. The Iroquois fought back but the Ottawas had French support in a few major, but inconclusive, encounters. Diplomacy was then followed with some success because after 1664 the Dutch, with the help of the English, offered lower prices for trading goods than the French. Iroquois as middlemen gained only limited success in these dealings, when the Ottawas resisted the peace overtures and trade did not greatly improve. In seeking more trade the Iroquois turned to other French tribes for furs and intensified their trappings in Ottawa territory. In trying to monopolize the beaver trade as traders and middlemen, the Iroquois antagonized the French and brought themselves into the intense rivalry between French and English. In the 1689-1697 hostilities, known as King William's War in America, the Iroquois were repeatedly raided by Frontenac's army. The casualties were severe, and some Iroquois were confronted in 1700 with critical problems that they felt involved their survival as a people.

The beaver trade was important to the French Indians too; also important were cheap goods and peace on the frontier for the English-Dutch and French. Luckily, in 1700 the Ottawas arranged a peace conference to be held the following year in Montreal that gave the Iroquois important hunting rights in Canada; the Ottawas, in turn, won the right to trade directly with Albany. A second conference was held in July 1701 between the English-Dutch and Iroquois, in which the Indians gave England title to their lands in exchange for protection. The Iroquois thus also became dependent upon England, but they had protection, too, for their homelands. The treaties of 1701 at Montreal and Albany, in short, stabilized the frontier for Iroquois trade.

Albany became an important mart for the Iroquois fur trade in the years after 1660. The town remained largely Dutch in population: probably not more than several hundred people were living in the town, and the merchants were almost all Dutch-speaking. The trade can only be estimated, but furs generally declined in numbers from a height of 46,000 in 1656 to 14,000 in 1686. Prices also declined because Europeans were less interested in wearing beaver hats. Even so, prices were two to four times better at Albany than at Montreal. The economy, however, was stagnant in 1700 and few Albany merchants were prospering. The fur trade brought the Indians sufficient business to buy guns, powder, and repairs for their muskets, and helped the merchants keep their warehouses and shops busy.

The West Indies

While English colonies were struggling for existence on the north Atlantic mainland, other colonies were founded on islands scattered all over the West Indies. The first explorations, however, were conducted in Guiana in 1604 on the north coast of South America, but heat, bad luck, and poor location contributed to its failure. Some English merchants repeated the effort in 1620, but protests from Spain caused withdrawal of the expedition. Guiana as a site for a colony was attractive, nonetheless, and English merchants in the mid-century established plantations there.

Some of the promoters of Guiana turned to the Caribbean islands when their project failed. A group of merchants headed by Ralph Merrifield backed a colony on St. Christopher in 1624, and a year of experimentation proved to them that tobacco could be easily grown. Other merchants, impressed with the possibilities of crops on Barbados, particularly its good soil and dyewoods, formed the "William Courteen Associates" and sent out an expedition in 1627. The success of their project attracted enough adventurous people in five years to give Barbados a larger population than Virginia's. Tobacco, sugar and dyewood found good markets in London.

The amazing success of Barbados encouraged Englishmen to settle Nevis, Barbuda, Anguilla, and Montserrat. People in great numbers came to the islands, and Barbados in the 1640s had a population nearing forty thousand. In these crowded conditions not everyone lived well, and a few sought relief as smugglers against the Spanish mainland and a few more left for less crowded Virginia. As the islands developed, sugar replaced tobacco as the principal crop and English eagerness to build her market led to the conquest of Jamaica in 1657. The spread of sugar as the important crop on these islands had economic consequences that changed greatly their relations with New England. It required much capital, large acreage, and a cheap labor supply. The islands in a few years were dominated by plantations which grew sugar almost exclusively, and the labor supply became primarily black slave. Surplus food supplies from the North American colonies now became essential to the survival of the island peoples.

There developed with New England a provision trade, which took fish from the fishing banks and grains from the other colonies to the West Indies. In exchange, New Englanders took cargoes of molasses and sugar to home ports where the molasses was turned into rum. The trade was quickly widened to include visits to the Dutch colonies of Surinam and Curacao, the French colonies, the Danish island of St. Thomas, and the Spanish ports in Mexico, Cuba, and Central America. The sea captains collected not only a wide variety of exportable products, but also foreign coin and bills of exchange. Prices were favorable, and some New England merchants established factors on important islands in order to regulate the activities of their sea captains.

It would be difficult to overestimate the importance of the West Indies to New England trade and prosperity in these years. The foreign islands and coastal colonies, in time, would be even more important than the English colonies in providing opportunities to buy cheap molasses and to sell North American food surpluses.

5

England Discovers the Colonies

For nearly one hundred years England suffered many sharp changes in government. Continuing agitation and violence in politics and religion had disrupted her people long before revolutionaries beheaded Charles I in 1649, and remained to influence the nation well after parliamentarians sat the Hanoverians on the throne in 1714. One thing became clear, moreover: whoever in England controlled policy toward the colonies developed an imperialist attitude that took the form of navigation acts, boards of trade, and colony development. Reports on commerce were frequently required of the colonies, and English officials were occasionally sent out to investigate politics. A time or two the ministers even dispatched warships to colonial ports to enforce regulations upon reluctant colonials.

Before 1649

Politics in Virginia, Maryland, and New England before 1649 were distant from the minds of the king and his ministers. They granted charters and exercised some continuing interest through the Privy Council, but they had problems aplenty at home and thus welcomed the departure for America of troublemakers. There were annoying colonial problems, however, and committees were assembled to study and discuss them.

The colonists reacted to any sign of unusual English interest in their affairs and tried to maintain a low profile. They emphasized purity of worship instead of separatism for their church and worried about the reception of Roger Williams' political ideas, especially his contention that the Indians alone had the rights to grant Massachusetts title to the land. Most of the colonists, however, wanted sufficient freedom to set up their own way of life, and they realized that this was possible only as long as the government was distrusted by opposition at home.

The colonists were not anti-English in their government, but were developing in America a religious haven and a new economic base. They brought out law books, sermons, and treatises, maintained commercial contacts, and kept up a correspondence with family and friends. They followed avidly the discontent in their home towns, and in the revolution of the 1640s a few of their leaders returned home to fight. They remained emotionally loyal to England—to a homeland that was to be purified of its sins. They were relatively moderate in their political and social ideas and shaped thus their institutions by their knowledge of the common law. Institutions often reflected frontier conditions, which were raw and challenging, but had much in them that was English and little that was utopian.

The Puritan revolution that broke out after 1640 exposed layers of dissatisfaction. Reformers, Levellers, Fifth Monarchists, utopians, and a variety of religious groups sprang forth to urge changes in society. Some would redistribute the land; others would rid the nation of aristocrats; still others would root out the Anglican church, its bishops and priests. The Society of Friends (the Quakers) offered a religious experience that was simple as well as mystical and attacked current dress, language, manners, intolerance, and norms of conduct. Other theorists speculated as well on the origin of society and government. Thomas Hobbes in his *Leviathan* argued that government had a human origin because people were unable to live together peaceably. He believed that people were mean, nasty, and brutish and had long ago turned to government to provide them with security. Hobbes thought human rights arose out of the creation of a powerful government. His attack, therefore, was waged against vested rights, religious rights, or some kind of a divine foundation for rights. James Harrington, also a very wise man, speculated on the origins of government. He asked in his *Oceana* what created the insecurity and instability that Englishmen were then experiencing. The source of evil, Harrington thought, rested with the distribution of land. In a wide distribution of land, he felt, lay the basis of a commonwealth, and land ownership should be severely regulated to keep it in an appropriately large number of hands. Harrington emphasized sufficient statecraft to insure a well-regulated state, which he compared to the circulation of the blood. He believed particularly in a rotation of offices, a ballot, a separation of powers, and a written constitution, but he also emphasized the need of religious freedom. His colleague in the revolution, John Milton, also defended religious toleration but excluded its extension to Roman Catholics, whom Milton condemned as idolaters and internationalists. Otherwise, he defended the truth of the Bible and the human ability to find truth. Government he saw as a source of corruption when it supported the clergy, and he advocated separation of church and state. In the *Areopagitica* Milton extended his concept of freedom to include publications: truth, he said, "needs no politics, nor stratagems, nor licensings to make her victorious."

None of these theorists was a Leveller, but all shared some of the ideas of John Lilburne and Richard Overton. Levellers were left-wing revolutionaries, a small but influential group mostly in Oliver Cromwell's army, who had helped overthrow both Charles I and the Presbyterians. Unlike Cromwell, who desired few actual changes in the social system, the Levellers were less conservative, less practical, and less cautious. They advocated equality of representation in Parliament and wide suffrage, and hoped for some major changes in land distribution and in the social structure.

Between 1649 and 1660

Oliver Cromwell and his colleagues possessed most of England's political power after 1649, but it was like a hot potato which they were unable to throw away. They tried repeatedly to create a representative government, only to have it fail on every occasion. Government initiative resided eventually in the military, who proceeded to require full allegiance of all parts of the empire. Military pressure was applied to Ireland, which required conquest and oppression, sieges and forays that lasted until the capture of Galway in 1652. Though brutal at times, the conquest ended with Ireland's being incorporated into the English economy. Scotland, like Ireland, offered stiff opposition to Cromwell, only to be easily conquered at Dunbar with casualties of three to four thousand and the loss of an army of ten thousand.

Cromwell then turned to the colonies. During the revolutions of the 1640s they had depended upon Dutch trade and had shown much independence in their politics. At the execution of Charles I, some colonial leaders in Virginia, Barbados, Maryland, and Bermuda had revealed their royalist sympathies by proclaiming Charles II as king. New Englanders, in general, refrained from expressing any sympathy for Charles II, but hesitated in joining Cromwell's cause. In 1650 Parliament insisted on having all the colonies express their loyalty to the new government and passed a coercive act to give reality in law to their feelings. They first prohibited the trade of certain colonies which they felt were rebellious, but then regulated as well the commerce of the other colonies as a matter of right belonging to the home government. Licenses would henceforth be required for foreigners to trade in the empire.

Parliament followed this legislation with the Navigation Act of 1651, which provided that goods of the empire must be conveyed in English ships, manned by a captain and a crew who were English. It required likewise that foreign goods must be taken to England only in the shipping of the country producing the products. It prohibited the importation of such products as fish, fish oil, and whale oil and bone on other than English-owned ships.

The act was an assault upon Dutch shipping, but also it was intended to stimulate the British merchant marine. Opposition was intense in the colonies, and few ever observed the law when they could avoid it. Open violations in contempt of the government occurred especially in Virginia and Massachusetts. Only the threat of military occupation kept the colonies relatively quiet.

Charles II

After Cromwell's death in 1658 and the inability of his son Richard to unify the many factions, their former supporters asked Charles II to return home. His "Restoration" in 1660 brought to the throne a person of much spirit, flexible morals, and political astuteness. In seeking stability Charles turned from Puritanism and religious radicalism to Anglicanism in a hope that its moderation would bring peace. But a severe code to enforce religious conformity was formulated by Parliament, and those who dissented from it were roughly treated with penalties ranging from fines to execution. In desperation many dissenters escaped to America where they found homes in the new colonies of East and West Jersey and Pennsylvania.

This religious anxiety did not please the wealthy merchants and courtiers who had flocked to the new government. They were investors and speculators, and some were imperialists who were ready to develop the empire. Turbulence at home reminded them of the dog days of the past and they tried to obliterate the memory of Cromwell. These persons were nervous and sometimes reached pathetic lengths as they sought to stamp out dissent. They had little humor for the foolish or inept, which may be seen in the following example: a crack-brained wine trader named Thomas

Venner, who pledged his support to the reign of "King Jesus" and attracted fifty followers to London, was captured and hanged as a mischief-maker, and justices of the peace then swept the countryside for Quakers and like-minded people and imprisoned more than four thousand people within a few weeks.

During this insanity, Charles II himself pursued a moderate course whenever he could. His memory of the Civil War was much too vivid for him to enjoy the repressive folly. From time to time he relaxed the law and freed dissenters from prison. Later in his reign he granted to William Penn, the only son of a loyal supporter and creditor, the spacious country now known as Pennsylvania, as a religious haven. Penn had been converted to Quakerism, was frequently in prison for religious activity, and was generally an embarrassment to friends for his offbeat religious opinions.

Penn was an unusual person. Both an aristocrat and a religious enthusiast, he joined a despised sect that was drawn from the working classes. Though he had the benefit of an Oxford education and European travel, he forsook those advantages of class for the humble experiences of an itinerant preacher. He accepted the Quaker beliefs in human equality, separation of church and state, the uselessness of war, and the constant presence of God in the actions of persons.

Penn's princely colony of Pennsylvania in 1680 was dedicated to these Quaker principles, and he proceeded to draw up a constitution that provided for representative institutions, adulthood suffrage, toleration of religion, and reasonable prices for land. He involved many merchant friends in his enterprise, and together they advertised its opportunities. He even went out to his colony on two separate occasions, acting as lawmaker, city planner of Philadelphia, and father of his people. His enthusiasm was infectious, and the colony won amazing success in a few years as thousands of settlers broke land with a minimum of misery and produced bountiful crops, to make themselves self-sufficient in food supply. By 1699 approximately twelve thousand people were already living in the colony and Philadelphia was thriving as a center of trade.

From the beginning Pennsylvania was a mix of religious groups. Huguenots from France accepted it as a refuge; Germans from the Rhineland, some known as Mennonites, were settling in villages. Welsh, Irish, Dutch, and Scottish peoples also sought homes in the colony. Control of government, nonetheless, remained in the hands of the Quakers, who were not always true to Penn's instructions but managed to maintain enough peace in the colony to permit everyone to share in its prosperity.

Pennsylvania's success may indirectly be attributed to the wisdom of

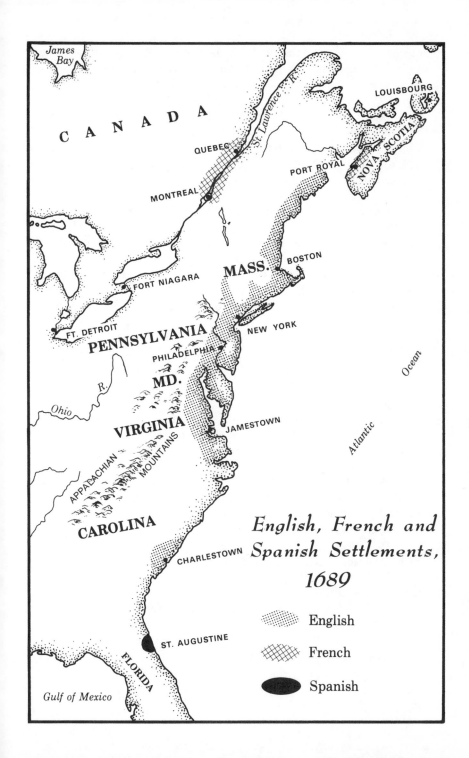

James
Bay

C A N A D A

St. Lawrence R.

LOUISBOURG

QUEBEC

PORT ROYAL

NOVA SCOTIA

MONTREAL

BOSTON

FORT NIAGARA

MASS.

FT. DETROIT

PENNSYLVANIA

NEW YORK

PHILADELPHIA

R.

MD.

Ohio

VIRGINIA

JAMESTOWN

Atlantic

Ocean

APPALACHIAN MOUNTAINS

CAROLINA

CHARLESTOWN

English, French and
Spanish Settlements,
1689

English

ST. AUGUSTINE

French

FLORIDA

Spanish

Gulf of Mexico

Charles II in letting Penn go forth to America. But the king and his merchant friends had an imperial interest that was probably based on trade. One of Charles's first acts was the establishment of dual bodies, the Council of Trade and the Council for Foreign Plantations. These advisory commissions were intended primarily to investigate colonial opportunities, but they had very little power to do anything. They pondered, recommended, and popularized colonial problems. In time, they evolved into the Lords of Trade which had enough authority to develop and enforce policies through the colonial governors and commissioners.

For the merchants these policies had great value when they related to commercial regulation. The policies inspired the Act of 1660, which restated in general terms the provisions of the Navigation Act of 1651. Trade again was to be conducted in English vessels, with English captains and mostly English crews, and foreign ships were not to be excluded from internal trade. The merchants appreciated also the Staple Act of 1663, which made England the center of trade and required all European goods destined for the colonies to be shipped to English ports first. Some direct trade in wines, salt, horses, and provisions was permitted if the merchandise were shipped from Ireland, Scotland, Madeira, the Azores, and Cape Verde Islands. Other laws refined these provisions restricting trade in foreign ships, but the navigation acts encouraged shipbuilding, seamanship, and domestic trade in an economy that was expanding at a good rate.

The merchants were especially interested in exploiting distant markets, and they quickly formed or reorganized companies so that they could exploit the Hudson Bay for fur trapping and engage in slaving along the west African coast. Old companies like the Levant and East Indian were recapitalized as merchants pushed the search for markets, trade routes, and opportunities in which textiles, finished products of all kinds, and bulky food items found markets. Eager merchants thus scanned the horizon for ways of turning profits.

Two areas appeared most engaging: the Dutch colony of New Netherland and the last unsettled area south of Virginia. In association with Charles II, who agonized for additional money, groups of merchants and courtiers speculated on colonization as a way of making money and of taking over and developing the Dutch colony. They represented leading men in the government like the Earl of Clarendon, the Duke of York, and Anthony Ashley Cooper. New Netherland was considered ripe for annexation. Its people were discontented by Dutch rule and its defenses were weak. Further, Englishmen had never accepted the idea of a "foreign colony" on their North American shores and had repeatedly planned its seizure. Dutch traders, too, were a nuisance as smugglers who often took the cream of colonial trade. The argument is a bit specious because the promoters wanted the land and were determined to seize it. When the king agreed and Parliament contributed funds, a small expedition in 1664 captured the colony without much ceremony. The Duke of York was given the proprietorship, and he in turn gave authority to Governor Richard Nichols, who was instructed to promote immigration and trade. Tactful and intelligent, the governor desired to make the transition to English rule painless, and he encouraged the Dutch to join the conquerors in transforming the colony. Laws were promulgated that were realistic and liberal in the sense that they created some representative institutions like the jury system and town government.

The Duke's interest, however, was primarily financial, and New York certainly was no disappointment. Rapid progress was made in agriculture, as the new settlers turned thousands of forested acres into wheat and corn fields. The colony soon became an exporter of food stuffs, and New York City emerged as a small but cosmopolitan center of population where people of many religions could worship, build homes, and live happy lives.

The lands across the Hudson and south to the Delaware River the Duke presented to a few proprietors, his close friends and fellow courtiers interested in colonization. In offering liberal attractions to prospective settlers, the proprietors quickly placed a few hundred people on farms of 150 acres or more, and the process of clearing the land proceeded rapidly. This colony of New Jersey eventually divided into several parts: the colonists living near New York were economically dependent upon that colony, while those living near Philadelphia were Quakers who looked to the city as their cultural center. Over the years the Jerseys experienced a hectic, argument-ridden existence that eventually led to their division, but for the three thousand people residing there in 1702 life was generally rural, healthful, and easy. The Quaker spirit tended to influence the pattern of life for these simple, humble folk.

This pastoral setting probably indicates that the London merchants and courtiers made little real money from New Jersey other than to found another base of empire. A similar experience, but with more potential, was the settlement of Carolina which was given to eight Englishmen in 1663. Most of these men had already invested in New York and New Jersey, and now had hope of developing plantation projects in Carolina. They wanted to develop estates which would grow fruit, mulberry trees (silk), and vineyards, and possibly other semitropical products and naval stores.

The first expeditions to Carolina in 1663 and 1665 concentrated upon the area near the mouth of the Cape Fear River. They drew potential settlers from Virginia, England, and Barbados, but life proved to be brutally hard and the colony was soon abandoned. Renewed attempts in 1670 finally succeeded in planting the settlement of "Charles Town," probably because the new colony was located sixty-five miles from the ocean, upon a sheltered peninsula between the Ashley and Cooper rivers that had the advantages of transportation and climate. There was, however, some controversy about the exact site for the permanent town.

Another colony was already founded in the Albemarle Sound near the Virginia border, where some settlers had flocked as early as 1653. They had discovered an unusually fertile land for tobacco, corn, and pasturage. By the time Charleston was being settled this area was already prospering.

When the permanent site for Charleston was finally selected in 1679, the building of port facilities proceeded rapidly. The town quickly attracted an amazing assortment of people—Huguenots, Germans, Scotsmen, and Englishmen, both directly from England and from Barbados—and the population grew into the hundreds. The surrounding country was fertile, like the lands in Albemarle Sound, and corn, dairy products, and tobacco cultivation occupied many hands. Rice, however, was soon discovered to be the staple crop, and by 1700 lands along the tidal streams and marshes near the coast had rice growing upon them. Like Albany in New York, Charleston became a center for Indian trade, with thousands of deerskins being exchanged for muskets, powder, and other products.

Life for these traders of South Carolina was well rewarded. Food was easy to come by and land was reasonable. The proprietors had hoped to establish the trappings of aristocracy with titles, landed estates, and governmental privileges, but there was never enough money or people to accomplish these policies. Government resided in a governor, a legislature with two houses, and local officials, and disputes over politics in the colony were frequently the business of legislative sessions. In 1691 North Carolina separated from the South, with its own governor and legislature. The northern settlements may not have been much different in economic pursuits, but they were filled with small farmers and poor people from Virginia and elsewhere, who often were smugglers and pirates. Historians make much of the differences between North and South Carolina, pointing to the North as a frontier for Virginia, a land of fiercely independent people. The South, too, was a frontier for Barbados and other American colonies, and it may have been more prosperous and cosmopolitan than the North, but hardly less fierce in its demands for individualism and liberty.

The Older Colonies: Virginia

The Restoration had a bewildering impact upon the older colonies because they had to conform in various ways to a new political order in the homeland. Virginia rejoiced on hearing news of Charles II's accession to the throne. Sir William Berkeley, the old royal governor, was restored to office, and he left almost immediately for London to make a personal judgment of politics. In his absence, subtle changes occurred in the government as the laws were codified, old royal routines were restored, and the wealthy landholders in the counties were confirmed in their places of influence. The governor's return in 1662 put him in the position of the chief landholder, the first among equals, a planter, friend of the king, courtier, and speculator. The luster of youth which had characterized his rule in the 1640s had worn off: he was wealthy, irascible, and inflexible, perhaps even dictatorial.

The rule of Virginia fell to local planters who made decisions along with the governor about day-to-day problems. The assembly met infrequently, and no new elections like those in England were called for many years. Even so, the franchise was tightened by raising requirements. This lessening of legislative activity, however, does not mean that the colony was quiet. Reaction to English trade regulations had caused bitterness, and the regulations had restricted the market for tobacco, lowered prices, and hurt many small planters. This was occurring at a time, too, when tobacco production was rising and more planters were entering the market. To add to the misery, a hurricane hit Virginia in 1667 and wiped out the production for a year. Destruction of buildings, wharves, and equipment, not to mention the occurrence of a few deaths and injuries, looked like the hand of God was punishing the colony. Worse was to follow, because the planters tried to make up for their losses of tobacco in 1668 by producing a bumper crop.

Much could be added concerning crop surpluses and shortages, rising food prices, and Indian hostility. While all Virginians were thoroughly shaken by their experiences, the small farmers accused the governor and assembly of causing some of the distress. Their protests became sharper in 1675 when Indian raids intensified, and the governor urged moderation and caution in the face of widening popular anxiety.

At this point of mounting crisis a daring English figure entered Virginia politics. This young aristocrat, Nathaniel Bacon, offered to do something drastic about the Indians. He had only recently come to Virginia but his wealth, social position in England, and education gave him an instant influence. With the additional help of a good marriage (to a wealthy widow), he even won a seat on the prestigious governor's council. In this crisis over Indian affairs Bacon snatched the initiative for making a raid on the Pamunkeys with a band of recruits. Though warned by the governor against any impulsive action, Bacon went ahead with his plan. The governor angrily responded by threatening to hang him. But Bacon continued his raids with little regard for the law, and the governor, in some desperation, called elections for a new assembly, probably in the hope of distracting Bacon's actions as an Indian fighter and winning some popular support for himself.

To the governor's embarrassment, Bacon won a seat in the new assembly and entered the capital with an armed guard. The governor responded, and in the confrontation that followed, Bacon was easily captured. Although Bacon was much too popular to be hanged, the governor used strategy and offered him a pardon in exchange for a public confession of guilt. Bacon sized up his situation and agreed that an expression of humility was better than being jailed.

Once freed, Bacon left Jamestown for his plantation and another encounter was soon in the making. In the meantime the assembly passed many bills to correct the abuses of the past ten years, and they won the governor's formal approval. The new encounter with Bacon brought another denunciation from the governor, but this time Bacon had the general backing of the people. In a proclamation he accused the governor of tyranny and asked the people to take an oath of loyalty to him personally while they awaited action from the king. Bacon then went off to the frontier to fight the Indians. The governor reacted to this disloyalty by crossing the Chesapeake Bay to Accomac, where he soon raised forces and tried to retake Jamestown. In their defense Bacon's people seized ships in the rivers, engaged the governor, and turned him back.

Something happened at this point. While Bacon was fighting on the frontier against the Pamunkeys, the governor regrouped his forces. In a short time he recaptured Jamestown and forced some lukewarm Bacon supporters to give him help. Bacon responded by returning to Jamestown, but in the exertion of fighting and travel he died of dysentery and his army quickly melted away. The governor counterattacked by using the hangman's rope to punish thirteen of Bacon's friends.

The rebellion was all but crushed when an English fleet of eleven vessels and over a thousand soldiers arrived in January and February 1677. News of the rebellion against Berkeley had caused a serious reaction in London, and a relief expedition was ordered in the dead of winter to sail to Jamestown. Commissioners had been sent along to investigate and bring the colony to terms. By the time the full fleet arrived a new assembly was sitting, who not only had voted a pardon for most revolutionaries but had also revoked some of the reform legislation of the past June. In place of Berkeley the Crown appointed an acting governor, and the business of finding a basis for peace was underway.

Britain exercised a rather firm hand upon the assembly in the 1680s. Under Thomas, Lord Culpeper, the legislature could not meet without consent of the Crown and had to send drafts of proposed legislation. Although Culpeper and his successor, Lord Howard of Effingham, evaded the instruction, the threat was still present, often taking the form of controlling assembly officers and membership. The colony, however, settled down in the 1680s. Population grew, and because of the shortage of available land many people moved beyond the fall line into the highland area where they raised cattle and food crops. Tobacco remained the principal crop of the lowland farms. Unfortunately, the governors encouraged large-scale production and prices were unstable. Discontent thus persisted from the 1670s, leading to a few riots and to demands to cut production. Too much may be made of the people's grumbling and the governors' controls because there was plainly more security from Indian attacks and more comfort and luxury than in the past.

Maryland

Traffic in the Chesapeake Bay grew each decade as tobacco and foodstuffs went to distant markets. Perhaps as many as fifty thousand hogsheads of tobacco were sent to England each year in the 1660s and 1670s. Plantations now spread along the Potomac River and the Chesapeake Bay, and black slaves in increasing number were becoming the work force. In a population of thirty thousand in 1690 nearly eight thousand were blacks.

In spite of these conditions of prosperity, Marylanders were not happy over the Navigation Act of 1660. They felt the regulation of their trade had affected tobacco prices so that profitable production was more and more difficult to achieve. They attempted to provide their own legislative control of production, but fellow planters divided on its practicality and the proprietor was hostile to controls because he reaped huge profits from port taxes and legal fees.

These burgeoning profits for Lord Baltimore only enhanced the position he now enjoyed as proprietor. For the first time since the colony's founding he was making a measurable profit. In 1660 Charles II had confirmed Baltimore in the proprietorship with enormous power and had allowed him to create an upper house of the legislature that represented primarily wealth, as the members of Baltimore's friends, relatives, and brothers in the Roman Catholic faith shared privileges. The lower house was more representative, mostly Protestant and, predictably, opposed to the proprietor's policies. Bickering between the houses persisted at every legislative session and grew bitter as the years passed. In time a climax occurred, with the assembly's making demands upon the proprietor. In 1676 during Bacon's rebellion in Virginia, a minor rebellion occurred in Maryland, but the governor moved swiftly against the leaders and had them hanged. Other rebellions broke out but they, too, were put down.

The discontent persisted. Rising to be a major leader of the Protestant Association in the 1680s was the rather unpleasant John Coode, caricatured as an ugly, deformed, clubfooted, and cowardly little man. Often shown as a baboon or monkey, Coode was in no way uncivilized but was a skillful agitator; he finally mobilized sufficient support by 1689 to lead a successful rebellion against Lord Baltimore and force the calling of an assembly which petitioned England for a royal government. The rebellion was undoubtedly against the monopoly of power held by the proprietor, the show of favoritism, the lack of forceful policies against the Indians, and the dominance of the Roman Catholic minority in the council. The colonists in a positive way were demanding the rights of Englishmen—to live under modern representative institutions in which executive power was limited.

Coode's rebellion coincided with plans of the Lords of Trade, who had worried about the continual disorders in the colony and also suspected violations of the Navigation Acts. The proprietor's rights to govern the colony were thus taken away in 1691, and the colony became a royal province for the coming twenty-five years.

New England

The restoration of the monarchy in 1660 was not warmly celebrated anywhere in New England. But the younger John Winthrop, who was then governor of Connecticut, realized the importance of securing a royal charter. With the support of the legislature he hurried off to London in 1661 and conducted negotiations for the better part of six months. In approaching the king and his council in February 1662 Winthrop used personal charm, "precisely the right phrases," and much political maneuvering to win the charter. He then helped the agent for Rhode Island to petition for that colony's charter. In both negotiations, Winthrop was unusually successful, and in record time won not only the charter for Connecticut, but an enlarged charter which added New Haven to

Connecticut's territory and even parts of Dutch New York and Rhode Island. The grant of religious toleration in Rhode Island is also attributed to Winthrop's persuasive ability.

Perhaps because Massachusetts did not have Winthrop's tartful services, the colony's experiences with England were less satisfactory. The colony was unwilling to accept the Navigation Act of 1660, and open smuggling and trade violations were notoriously visible. A royal commission in 1664 collected enough evidence to document colony disobedience in these matters, and in religious affairs it accused Massachusetts of violating the rights of Englishmen. The colony had treated Anglicans harshly and had put Quakers to death. In an arrogant spirit, Massachusetts had acted as if the colony were independent and refused to defend or justify its actions. Finally, in 1675, the Lords of Trade sent an agent, Edward Randolph, to Boston, and he undertook with equal arrogance an intensive investigation of the colony. Coolly received, insulted, and berated, Randolph felt the hatred of some leaders, and in disgust he lodged formal charges against the colony. Massachusetts finally answered these charges by sending to London two envoys, who asserted that English law did not apply to Massachusetts because it did not have representation in Parliament. Although the colony in a conciliatory gesture enacted the Navigation Acts for Massachusetts, its stiff-necked position irritated the Lords of Trade who insisted that the colony must recognize English supremacy or face the consequences.

Massachusetts was suffering much from growing pains. The second generation was taking over church and state in the 1660s, and all sorts of issues confronted the leadership. Perhaps the reality of being a peculiar people and living in a frontier environment hit them hardest. Their religious experience was not creating a unique society, but just another English one that had idiosyncrasies. They were not the vanguard of a new society that might inhabit the world; rather they were Englishmen who had chosen a Puritan form of religious worship. Worse still, the people were not certain of their religious discipline, and large numbers were not joining the churches or having their children and grandchildren baptized. Scruples were weighing heavily on their minds as they picked at issues. They wondered about themselves and whether they were truly saved; whether the members of their churches were fooling themselves and others about salvation; whether they should hang Quakers and exclude Anglicans; and whether they should permit luxury to invade the colony.

These misgivings should not disguise the fact that the colony, like its many neighbors in New England, was rapidly expanding in population and commerce. The population of New England in 1638 may have been

37,000; a decade later it was 48,000, and in 1676 it was approximately 80,000. People were breaking ground everywhere, new homes were being built or enlarged, and towns were dividing and new ones were being established. The sea coasts were alive with activity, and merchants were establishing networks of agents throughout the empire. Business had the appearance of being prosperous, and statistics gathered by researchers indicate much activity. Shipbuilding was excellent: perhaps 730 vessels were completed from 1630 to 1675, and the pace was quickening. Fishing, transshipping, distilling, and marketing were enterprises shared by most coastal people, with Boston, Salem, Marblehead, and Gloucester being the booming centers for Massachusetts Bay.

This kind of activity, good and commendable in itself, certainly challenged Puritan ideals. It enticed people from the community, turned their thoughts to luxuries, and put them into the mainstream of English life. As the hub of trade, Boston became for many people a town full of temptation, even of sin because it gathered a population of workers, merchants, and wealthy people who enjoyed the many taverns, the stores full of luxuries, and the markets loaded with choice produce. Its prosperity depended upon trading in the empire, and English regulations seemed threatening to its way of life.

In this period of misgiving, to be challenged by the outside force of the English government was indeed unsettling for everyone, but in 1675 to be also confronted with a serious Indian uprising seemed a sign from heaven. The causes of war with the Wampanoag Indians are disputed by historians: some cite the land hunger of the Puritans who provided impossible pressures upon the Indian king Philip and his associates; others think Philip concluded that his people were being corrupted by English customs and soon would lose their identity. Some were wearing English clothes, worshiping the English god, and using the English courts. Philip, moreover, was repeatedly humiliated by English arrogance when he was forced to pay tribute and acknowledge himself as an English subject. He gathered friends from neighboring Indian tribes, the Narragansetts, Nipmucs, and Pocumtucks, and tried to apply pressure to the so-called praying Indians—those that were living peaceably in the colony under its laws. Philip's coalition fell upon Swansea first, and the reaction in Massachusetts and Plymouth was instantaneously hostile to all Indians. The Marlboro Indians, for example, were assaulted by a local hero and fought back. Some were hanged and others were tried in the courts. To save the tribe many were taken to Deer Island, but a few escaped into the forest.

Philip's forces suddenly attacked exposed frontier towns everywhere in Massachusetts. Springfield, Northfield, Deerfield, Worcester, and many villages were entirely destroyed. Burned towns and farm homes, atrocities and murders, and frightened people, both Indian and white, were in general terms the results of this havoc. Retaliation by friendly Indians of Massachusetts and Plymouth and by the colonial forces themselves added to the devastation. The heat of war continued into August 1676 when Philip fell at the hands of an Indian marksman, but the bitterness of counterattack and retaliation lasted for another year or two. Estimates of white deaths were high—perhaps 10 percent of the forces—and one in sixteen of the population. The Indians may have lost five thousand people but, even worse, they lost their tribes and were scattered in the forests.

John Eliot, the great New England Puritan missionary, described the war in these sad words: "So that Satan improved the opportunity to defile, to debate and bring into contempt the whole work of praying to God." Other ministers interpreted the war as a trial of faith and a warning of still greater punishment.

Just as King Philip's war ended, Massachusetts faced another peril in London. Edward Randolph had already brought formal charges against the colony for its violations of English laws. The colony tried to deflect the pressure, however, but continued to disobey the law. Offense upon offense was charged against its traders, and the revenue laws were generally administered by colony officials without regard for Randolph or anyone else. Finally, the Lords of Trade could not tolerate this contempt of authority any longer and initiated legal proceedings in 1684 to declare the charter forfeit. Similar proceedings were also taken against the charters of Connecticut and Rhode Island. Parenthetically, one might add that Charles's government was making short work of charters elsewhere in the empire—Evesham, Norwich, and London—and the king was centralizing administration to combat local opposition to his rule. Before King Charles could establish the new government, however, he died of a stroke in 1685 and was succeeded by his brother.

James II

The new king as the proprietor already of New York and Maine wanted to unite the northern colonies into one great "Dominion." In 1686 he entrusted Sir Edmund Andros of New York with the responsibility of unifying all the colonies from New Jersey to Maine into one government, with Andros as the governor general. James did not provide for any representative institutions, but appointed a council which would make laws and levy taxes. News of this federation was explosive in Boston, but little was immediately done as leaders sought the wisdom of their friends. Their emotions were churned up, however, when Andros insisted upon having Anglican services in Boston and when he observed Christmas and legalized the use of the maypole.

Such evidence of Androsian popery was slight considering what James II did in England. He attended mass in his chapel at Whitehall and appointed Roman Catholics as officers in the army and as important officials in the civil service. Dispensing with the law against religious dissent, James both encouraged Catholics to enter the universities and tried to revise the Catholic hierarchy. The worst was to come, however, when his second wife Mary of Modena, a Roman Catholic, gave birth to a son in 1688 after fifteen years of marriage. The son was now heir apparent.

Enough people were bitterly alienated by these religious developments and other matters of law and order to seek a change in the kingship. They turned to William of Orange and Mary, James's Protestant daughter by his first wife, and William responded by invading England with a military force and pressing James hard. The king's forces quickly melted away and his position soon became untenable. In the early morning of December 21 James escaped to France, and the revolution succeeded for want of an opposition.

William used as his motto "the Liberties of England, and the Protestant Religion." With that motto known everywhere, minor revolutions broke out in England, Scotland, Ireland, and in most American colonies. William III and Mary II, the nephew and the daughter of James II, now began a joint constitutional reign that included declarations on rights, toleration, and military power. A new era for the English people was beginning, with regular meetings of Parliament, new charters for many American colonies, and a declaration by the philosopher of the revolution, John Locke, that government is created by people to serve their interests. On the hills of Charlestown in Massachusetts, bonfires blazed in celebration of the accession. Andros and his now-deposed colleagues were on their way home to England, but in their places other royal officials assumed office. Massachusetts became a royal province like New York, New Jersey, and New Hampshire.

6

Looking into the Eighteenth Century

The accession of William and Mary to the throne in 1689 marked the beginning of nearly twenty years of war. The first phase lasted until 1697, followed by a few years of uncertain peace and then another war in 1702. Eleven additional years of conflict occurred under Queen Anne, whose gentle disposition made her an unlikely warlord. But the Treaty of Utrecht, nonetheless, ended these bitter years of conflict with a great victory for British arms. The backdrop of European war had its sobering influence upon the colonies, who were touched by Indian warfare, military mobilization, and fighting along the frontier. Frightening attacks by Indians occurred frequently along the whole frontier, and the shrieking cry of Indians and the burning of homes and villages kept settlers close to the Atlantic coast.

By 1714 there were 350,000 Europeans and Africans in the twenty major American settlements from Newfoundland to Guiana. The third generation in many places had already taken power, and the population was more than half native-born. Most white people had traced their roots to England, but influences of soil, weather, crops, and religion in the colonies helped to mold different institutions, manners, and attitudes. Each colony, too, differed from England, perhaps most in traditions and social systems. The plantations of the Caribbean were remarkably different in their use of slave labor, but Puritan attitudes in New England also influenced the development of institutions. A generation was arising that was self-consciously American, but it was fighting the changes in culture and hoping to capture something of England in its daily life.

The Witch. *(Library of Congress)*

The Glorious Revolution

The new monarchs in England brought many constitutional changes. Parliament gained supremacy in the government at the expense of the Crown, but merchants also won power over the landowners. The nation seemed to put aside its Puritanism and its intolerance of Protestants who were not Anglicans, and loosened its controls over the press and speech. War, however, kept politics unstable, and a revolt in Ireland led to much bitterness.

In New England

New Englanders hailed the accession of the new monarchs as Protestants and saviors of the state and like them were Calvinists in religious emphasis and Puritan in politics. To their shock, the monarchs adopted the service of the Anglican church and favored toleration of all trinitarians except Roman Catholics. This decision deeply affected Increase Mather, a sophisticated minister, a traditionalist, and a pious gentleman, whom Massachusetts had sent over to London to negotiate a return of the charter. He argued well among the king's ministers for the cause of the colony, but gave way reluctantly to the new currents of thought, to a peaceful revolution that seemed to take away everything that was good in overthrowing James II.

Mather also swallowed hard when he heard that Massachusetts henceforth would have a royal governor and a charter that liberalized the franchise. All freemen now had the right to vote and all inhabitants had the right to freedom of conscience, except the hated Roman Catholics. The monopoly of the Massachusetts church was also broken even among Congregationalists, who would experiment with forms of worship by introducing instrumental music, inspirational sermons, and distinctive church architecture. The power of the ministers, however, remained visibly strong, and Mather served both as pastor of an influential church in Boston and for a time as rector of Harvard College. His prestige did not go unchallenged, however, most noticeably by unexpected events in Salem.

In the 1690s a contagion broke out in Salem in which widespread fear of witchcraft turned the community mad. The Mathers, Increase and Cotton (his son), were in the midst of the controversy as writers and interpreters of the phenomenon. Two little girls had apparently started the craze in 1691 by accusing townspeople of bewitching them. Emotional persons permitted themselves to be drawn into the hysteria, and in short order over fifty people confessed that they were witches. A wave of suspicion soon engulfed people even in high places. Twenty persons were hanged, many more were prosecuted, and the jails filled with people standing accused or awaiting execution. In this crisis the royal governor, Sir William Phips, ended the special prosecution, but not without the help of Increase Mather who questioned whether the devil was taking the human form of these accused people. According to Puritan tradition, however, their suffering was a sign of sin which needed repentance.

More to the point, as two recent historians have written, was the dislocation in Salem Town—its political uncertainties and rivalries—that may have caused the witchery. This local inflation may have reflected also the politics of the colony with the change in government, the war, and depression-like conditions.

Public reaction to the witchery damaged the reputation of the ministers and hastened the secularization of life in New England. Surrounding the new governor was a council of twenty-eight merchants, landholders, and wealthy leaders. Phips himself was interested in attacking French Canada and personally led attacks upon Acadia and Quebec, and his councilors, in turn, backed his plans to enlarge trade in Maine and on the fishing banks. Though Phips remained only a few years in the colony his successors were like-minded, especially Joseph Dudley, who used merchant aid to develop a long and successful rule.

The sons of these councillors, brought up in a secularized environment, chose merchant careers and gave service to government. While they chose Harvard College for their education, they asked more and more of the curriculum. They forced Increase Mather out of his rectorship, helped substitute the logic of Descartes for Ramus, and widened their reading to include classical authors.

Not all were happy with these changes, however, and many wanted less modern influences. They gave their support in 1704 to the establishment of Yale College in Connecticut, which became permanently situated at New Haven by the 1720s. The junior institution drew students from western Massachusetts as well as from Connecticut. A few of the graduates would join the merchant group in coastal Massachusetts and react to politics and religion as if they had attended Harvard College.

The secularization of Massachusetts is also reflected in the establishment in 1704 of the first colonial newspaper, *The Boston Weekly Newsletter*. It covered news of Europe, trade, politics, and the market, perhaps not very well, because the desire for more than a weekly report led to other newspapers in future years. Merchants read these papers in the taverns, and Boston had many inns and taverns. Taverns were popular meeting places for business, politics, and conversation, and men of affairs spent hours in them during any business week.

The other areas of New England enjoyed equal growth and prosperity. Rhode Island and Connecticut kept their charters, while New Hampshire had a separate political order save that the governor of Massachusetts would be their link with England. The old colonies of Plymouth and Sagadahoc and the district of Maine joined Massachusetts. The settled parts of New England were divided into townships that were self-governed and composed of people attached to their communities. Most people outside the coastal towns had little or no interest in the areas distant from them. Boston, London, Amsterdam, and Dublin were equally distant and equally strange. Secular influences in these frontier towns developed too, but at a slower rate than in the coastal communities. They can be seen in the larger homes, a few luxuries, emphasis on community service, and reverence for family. Each town was drawn to the colony legislature because of levies of taxes, the need of protection, and sometimes internal issues of maintaining local harmony. The towns, almost as a rule, were not greatly interested in sending representatives to Boston, Hartford, or Portsmouth. They regarded the representation as a right, however, and exercised it when local needs required outside help.

New York

News of revolution in England quickly brought an overthrow of the Andros regime in New York. The insurgents formed a committee of safety, but were bewildered by what they should do and sent explanations to neighboring colonies. Jacob Leisler was charged with the responsibility of local defense, and he proceeded to jail members of the Andros government and to call elections in the city. Acting on what he considered was power from the king, Leisler formed a council, reactivated old legislation of the years before Andros took over, and demanded a loyalty oath. For approximately a year Leisler guided the revolutionary government and waited for royal approval of his actions.

To his surprise the Crown rejected his government and appointed a royal governor. In the meantime, opposition grew against Leisler, and he compromised himself by disobeying immediate orders of royal officials that he step down from power. A minor battle ensued, some people were killed, and Leisler was captured. When the governor arrived in 1692 he ordered a state trial for Leisler, who was swiftly tried and condemned. His speech from the scaffold saddened those who heard his words, and his death left a lingering bitterness among his friends and partisans against royal authority.

In spite of this inauspicious beginning, New York developed rapidly as a colony. Both in population and economic activity it showed great advances. Dutch and English, in spite of mutual suspicions, managed to work together, even to intermarry and form business partnerships. By 1715, twenty-five thousand people lived along the upper Hudson and Mohawk rivers. Within a few years these prosperous farmers sent boatloads of grains, livestock, and lumber annually into intercolonial commerce. The town of New York itself took on the business of a port, and its merchants gathered the surpluses of neighboring colonies on its docks for shipment to the West Indies or to New England. The city had a work force of black slaves, estimated at 15 percent of the population, who handled the cargoes. Tensions between the black slaves and the whites were often great, and in 1712 a score or more of slaves burned buildings and killed nine whites. Retaliation was swift and left the city edgy for years to come.

The colony probably would have developed even faster had not vast tracts of land been monopolized by a few aristocrats. English governors like Viscount Cornbury after 1702 gave their friends and themselves estates ranging from a few thousand to a million or more acres. Settlers, therefore, had to bargain with the agents of the great landlords or to accept tenancies, and many times they squatted upon the estates and dared the authorities to remove them. Other times, they moved voluntarily up the Mohawk River along which they trapped furs and farmed.

The uneven distribution of land gave New York an unsettling element in its politics that kept the assembly in constant conflict. Unlike Massachusetts which enjoyed a flourishing community life, New York was divided often by conflicts with the governors and landowners. Frequently these conflicts were over privilege, which was not as much a battle of classes as a battle of the same economic group for sharing the spoils. Mixed in the conflict were the Dutch, who had intermarried and were prominent in most political groups. Undoubtedly ethnic and linguistic considerations also brought rivalries among merchants, particularly in the Albany area. Party reversals in the legislature occurred regularly, frequently with no more reason than a fight of the "outs" vs. the "ins," or a shift in the governor's patronage. Hatred for Lord Cornbury consolidated some of the factions as they fought his avarice and spendthrift policies. The assembly raised issues of its rights to pass money bills without council interference, and appointed a treasurer to monitor expenditures. Pronouncements were exchanged between governor and assembly on issues of prerogative and popular rights, but little was settled in this quarrelsome atmosphere. Cornbury's successor in 1710, Robert Hunter, was a man of integrity whose reputation helped him weather many storms in the next decade, and New York gained in prosperity. The colony remained at heart a "factious province," and group warfare broke out again in the governorship of Hunter's successor.

Both Cornbury and Hunter in these years before 1714 faced minor border crises, and both urged Britain to seize French Canada in order to control the Indians. Their raids were less serious in New York than in Massachusetts and New Hampshire, but relations with the French Indians often were bloody. Deerfield in western Massachusetts was severely attacked in 1704, and raids in Maine devastated most frontier settlements. In 1709, the governors of the northern colonies mobilized thousands of men for attacks on Canada from Albany and the gulf of St. Lawrence. Most colonies quickly raised their quotas of recruits and supplies, and waited for the British reinforcements. But the summer had passed into the fall when the colonies finally learned that the British naval support had been withdrawn. Albany received, however, some protection from French raids by the presence of these colonials, and the Iroquois interpreted the mobilization in favorable terms. In 1710 Britain launched a successful attack upon Port Royal in Acadia, and the next year sent warships and transports into the St. Lawrence for an attack upon Quebec. When some transports foundered on the reefs of Egg Island the whole expedition was withdrawn. This abortive attack "stunned" some colonials who had suffered severe losses on the fishing banks. In the Peace of Utrecht which ended the War of the Austrian Succession (Queen Anne's War), both Acadia and Newfoundland became British territories.

Pennsylvania

In Penn's colony the Glorious Revolution brought an English scrutiny of its government by the Lords of Trade, who quickly decided to place the colony in the hands of a royal governor. The Lords reacted to many concerns: to widespread smuggling, to a need for defensive measures against the Indians, and to worry about the dependence of the people upon English laws. Most important in their view was the need that this occasion presented of changing Pennsylvania's government—to make it a royal colony like many of the others. The arrival of Benjamin Fletcher in 1693 evoked resentment especially among Quakers, who feared a loss of political power to other groups. With full authority to name a council and veto legislation, Fletcher exercised his prerogatives as opposition developed and tried to recast the leadership of the young colony. His tactics in governing the colony aroused most groups and politicians, who appealed to London for help. In the end the Lords of Trade handed the colony back to Penn as proprietor. Penn's restoration, however, was not without strings: he had to accept royal supervision of trade, admiralty courts, and endorsement of his governors. The Quakers returned to government control and their old ways of trade, which included smuggling. Their rivals, particularly Anglicans and Calvinists, fought for part of the spoils and were themselves smugglers. These groups used the assembly to battle one another. Reports of their behavior spread to royal officials and criticism of the colony mounted into a crisis. A hearing before the House of Lords in 1697 threatened the colony, and personal investigation by royal officials in 1698 forced Penn to make a second trip to America.

When Penn set foot in Philadelphia in December 1699, he discovered a colony far different from the one he had left in 1684. It had grown to nearly 20,000 people, who lived primarily on farms spreading from the rivers and also in the city as merchants, dock workers, and artisans. The rich soil and pleasant climate made life easier than in New England, and this attraction brought a constant flow of people to the colony.

Life was undoubtedly full of contentment in the rural areas. Quakers organized themselves into monthly meetings and proceeded to legislate on matters of morals and to dispense help to members. They hoped to create "the holy community" in which men looked after each other as seeds of God's love. Quakers had a peculiar concern for each other's welfare so that charity, a sense of community, brotherhood, and one's responsibility to others were daily interests. Since all secular problems were basically religious, the monthly meeting appointed "substantial" friends to visit families among them "where they think there is Occasion to suspect they are going backward in the World by Estate, and to Enquire and See how things are with them."

Quakers disputed with each other, but always were embarrassed by their human frailty. For solving problems they looked to the monthly meeting, which had developed an elaborate procedure; but in the end if all mediation failed, they hoped love would prevail. Resort to the law courts was discouraged and only Quakers cast from fellowship were permitted to use them.

Quakers developed tight little communities, woven together by religious fellowship, marriage, family, and association. Outsiders used Quaker arbitration services, valued their honesty and integrity, and admired their religious principles, but the Quakers were a stubborn people who did not win large numbers to their faith. They monopolized power in the colony, organized a party that challenged Penn's authority, and often treated with contempt any opposition, British or colonial, to their way of life.

Penn in 1701 tried to set Pennsylvania and Delaware on an even course so that he could return quickly to England. With some consultation, Penn promulgated a new "Frame of Government." Though preciously vague, it provided for religious toleration for those worshiping one God; the right to hold office; and the right to elect an assembly. The one-house legislature had great power, with the right to choose its own speaker, pass upon the qualification of members, and adjourn itself. It could nominate some local officials as well. The assembly in time thought of itself as a parliament and resisted any controls by the governor or proprietor.

Penn granted the people much autonomy in the hope that they would rule themselves well. In practice, the Quakers gained increasing power over other groups in directing the colony's affairs. Their leaders, known as the "Quaker Party" by critics, generally favored Quaker religious beliefs and were moderate, but some became slaveowners and prosperous merchants with less sympathy for the simple life and the humanity of their founder. During these years the colony revealed much immaturity because society was factionalized. A kind of political anarchy prevailed with which the Quakers could not always cope. Politicians were regularly divided on subjective issues, but often their divisions were no more than personal piques. They were contentious, intemperate in their speeches, and irresponsible. One politician likened his colleagues to "witless zealots who make [the Assembly] a monkey house." Perhaps the wilderness environment had something to do with the failure of society to coalesce. The rootlessness of the people, too, and their inexperience in ruling themselves were equally responsible in creating the malaise. Pennsylvania, in short, was outwardly prospering, but inwardly searching for stability.

Virginia and Maryland

The collapse of Bacon's rebellion in 1676 had left deep scars on Virginia's political life, plus much discontent and some distress. Reform was nullified by the resumption of English control of the province and the desire of wealthy plantation owners along the Chesapeake Bay to monopolize political power. The challenge of the frontiersmen to Governor Berkeley remained unsatisfied, and the colony was taking on the appearance of two colonies. Plantations were enlarging at the tidewater and using more and more slave labor, while small farms on the piedmont were self-sufficient and worked by individual farmers and their families.

The English revolution of 1689 had little effect upon Virginia. While leaders were in no mood to make changes in the colony's government, news of the revolution in England was welcomed in Jamestown. Virginia, nonetheless, was changing. People were arriving each year in good numbers and the birth rate was impressive. By 1720, the colony had 72,000 whites and 23,000 slaves, which more than doubled the population of 1660. Most of the white immigrants came from Pennsylvania and were Scots-Irish and Germans who differed in culture from the older settlers, particularly in their religion. They cherished the separate life of the piedmont. In 1716 Governor Alexander Spotswood, who was interested in this immigration, led an expedition to the crest of the Blue Ridge Mountains to look across them for western lands to settle.

The black immigrants of these years came in great numbers to the tidewater region, but they came almost always as slaves. Colony laws treated those persons as property and separated them from the white workers. These laws were gathered in 1705 into a "slave code" which attempted to regulate relations with the whites and restrain the rebellious actions of the blacks.

In the 1690s, Virginia established a new capital, Williamsburg, and a college, William and Mary, which soon became its educational center. Founded through the efforts of James Blair, the college, like Harvard, offered local students an opportunity for an education without risking the hazards of an ocean journey, the diseases of England, and the corruption of Old World society. Blair obtained both a landed endowment and English monetary support for his college and labored steadily to make it educationally respectable. Like the college, Williamsburg developed slowly as a town, and in time its buildings included a governor's palace, Bruton Church, Raleigh Tavern, mercantile shops, and a house for the legislature. The tree-lined streets of the capital gave it a delightful appearance, but the town always remained small, filling for legislative sessions once or twice a year and then emptying as the plantation owners left for their estates.

In these years before 1715 the owners grew wealthier as they amassed land and extended their acreages of tobacco. Families became important in the colony's life and family connections in marriages created a tight little society that became conscious of family names, education, offices and honors, and wealth. More contentment was realized as the plantation owners built large houses along the waterways, gathering around them in smaller dwellings the indentured workers and slaves. They developed gardens, formal walkways, and mansion houses, which were filling with the luxuries that could be transported to America.

The plantations, like the scattered farms on the piedmont, were isolated from each other by distances. Virginia remained rural in institutions and culture, and its commercial capital continued to be London, where tobacco was marketed and purchases were made. The Virginia-bound books, newspapers, clothes, luxuries, and some foods were anxiously awaited as ships navigated the streams to the wharves of plantations or market places. Virginia was rustic in 1715, but Robert Beverley was writing *The History and Present State of Virginia;* his brother-in-law, William Byrd II, was collecting books; and a few dozen clergy and teachers were spreading the culture of Western civilization to the young of the colony.

In Maryland life was turbulent and troubled by religious and economic differences. The Glorious Revolution in England gave the Protestants an opportunity to overthrow Lord Baltimore, and Maryland became a royal colony in 1691. Though the proprietor retained his title to the land, government was in the hands of the Crown and the Protestant legislature. In 1715 when Charles Calvert was converted to Anglicanism, he was able to secure a return of the proprietorship.

In spite of the instability of the colony's government, Maryland's plantation owners spread their fields of tobacco and attracted a good flow of people to the colony. By 1715 at least 45,000 people were living in the colony. Plantations were large in size, and labor was supplied by slaves and indentured servants. Like Virginia, the colony was rural in its institutions and culture, and the Chesapeake Bay and Potomac River were the principal lifelines to markets in England. For most people the good soil and weather made life pleasant, but isolation and rustic surroundings must have dampened the spirits of many people.

The Rim of Empire

Both Carolinas struggled as colonies against Indian attacks, but South Carolina was prosperous because it grew rice and indigo and raised livestock. In 1721 South Carolina's population was estimated at 9,000 whites and 12,000 blacks. It had the distinction of deliberately instigating black slavery, drawing planters from Barbados and using the slave code of that island as the inspiration for local institutions. Blacks had little or no rights and, as Winthrop D. Jordan has written, blacks had less human freedom in South Carolina than in any other continental English colony. The colony had an exposed southern border of frontier lands, partly inhabited by Creek Indians and often visited by Spanish traders from Florida. North Carolina was generally isolated by its poor harbors and land, and as a result developed few staple products which were attractive to English trade. Population remained small, perhaps less than 9,000 in 1721.

Compared to these struggling outposts, the West Indian islands were paradises. Most grew sugar for export, and some distilled molasses into rum. The Leeward Islands also grew cotton and ginger. Jamaica was by far the most important of the colonies; in addition to sugar it exported pimiento, spices, cocoa, cotton, and fustic, a wood that was used by dye-makers.

These colonies had limited numbers of permanent white settlers. Most were operators of plantations for absentee owners, workers, and commercial people. The labor force consisted primarily of black slaves who were imported in large numbers each year. Life for them in the isles was hard, and their life span was short if they were used on the sugar plantations. Many of the slaves who were rebellious or worn-out by work were sent to the continental colonies.

Most islands had little local food because sugar or other tropical products were too valuable to expend time on growing food. Necessary provisions were usually purchased from the continental colonies where surpluses were abundant and inexpensive. For British merchants the West Indies was the valuable part of the empire, especially for the sugar trade, but also for the slave trade. This commerce would not have been possible, however, without the provision colonies of North America. Various kinds of trade routes were possible, but England eventually became the beneficiary because the trade increased the demand for English goods. New England fish and Pennsylvania grains went south to the islands, where the sea captains picked up cargoes of molasses. The molasses was taken to New England for distilling, then the rum to England and Africa in the slave trade. Other New England trade went to the foreign islands to provide them with food, slaves, and English wares in exchange for bullion and molasses.

The planter population of the West Indies lived for long periods in England and operated their estates by overseers. These absentee owners, frequently wealthy men, also owned estates in England and sometimes were members of the House of Commons. Over the years they exercised much political influence in imperial affairs and gave to the West Indies a prominence in British policy that was powerful and out of proportion to their trade and population.

In the intercolonial wars many of the isles suffered from French attacks and shipping was severely disrupted. In King William's War (1689-1697) no territory was exchanged, but many islands suffered from impoverishment, piracy, and depopulation. St. Kitts was taken early in the war, recovered in 1690, and attacked repeatedly in later years. Jamaica was invaded in 1695, but the local settlers ejected the French in a few weeks. Damage was severe, nonetheless, and the plantations were put out of production for some months. In Queen Anne's War (1702-1714) the French brought a fleet of forty ships of the line into the Caribbean and disrupted trade. Attacks were also made upon the Bahamas and St. Kitts, which were occupied for a time, and British forces in retaliation then devastated Guadeloupe. Continual raids and counter raids throughout the war left the islands of all the European powers in a sad condition, in which no power seemed to have benefited much from the war.

A peace conference was finally held at Utrecht in 1712 and 1713. The major issue of the war—the union of the thrones of France and Spain—was resolved with a declaration that the two nations would never be united. Lesser issues included distributions of territory, with Britain getting major territorial acquisitions: Gibraltar, Nova Scotia, Newfoundland and the Hudson Bay. Britain won from Spain, moreover, the Assiento which gave her the right through the South Sea Company to transport annually as many as 4,800 slaves into the Spanish empire. This prize was granted for thirty years and included also the privilege of sending one merchant ship a year to the great fair at Porto Bello.

The Treaty of Utrecht created an equilibrium among the powers that would exist for nearly twenty-five years. In addition, everyone was tired of war after almost twenty years of fighting, and welcomed the peace. New monarchs and new politicians took their places in the new order, determined to find ways of keeping the peace. Britain experienced a minor yet serious succession crisis in 1714, when Queen Anne died without heirs and distant relatives from Hanover took the throne. Most politicians who had engineered the succession of 1689 backed the compromise of having the German-speaking monarchs rather than having a return of the ousted relatives of James II. The choice between a Protestant family and a Catholic one was still important in politics. The choice also meant that the Revolution of 1689 was reconfirmed. The middle-aged monarch George I was welcomed to the throne, and Britain settled down to the new era with a promise of peace and stability.

7

The Anglo-Americans

Englishmen loved to use the symbolism of "mother" England and "children" colonies. The symbolism was appropriate, but irritating to the colonies as the eighteenth century unfolded. English politicians worried about the children colonies' growing up, and believed the colonies were already showing too much independence in their governments, their religious observances, and their trading practices. Some members of the Board of Trade, the English supervising agency for the colonies, wanted to tighten the reins of authority and observe the colonies closely. Most British ministers of state, however, were content, though often worried, to let the colonies rule themselves with a minimum of interference. The great man of the day, Sir Robert Walpole, had little interest in irritating anyone, and was often quoted as advising his associates "to let sleeping dogs lie." Walpole believed that the empire was a self-regulating unit and that the profits of trade would eventually fill the pockets of his merchant friends. What more was desired, he asked?

Those years in England after 1715 saw the consolidation in power of the revolutionary party of 1689. They gained control over the monarchy after Queen Anne's death in 1714 by making George I, the elector of Hanover, their king. His son, George II (1727-1760), and great-grandson, George III (1760-1820), would give the nation years of uninterrupted but mediocre reigns. The power of ruling fell into the hands of the revolutionary party, the Whigs, especially during the reigns of the first two Georges, when the kings had language handicaps and limited interest in England. The Whigs used Parliament, their presence in the aristocracy, church, military, and business, to mold the nation into their image and likeness.

The party in time took on a conservative cast, in which its leaders used their positions and wealth to keep themselves in office and enjoy their privileges. The House of Commons became a kind of private domain for them because they did not redistribute seats. Sometimes they owned seats outright or could control the few voters in a borough, or could dominate a small village which had a seat. A network of relatives and friends was thus formed. Influence also extended to military commissions, to places in the Anglican church, to government offices, and to some offices in the colonies. The state became a web of alliances, in which spoilsmen offered loyalty to their patrons in exchange for jobs. The boards of directors or governors of the business companies were likewise filled with these leaders, their relatives, and clients, and frequently the boards were treated as their private preserve.

Most of the leaders developed country estates where they spent most of their free time away from government or business. These well-furnished houses were filled with the luxuries of the day and surrounded by formal gardens, riding paths, game preserves, and fields of grain. Of course, there were degrees of opulence, but a pattern of conduct was set and imitated by high and low alike according to their talent and taste. Good tables were set; fine food was valued; fashionable clothes and hairstyles were appreciated; and a coach, footman, and servants added the finishing touches.

For this exhibition of style London became the imperial center. Its fine homes and palaces gave the rich and the not-so-rich opportunities to be seen and to meet the Whig politicians. Its shops were filled with the raw materials to make this display possible. London, moreover, was a cultural center of artists, scholars, and writers; of publishing houses, newspapers, and bookstores; of discussion and philosophical societies; of concerts and the theater. There was much hustle in the streets as merchants and consignment people handled the business of the worldwide empire. Some specialized in the sale of West Indian sugar, or in Virginian or New England tobacco or rum. Others had warehouses, docks, and shops, and letters poured out in a stream to clients who were advised on market conditions.

London, too, was headquarters for colonial agents, travelers, and politicians, who interpreted the town's gossip and peddled their reports to the colonies. The agents, frequently resident colonials like Christopher Kilby of Massachusetts, were commissioned to represent one or more colonies, and made the rounds of the public offices, the merchant establishments, and the docks as they managed business affairs. They appeared sometimes before the Board of Trade, occasionally before the committees of the House of Commons, and frequently before ministers of state. Their interpretations of local affairs often determined the policy of the imperial government, and also would win a military contract for a lucky merchant, place a colonial in office, or remove a hated governor.

This London response to colonial affairs best came from the merchants whose trading interests were vitally related to most colonial grievances. But there were religious groups hostile to the Anglican church who reflected colonial fear over the possible establishment of the English church in America. Their cry against bishops frequently was heard in ministerial circles, and their letters to Americans served to alert dissenting Christians of the Anglican peril. College people, like merchants, clerics and officials, exchanged news and gossip and performed acts of kindness which kept avenues of empire well traveled by correspondence.

Ideas in the form of books also spread from England. Books by the thousands left London and Edinburgh yearly and covered any questions which concerned humankind. Britain had a free press, with many contributing essayists, publicists, translators, poets, playwrights and novelists, and a substantial literature that reviewed time and again the ideas of the English revolutions. Though England had become reactionary in political doctrine and practice, there remained spokesmen who commented in magazines and books about problems of representative government. Thomas Gordon and John Trenchard, authors of *Cato's Letters* in the 1720s, attacked Whig politics and those who served as clients of patrons. "No Men upon Earth have been more servile, crouching, and abandoned Creatures of Power, than the *Whigs* sometimes have been."

Gordon translated *Tacitus* and *Sallust* and joined others who commented on the virtues of republican Rome. Charles Rollin's *Ancient History* extracted writings of the Greeks and Romans, with the hope of being "instructive." Edward Montague blamed the fall of Athens upon luxury and immorality, but outlined principles of government for his readers. Colonial exposure to Cicero, Tacitus, Thucydides, and Polybius gave Americans information on ancient empires and the rise and fall of many, and a familiarity with civilizations that made them ponder problems of liberty and tyranny.

Not all this literature that traveled the ships to America was serious in a philosophical sense. Some was instructive and had a utilitarian purpose. Thomas Chippendale's *The Gentlemen and Cabinet-Maker's Director* gave appropriate advice to craftsmen. Other books helped those who worried about their conversation, their dress, their style of horseback riding, and their approaching deathbed manner. The "Art of Dying" may not have been entertaining, but it was instructive, perhaps even popular. In addition, there were books on architecture, gardening, household management, and law. In short, Britain transported by words and pictures its civilization to the colonies. The demand, moreover, was a colonial one, because Americans were painfully aware they were living on the rim of civilization; they hungered for English culture.

In America

Life in America varied almost as much as it did in the United Kingdom. Perhaps the spread of wealth was not as great, nor did America have the display of wealth or the depths of poverty. Each seaport town had an area of fine homes—Boston's Roxbury took form in the 1730s and Charleston's bay front years later. Philadelphia probably had more beautiful homes than any other town, because the city grew in mid-century to be the largest city next to London in the empire and had a most pleasant site for residential housing. Though the city had a mixed population of British and German peoples, both the language and the customs were English. The city was developing urban institutions like a library, hospital, college, social and intellectual societies, and a professional group of medical doctors, scientists, house-builders, and teachers. It had people who enjoyed enough leisure time to form a philosophical society, to support lectures, and to be patrons of music and the theater. It had tailors, dressmakers, hairdressers, and other services for the cultivated gentleman and his wife. Finally, Philadelphia had Benjamin Franklin, who had arrived from Boston as a young man and given his talents to the cultivation of urban life in a remarkable manner. A printer, newspaper editor, inventor, and promoter of good causes, Franklin retired in the mid-1700s to serve as a politician and representative of the colony as occasions presented themselves. He had amateur interests in science, colonial organization, Indian affairs, and currency reform, and drew to himself able people who shared often his wide interests in society and politics. In a city with a Franklin there was little need for any other luminary, but Philadelphia had as well David Rittenhouse, the mathematician, and John Bartram, the botanist.

Boston was a rival of Philadelphia being the center of a metropolitan area that included Charlestown, Cambridge, Newton, Roxbury, Dorchester, Milton, and several other towns. It was as much a melting pot as Philadelphia, but was primarily filled with British peoples who were interested as much in religion as in trade—although perhaps trade at times consumed more of their attention than religion. Boston occupied a narrow

Hancock House, Boston. *(Library of Congress)*

peninsula that had little space for much expansion of residential areas, except off from the city into Chelsea, Charlestown, and Cambridge. As the century wore on, the city became a business area and had many of the problems of a modern inner city. People with moderate wealth and riches moved to the suburbs, and the city's population had more working or business people as a result. Boston never developed the urban elegance of Philadelphia or its sophistication and diversity. But it had fine churches, a few public buildings, a variety of merchant establishments, and some fine homes. Probably Boston was known more than other towns for its people, who had developed early and well the art of governing themselves. They had clubs, both literary and scholarly, and all sorts of organizations where they could chat and argue.

Like Boston, the town of New York was packed with merchants, their warehouses and shops, but unlike Boston the town had a superhighway into the interior. Travelers praised New York as the "pleasantest and best built City in British America." Its skyline, or harborline, was crowded with warehouses, sugarhouses, distilleries, and the occasional spire of a church. The shortage of residential houses was severely felt, however, and residential building boomed at mid-century, more than doubling the number of houses from 1,140 in 1743 to 2,600 in 1760. Up the river were a few trading ports, but Albany was larger than all of them together. A few thousand settlers were living in and near the town, engaged in agriculture and trade with the Six Nations of Iroquois. Hundreds of additional settlers were living in and around Schenectady on the Mohawk River. From their frontier towns traders traveled westward to Fort Oswego on Lake Ontario where they maintained a major commercial base.

Many of these farmers and traders were descended from the early Dutch: they were often clannish and suspicious of the "foreign" English, and held most of the appointive offices in the region. To take advantage of these fertile lands, many New England settlers migrated into Albany County. The most politically powerful of the newcomers was William Johnson, who had come from Ireland and had established his influence among the Mohawk Indians by the late 1740s. He became the proprietor of a large estate in the Mohawk Valley and won a reputation for honest dealings as a trader. Until his death in 1774 Johnson was present at most Indian conferences where he acted as mediator, interpreter, and merchant.

The river trade not only gave the colony a continuing source of prosperity, but also its chief city became the headquarters for the British military after England entered the war against French Canada in 1756. British warships and troop transports used the port, and the flow of direct trade brought boom times. In 1744 imports were only £54,957, but in 1760 they rose to £480,106. The prosperity brought luxuries, a large leisure class, interest in science and the arts, and a wide assortment of amusements. A significant figure among the learned of the city was Cadwallader Colden, medical doctor, scientist, and merchant who served as lieutenant governor and often as acting governor. The variety of his interests, like those of Benjamin Franklin, were truly astonishing. Besides his research interests in medicine and physics, Colden described the flora of New York for Linnaeus in Sweden and wrote a history of the Five Nations of Iroquois. Other scholars joined in the new educational enterprise of King's College, which was then struggling for survival under Dr. Samuel Johnson, and still others sponsored lectures or kept up a correspondence with like spirits in Europe.

The southernmost town of the colonies, Charleston, South Carolina, developed more slowly than Philadelphia or New York, but warehouses, docks, and shops appeared in great numbers in the mid-1700s as the population and agriculture of the colony supported large activity. The town became a cultural center, with some urban elegance from the beautiful mansions, the tree-lined streets, and the large churches, and it was also a retreat for the planters from the hot interior during the summer months.

Charleston developed into a small but sophisticated town, with considerable wealth from the trade in furs, indigo, and rice. Some critics estimated the wealth to be greater than any other town in America, and the townspeople reflected their opulence by imitating the fashions and manners of the English gentility. They supported a theater and concerts, and imported the latest books, furniture, and clothes from London. And like Philadelphia they had their scholars. Alexander Garden, a Scottish physician who came to Charleston soon after receiving his degree from Aberdeen University in 1753, studied the plants and animals of the colony and exchanged information with Colden and Bartram while on a trip to the northern colonies.

During the years from 1715 to 1760 most colonies developed a leisure class who either cultivated or just appreciated the arts. The towns became centers for artists and philosophers to meet, but in many rural areas libraries were collected, country places were planned by architects, and musicians gathered for concerts. America remained rustic, or distant from cultural centers, nonetheless, and reflected the sophistication of Great Britain or the Continent.

Two border colonies were founded in this period: Georgia and Nova Scotia. Both served to restrain penetration by either Spain or France into the older areas of the empire. Georgia's promoters were also interested in taking care of English debtors and creating for them a colony of small landholders who could live under idealized conditions. No slavery or traffic in liquor was permitted, and the resident governor, James Oglethorpe, looked after most problems of government. English philanthropy made taxation unnecessary, but all male inhabitants were expected to serve in the military forces. Even so, discontent arose over arbitrary government and the lack of slavery which made labor costs higher than in neighboring South Carolina. In 1752 the colony was given the status of a royal colony, with British governor, assembly, judicial system, and local self-government. The other border colony, Nova Scotia, was settled as an outpost of the empire in 1749. About 2500 settlers were sent by the English government to found Halifax. They were enticed by free transportation, land, tools, subsistence and protection. They were to be a counterweight for the French Canadians who were living there in greater numbers. Some were moved out of the colony, but most remained as settlers. By 1756 the governor called an assembly and gave the colony a large measure of self-government. In time, it became an extension of New England as people migrated to the north.

Government in the Colonies

Everyone in the British colonies enjoyed self-government. The form of each government varied somewhat because of the economic system, state of development, or religious emphasis, but all shared in a common British inheritance that made home rule an essential part of life. White Europeans generally attributed to themselves certain natural rights which became clearer as the eighteenth century progressed. These rights included the right to own property, to worship God, to have a voice in their government, to marry and have a family, and to pass property along to their children. None of these rights was absolute, but in their practical wisdom Americans worked out legal and social relationships that were changed from time to time as the colonies matured.

The right to own land was generally observed and most Americans held from a few to thousands of acres. Recent studies of land ownership, however, reveal a landless class of tenant farmers, workers, and town dwellers, and the children, too, of landowners. Landed property was widely held, highly regarded, and attached to citizenship as a qualification for office. Those possessing land, in the eyes of many people, were superior citizens and attributed to them were such qualities as stability, wisdom, and certain natural gifts of insight.

The franchise in most colonies was also determined by residence. Landed area was divided into townships, counties, and parishes, and those owning land and residing in these subdivisions of the colony had the right to vote. Local offices were as wide as the needs of the community, and included the usual law enforcement jobs, road and bridge maintenance tasks, church and court duties, and military service. The impression is easily gained that early Americans were far more interested in local affairs than in colony-wide or imperial affairs. In New England, townships held annual elections which thrust burdens upon twenty-five or more citizens who often tried to beg off or pay a fine in order to escape the obligation. But tasks frequently did not get done without the cooperation of able-bodied persons. The vote usually carried with it duties, or a tour of service, and direct involvement with community matters. There were few professional officials, though some people served longer in public offices than others.

Most people battled for some kind of representation in government. Their agitation usually won guarantees for home rule, accessibility of law enforcement and civil courts, and proper defense. For most people counties or colony-wide representation was not valued as much as home rule, but there were times when local officials became so embroiled in their own politics that neutral observers from larger jurisdictions were asked to find a solution.

In Massachusetts the townships were the primary agency of government. The selectmen handled most issues of local importance. They shared responsibility in military matters with the company of militia, which was semi-independent and conformed to rules set down by the colonial legislature. In addition, they cooperated also with the deacons of the Church of Christ, helped choose the minister, paid his salary, and looked after the moral life of the community. The town's leaders had little to do with law and order, in the larger sense of enforcing colonial laws. The constables, the justices of the peace, and the inferior courts of judicature operated on the county level, and officials moved from town to town as problems arose. The shire town, or county seat, was a record center, a gathering place for regional officials, and an assembly point for the regiments in times of emergency.

On both the township and county levels there developed a body of leaders who were distinguished by experience, wealth, and family ties. These people are fluid on the local level, for the base was broad and many offered their services. On the county level there were important families, sometimes in good number, but certain families seemed to dominate regimental, judicial, and law enforcement posts. The Chandlers of Worcester, the Stoddards and Williams of Northampton, and the Hutchinsons of Suffolk were regularly in the county offices.

On the colony level the House of Representatives was annually elected, with members drawn from the townships. Each could send one or two members depending upon population, while Boston was permitted to send four; but almost no town except Salem and Boston took advantage of its privilege to have larger representation. In general, representation was well spread—perhaps the interior areas were better represented than the coast, but many towns in the interior did not exercise their rights or force their delegates to attend the sessions. In legislating the House shared its responsibility with the Council, which was chosen annually by the House with the approval of the governor. Council members tended to be county officials or persons of prominence and wealth in colony affairs. The houses of the legislature carried out the expected functions of government: they passed the usual budget, oversaw the defense needs, apportioned land, and regulated trade. Much of their work, too, was investigative. They heard petitions by the hundreds and dispatched agents to seek information.

The representatives met about four times a year for varying periods of a few days to a few months, depending upon business and relations with England. The Council in its executive capacity met semi-weekly with the governor, and shared the executive authority by giving its advice and consent. The governor had little independent initiative as an executive; although he could nominate officials and veto legislation, the houses held the purse strings and drew their power ultimately from the people.

The governor was an appointee of the English government. Often an Englishman, frequently inexperienced in administration, and generally lacking in wealth, he cut an uncertain figure and battled to find a prestigious place. Most governors of Massachusetts were talented men—lawyers, military personnel, or public servants—and a few were natives of the colony, as were Joseph Dudley and Jonathan Belcher. Even if governors had the talent, their office was weak and they were frequently caught in disputes over the limits of British and colonial authority. Their position was symbolic; they were innocent victims occasionally of a poor constitutional arrangement with Britain.

The governors were the executives, however, in a government of law. Bills were signed into laws, which in turn were enforced by a well-developed court system where penalties or solutions were provided. The courts were used for suits and prosecutions, and if the bundles of legal documents measure anything about Massachusetts life, its people were litigious and contentious. Only a few trained lawyers or judges were available, but enough enlightened amateurs were present to help most people win a day in court. Justice was mild by the standards of the age; fines were frequently heavy; and litigation often lengthy. In cases of murder or other serious crimes, the trial-by-jury system was used; hanging was given the condemned without much delay. Even so, surprisingly few people merited the death penalty and were hanged.

Other colonies had in spirit similar, if varied governmental systems. Most everywhere in New England the urbanized township system prevailed, with a vast number of people tasting the fruits of representative government. Elsewhere rural conditions made the county form of government more practical, but urban communities had self-government where it was practical to give them these institutions. The difference between New England and the other colonies was the degree of popular participation. When one can join others in a discussion of issues, it is personal, direct, and exciting, but government by delegate at a distant courthouse, with a report by word of mouth or newspaper, may have been no less representative than the confrontation of the town meeting. It often drew into office persons of education who gave their lives to public service, and people like George Washington who sacrificed personal comfort for the Virginian commonwealth.

In Pennsylvania colonials failed to establish townships as William Penn had hoped, and counties became the basic unit of government. By 1755 only eight counties were erected for the whole colony of 150,000 people, and most county seats were distant from the majority of the county population. Services such as registry of deeds, civil court actions, criminal prosecutions, and probate often required long journeys and costly trips; as one critic complained, "the benefit of many good and wholesome laws was almost, if not entirely lost." Most of the county personnel, though fellow citizens as a rule, received appointment from the governor. Their offices stood at the center of county affairs and were coveted for the opportunities that they brought the incumbent. Other offices such as sheriff, the commissioners, and assessors were elective, and by tradition sheriffs served three one-year terms and did not succeed themselves.

Choosing candidates was not a completely open affair where citizens voted for men who "caught their fancy." Instead, influential men of weight and substance formed most slates, and deference played its important role in the voters' choice. Religion, wealth, family, and prior elective experience were also decisive influences. Non-Quakers learned early to cooperate with the Friends, and voters chose personalities who had gained some local prestige. With this understood, the voting statistics should not be surprising when they give a remarkably dismal account of popular participation. Less than 40 percent of the voters turned out for most elections. Pennsylvanians failed to vote because they lacked stimulation, because of the hardship of distances, and because of many petty excuses. Maybe the voters' conduct is more indicative than the excuses that they often gave in their letters—the election managers did a good job, and the indifference of the freemen "was the indifference of the satisfied."

The single-house legislature performed in many ways like the two-house Massachusetts General Court, but in two specific ways it was different. The Pennsylvania legislature adapted itself to the Quaker habit of silence and compromise. Governor George Thomas described the Assembly as a "conclave" rather than as a body of persons who were "accountable to their Electors." Most of its work was done off the floor, in committee rooms where there was less meditation and more confrontation by members. Unlike the Massachusetts assembly, the turnover of members was slight, and they were drawn from a narrow group of people who were part of the upper strata of society.

The legislature's relations with the governor always reflected an inherent tension. The governor represented the proprietary interest, the financial, landed, religious, and family interests of the Penns and their associates. The tension occurred in appointments and legislation, especially in taxing proprietary land and providing for defense, and the tension sometimes appeared in the elections when separate groups represented the two interests. When bitterness erupted, it often brought riots and bloodshed, and always much acrimony.

By comparison, politics in Virginia were tranquil. Most powers of government resided in the hands of the great planters, their relatives, and friends. To some extent their presence was most visible in the counties where they lived and held the offices, but they exercised intellectual and economic leadership throughout the colony, and it reached to the highest levels of authority. The Council and House of Burgesses provided opportunities to display their power as they met at Williamsburg, participated in the periodic ritual of considering the state of colony politics, socialized with their equals, and attended to legal and personal problems.

Power also was displayed at the planters' country seats: in their amassing of landed estate, the number of slaves they owned, their family connections, and their personal achievements. The gentry were a hard-working, ambitious people, with a tradition of independence already well-grounded; they were also "haughty and jealous of their liberties," as one observer noted, and were impatient of restraint and unable to "bear the thought of being controlled by any superior power."

Nevertheless, the planters had to face reality. Their God-like existence had its limitations. The major market for the tobacco crop was in England, and financial problems of surplus and sales often plunged the planters into serious debt. Besides, their crops were primarily worked by black slaves, whose numbers had increased by 1750 to nearly one third of the population of 300,000. The black slaves were generally docile, but maintenance of security caused tensions. To safeguard themselves the gentry developed black codes to regulate slave conduct, and reacted with harsh penalties when offenses occurred. Virginia, unlike New York, had little organized violence even though it had a greater number of slaves.

The power of the gentry was also challenged by the coming to Virginia of vast numbers of immigrants who took up land on the piedmont. Their small farms, mostly subsistence, brought into politics a new kind of Virginian who was frequently Scots-Irish, Presbyterian, and demanding of representation in county and colony government. New counties were erected to satisfy the needs of these settlers, but their uncultured voices in the House of Burgesses raised additional questions regarding legislative responsibility and popular rights.

Virginia was, nonetheless, well governed by its people, and British control was exercised through influence of culture and market. Much the same can be said for the planter-merchant aristocracy of South Carolina. Persons such as Charles Pinckney and Andrew Rutledge were usually members of the council and assembly, which kept out ordinary folk by high property qualifications. In fact, the Commons had the highest property requirements in the colonies, and seats were distributed in such a way as to severely limit representation to the tidewater and plantation areas. The Commons, thus under the control of the Charleston merchants and planters, had their hands upon finance, Indian trade, and local administration. Their conduct was informal, and as a traveler from Massachusetts observed, "the members conversed, lolled, and chatted much like a friendly jovial society."

Like other colonies, only the legislature could pass bills, and these became law only with the signature of the governor. Most governmental control also rested with the legislature, governor, and courts. Local government was surprisingly weak, but parishes of the Church of England had some power to handle their own affairs, and the road commissions oversaw the maintenance of public roads, bridges, and waterways within their districts. The most irritating aspect of government was the lack of proper governmental facilities in the back country, where courthouses, with their much-needed registry bureaus and courts were often distant. Officials frequently were the appointees of the distant planters or the royal governor, and had a different social background and religion.

For South Carolina, and for most other colonies, the people of property or business had the responsibility to govern. Such persons came forth in every colony to offer their services, frequently at a sacrifice of personal comfort, and there was a feeling of obligation to serve one's neighbors well. Most colonists regarded those who were born of respected families, Protestant in religion, and wealthy in land suitable for these responsibilities, and pledged their allegiance willingly and without much thought of equality or democracy. All colonies had representative governments whatever the state of the franchise. All drew their power from England by charter, by instructions to the governor, by an order from the Board of Trade, or by an act of Parliament. Though the power granted was modified from time to time, most people regarded their government as a right of Englishmen, and the legislatures were bold enough to wage battles with the governor or directly with the home government when they sensed restrictions were oppressive to liberty. Little was done, however, to establish regular constitutional limitations, probably because the issues did not touch a sufficient number of people.

Economic Affairs

In general, most North Americans were engaged in agriculture or in taking fish from the sea. Vast surpluses of grains, ores, tobacco, indigo, timber, and fish gave colonials sufficient products to exchange for other necessities so that they had a flourishing economy. Trade, however, was carried on with the English Caribbean isles in order to sell food surpluses and secure additional products for European trade. Commerce also with the Dutch, Spanish, and French empires—trade that was mostly illegal—brought in a supply of coin which was used to settle unfavorable balances.

The agriculture of New England provided subsistence living, but necessitated much effort almost everywhere. Its rocky lands had to be cleared, and its thin soils required loving care, but the rewards of good crops were possible if the capricious climate cooperated. Many colonials had thus to engage in other pursuits for a living. Some cut timber for masts or ships, others signed on for fishing voyages to Nova Scotia and Newfoundland. Many spent years on trading voyages to the Caribbean and Europe. A modest amount of manufacturing or processing also took place such as the processing of molasses into rum, salting of fish, and cutting of timber. Ships by the tens were always under construction, primarily for fishing and commerce. One has the impression that the growing New England population of 350,000 in 1750 was then pressing on the land supply, and there was a struggle to find food and employment. Some people drifted among the towns looking for work; others sought relief by migrating to Maine, Nova Scotia, and western Massachusetts. Thousands of farmers were tenants, sharing their crops to pay rent, and there were many day laborers. Overall, however, New Englanders were a hard-working, industrious people whose standard of living was good.

Some of the necessary foodstuffs came from New York, which was prospering because of the advantages of good land and climate. Grains, furs, and livestock were exported also to the Caribbean. Monopoly land ownership by the proprietors held down colony development, but by 1750 New York City had still become a major center of population, with nearly 15,000 people drawn from many nations. Its large black, servant population, numbering over a thousand, was restless and caused the white population much fear. In 1741 a revolt of some blacks brought fires and destruction, and a witch-hunt by white authorities caused many executions of whites as well as of blacks. Tempered always by these prevailing fears, whites lived well in their beautiful homes and large shops and the city was booming in appearance.

Contrasted to the fears and restraints of New Yorkers, people flooded into Pennsylvania, Delaware, and West New Jersey, making the area extraordinarily prosperous. Looking at the trading charts, one cannot help feeling that the area had balanced exports and imports. Its fine agricultural lands, good climate, and iron deposits, plus its thrifty, industrious people, gave the colonies enough of the trade balance that their merchants did not need to seek debt relief. Taxes were relatively low, and government was less a burden than anywhere in America. Luxuries were certainly most visible in Philadelphia and its surrounding areas. Fine homes, beautiful furnishings, and well-adorned carriages were enjoyed by the leadership groups, and the city itself was able to support many institutions that were commonplace in London—a hospital, libraries, societies, shops, and paved streets. Of course, in this paradise there were some imperfections. The trade with London drained the colony of hard currency, as it did elsewhere in America, and various kinds of expediencies were used. A local paper currency was tried, but it was subject to some fluctuation. The flood of immigrants, too, brought rewards as well as uncertainties because many pushed into the frontier where they and the Indians vied for the lands. The violence sometimes spread deep into settled country and brought demands for improved frontier defense. People suffered from these attacks; insecurity was often widespread.

Further south, Virginia enjoyed both the imperfections and the advantages of its plantation economy and temperate climate. Tobacco was the major money crop, though the colony grew wheat and other food crops and raised cattle and poultry. From the 1640s food had always been abundant in ordinary times; the surplus was sold to newcomers and traders. Tobacco had a primacy, however, that is difficult to appreciate. It grew so well and luxuriantly that oversupply depressed prices on the English market and growers were never certain of their profit margins. They were caught up in the problem of distant, advance credit, and dependence upon factors. Considering the uncertainties, one must judge that they did very well in the market and that they were generally satisfied with the profits. While the annual returns were nearly always doubtful, growers took their profits and put them into clothes, furniture, and household luxuries, bought slaves, and built spacious mansions. They used their free time, moreover, to develop a responsible type of society that appreciated order, education, religion, and family.

The tobacco crop was wearing upon the soil. Growers in marginal areas always faced the prospect of finding new land. The colony had thus a restlessness in its economy as growers amassed vast lands and searched out the Appalachian West for additional plantation sites. Some owners controlled well over 100,000 acres and formed companies to win additional grants of many millions of acres.

Land was an investment, but it also was a means of speculation. With thousands of immigrants coming yearly, Virginians sold lands, equipment, food, and services, and often rented their black slaves to help clear the forests. From this additional revenue, they received enough coin and credits undoubtedly to offset losses from the tobacco market.

Many of these immigrants were destined for Maryland. While the colony had less land to sell, its growers and the proprietors exploited their opportunities and made a good living. They engaged in trade with the Indians and divided the profits from a vigorous agricultural and trading economy, which developed in mid-century and led to the evolution of Baltimore as a seaport. Over the years they turned some tobacco lands into wheat acreage and the town became a center of flour mills. Vessels traveled through the Chesapeake Bay and to ports in the Caribbean and the British islands as they distributed the products of the region. Profits were good enough to attract an ever-increasing population.

Even though Baltimore had some characteristics of an urban area, both Maryland and Virginia remained generally rural. Little capital went into ships or trade facilities. The planters were agriculturalists who used tobacco as their principal money crop. It provided sufficient revenue over the years to give them a high standard of living, and even a comfortable living for those owning only small patches of tobacco. Much debt accumulated because of marketing practices and crop prices, but it apparently never unduly upset the planters who looked to a future of better crops and prices.

South Carolina was even more fortunate in the sale of rice, indigo, tobacco, and forest products. The economy was less troubled by surpluses in meeting English market conditions. The flow of profits was more predictable, and debt was not greatly burdensome. Indian trade, too, was a source of ready money with the exchange of furs for English products and services.

In all the colonies prosperity depended upon some trade outside their territories. New Englanders traded along the coast, to the Caribbean, England, Holland, Spain, and France. Some commerce was illicit, but it brought sufficient profits to settle accounts in England, and it also saved merchants from accumulating large debts. Products of other colonies found their way into the illicit market and all benefited by the aggressive merchandising. The tobacco trade also enjoyed an extralegal relationship with Europe, with seamen of New York, Pennsylvania, and New England participating. Tea, cloth, wines, and furniture were often exchanged.

The Caribbean was an essential part of the economy. The sugar isles rarely had enough food for their inhabitants, and surpluses of the northern colonies thus had a ready market. The French isles were handicapped by commercial restrictions that prohibited the importation of molasses or rum into the home market. These products were exchanged for wheat or fish which were transported by British colonials. Sometimes trade extended to the Spanish coasts of Central and South America, where profits were good but the dangers of seizure were great.

In managing this trade, colonials developed networks of associations. Sometimes New Englanders went to the Caribbean, Nova Scotia, or Newfoundland and acted as managers of businesses. Other times the enticement of profits brought them to Charleston, New York, and Albany. Frequently members of the family settled in London, Bristol, or Plymouth. The Livingston and Wendell families, the Hutchinsons and Temples, the Vassells and Hamiltons had family arrangements in distant ports. Americans, in brief, were energetic and commercially minded partners in the gigantic British empire.

The Anglo-Americans

Not all Americans were Englishmen, Scotsmen, or Irishmen, for there were also Germans, Swedes, Dutch, and Africans. But more than half of the two million people in 1750 were originally from the United Kingdom. Since the founding of Jamestown four or five generations had passed, with less time passing for the newer colonies like Pennsylvania or Georgia. Certain patterns of development were readily apparent regardless of land conditions or time of settlement. Most Britons were family people who believed in marriage, loved (or tolerated) many children, and made homes for themselves. The size of their homes depended upon their success, but they took up homesteads, planted orchards and fields of corn or wheat, raised cattle and poultry, and added to their acreage as sons came of age to help them. Most were God-fearing Protestants, Bible readers and sermon-tasters, and tinged with Puritanism. They passed laws against swearing, supported religious worship, and called often for days of fast and thanksgiving.

Their homes they called mansion houses. The buildings were simple at first—only a few rooms downstairs and a couple of bedrooms upstairs. Time and fortune often permitted extensions of the house, with bedrooms, a parlor, large kitchen, and additional fireplaces. Sometimes in Virginia and South Carolina the urge for beauty came early, and truly well-constructed homes of brick were built, with splendid staircases to upstairs rooms; spacious, airy rooms; outside kitchen and pantry; and views and walkways. New Englanders may have been a bit slower to react to the desire for beauty, but their houses on the bluffs of Milton, along the rivers, and on hilltops overlooking the ports had breathtaking charm. Decorated as they were with some fine furniture, carpets, and portraits, these homes gave much comfort to their owners.

For most Americans there was more simplicity. Their homes with floors, windows, and handmade furniture were less luxurious, but there could be a print of the governor or king on the wall, a handful or armload of books on the table, changes of clothes in the closet, and an assortment of pots and pans in the kitchen. The house, being small, had the press of people, the noise of children, and little privacy. People were hardy and lived on wholesome food. If they were lucky, they could live a long time. But childbirth, infant diseases, ruptures, accidents, and ordinary ills took their toll.

Americans multiplied, nonetheless, and the colonies were generally a healthful place to live. The isolated areas, even though subject to hazards of the frontier, seemed even more healthful than the sea coast. They were less ravaged by the epidemics that passed through the cities, and commonsense precautions increased life expectancy often by decades. In the Massachusetts town of Andover (studied by Philip Greven) successive generations of men seemed to live less on an average as the town made contacts with its neighbors. The second generation lived to an average age of 64.2 years, while the third and fourth generations declined respectively, to 62.4 and 59.8 years. Still, a goodly number (39.4 percent) lived past seventy years even in the eighteenth century. Compared with Boston's mortality rate for men and women of 21 per thousand in 1701 and an average of 31 to 46 per thousand in 1744, Andover's rate of 16 per thousand in 1715, 19 in 1725, 9 in 1735, and 15 in 1740 should be regarded as excellent. Other inland towns may have matched its record of healthful living.

To generalize about the age of marriage in America after 1720 may be futile, but in Andover after 1720 men married about the age of twenty-six years and women a year or two younger. In Bristol, Rhode Island, women married as they turned twenty. For most couples, children arrived in proper time and then fairly regularly in the fifteen to twenty years after marriage. In Andover families averaged about eight children. Studies of members of the Massachusetts legislature would indicate that the experience of Andover was the experience of its colonial leaders.

Aged parents or relatives usually lived in the home of a son or daughter or relatives, which earlier may have been the family home. In a will husbands provided for their widows a room of the house, firewood, horse, cow, and transportation to the church and town. Most widows often received a share of the family property and a return of what they brought into the marriages. The wife (and widow), however, was dependent upon her husband who might distribute most of the family

A New England kitchen. *(Library of Congress)*

property to the children as he became older. She would not be destitute because families took care of their own, and social consciousness imposed a responsibility upon the children.

Religion in America

Colonial America was primarily Protestant in religious belief. Some Catholics lived in Pennsylvania, Maryland, and Rhode Island, but only a few were visible in colonial life. A lesser number of Jews settled in America, primarily in Newport, Philadelphia, and Charleston. They worked as artisans and merchants in the towns, though some became farmers in the country. New England remained primarily Congregational, with many Baptists in Rhode Island, a sprinkling of Presbyterians everywhere, and a few Anglicans in Boston and Cambridge. In New York the Dutch worshiped in the Reformed Church, but most English were Anglicans or Congregationalists. Pennsylvania had the largest mixture of religions. Though Quakers founded the colony and dominated the government, they were a minority in a population of Presbyterians, German pietists, and Anglicans. Quakers also spread into neighboring Delaware and New Jersey, but here, too, Anglicans and Presbyterians were probably the majority group. The southern colonies were primarily Anglican, but local control and ministerial selection gave their churches characteristics of Congregationalism.

By the fourth decade Americans were restless in their religious practices and beliefs. In frontier Massachusetts Jonathan Edwards at Northampton was experimenting with a form of revivalism. He was worried about the rigidity of worship, the lack of commitment, and the historic way of admitting people to church membership. At the same time missionary bands of Anglican enthusiasts were moving through the colonies, using preaching, exhorting, music, and emotion to awaken people's sense of duty to God and the peril of damnation. Leaders like George Whitefield, Charles and John Wesley, and Gilbert and William Tennant, in England and America, spread their messages, and surprisingly large groups pledged their souls to God.

Popular reaction to the revivals was unlike anything the colonies had ever seen. Almost everywhere crowds turned out; great religious displays occurred; and a religious revolution of a sort resulted. Congregationalism in New England was shaken to its roots, and "New Light" churches were established in many communities. Old congregations also re-examined the basis of their beliefs, with some modification of worship and doctrine resulting. Americans undoubtedly became more tolerant of each other than ever before, and the power of the old ministerial group in New England was lessened. Perhaps more Americans had greater regard for each other as human beings than in the past, accepting the concept of natural rights philosophers that all persons had human rights of life, liberty, and property.

As the century unfolded the colonists were content to build in a modest fashion their homes and churches. In their opinion worship of God did not require cathedrals or social institutions. Nor were they monument builders in a religious or secular sense. Even the buildings at Harvard and Yale colleges were modest, and there was nothing that represented a capitol building which was truly impressive. Their only monuments of a sort were their own tombstones, but even these were less impressive as markers than for their word-messages to future generations.

8

Frontier America

All colonies in British North America lined the Atlantic coast and reached inland in a few places from one hundred to one hundred and fifty miles. Exceptions were the lines of settlement up the Chesapeake Bay and the Hudson and Connecticut rivers. The spread of settlers almost everywhere was thin, and forested and unsettled country separated and isolated communities everywhere. West of the farms was mountainous country that was an effective barrier for years to settlement and travel. In several places along the frontier there were natural pathways into the West, or the North, but otherwise, the mountains, trees, brush, and the dangers from Indian attack made travel slow and hazardous. The Cumberland Gap, the Mohawk River and waterways of New York, and the water route across lakes George and Champlain are examples of breaks in the barrier.

For most Anglo-Americans there was a mystery and excitement about the West, and they claimed vast areas of this unknown region for future settlement. Virginia had charter claims sweeping across the continent to the "isle of California"; Massachusetts looked to the Mississippi River as a possible boundary; but almost all the colonies had interest in the West as a place of expansion for their people. Perhaps New York alone had the most extended western reach when it established Oswego on Lake Ontario as a trading post. Governor Alexander Spotswood of Virginia in 1716 took a band of adventurers into the Shenandoah Valley, and other Virginians followed his exploits by breaching the Appalachian mountains in the 1720s and 1730s.

These exploratory ventures were followed by the spread of

immigrants into the area. Germans and Scots-Irish moved from the port of Philadelphia into the West in large numbers, and some settled around Harpers Ferry in 1726. Others went across the piedmont area of Virginia and into the Shenandoah Valley. Their success convinced members of the Virginia government that they could establish colonies and trading posts on the upper Ohio River. Under the leadership of Thomas Lee of the Virginia council, the Ohio Company was organized in 1747. Other land companies then followed until there was an involvement of nearly every important Virginian in these ventures. The Washington family was among these families who had significant landed claims and who felt the excitement of the West.

Farther South immigrants were pushing into the piedmont area of North and South Carolina. Defeat of the Tuscarora Indians allowed thousands of Scots-Irish to spread into their hunting area, and the population multiplied impressively. Speculators in both colonies also secured vast tracts of land, and they offered, in turn, to sell the land in small parcels. Similar conditions, if not exaggerated, prevailed in Virginia, Western Massachusetts, and Maine. Land hunger affected most of these people, but speculation was also a way of gaining riches.

French Canada

The western area of New England, New York, Pennsylvania, Maryland, and Virginia was French territory. Most irritating to these Americans was the French influence with the Indians, their claim to lands which Americans thought were theirs, and their Roman Catholic religion. Rivalry, too, was intense in the northern fishing banks of Nova Scotia and Newfoundland. The Canadians did not pose much of a threat because their population was small and the colony struggled for survival. But it was an area, nevertheless, held tenaciously by France, and in the many bitter disputes between England and France in Europe the empires clashed also in America. For the home countries the border disputes were regarded as minor issues compared with territorial gains in Europe.

The clashes first began with King William's War in 1689 and lasted until 1697. Perhaps the greatest impact for Americans was felt in organizing campaigns against Quebec. Drives were eventually made up the lake route in New York and through the St. Lawrence Gulf and River. Both campaigns failed miserably, though William Phips, the commander of the St. Lawrence expedition, actually reached Quebec City. Most of the hostilities, however, were frontier raids, primarily by Indians, that accomplished nothing strategic except to bring heartaches and suffering to those living in exposed areas.

The war increased the awareness of France at Quebec, nonetheless, and awakened particularly the hostility among Puritans of the Catholic presence there. When another chance came to attack Quebec, the New Englanders understood their objective better. The Queen Anne's War (The War of the Spanish Succession) took place first in the Caribbean, where the British navy not only drove the French from the Bahamas and St. Christopher Island, but also destroyed most of the French fleet and merchantmen. In the northern colonies the rivals exchanged raids along the frontier, often with bloody consequences. The massacre at Deerfield in 1704 was the most serious. Attacks on the fisheries of both nations were devastating and brought fishing to a halt. But British control of the seas in the end led to successful seizure of Port Royal in Arcadia (Nova Scotia). An expedition against Quebec City floundered when transports through carelessness ran on the reefs of Egg Island.

The peace conference at Utrecht in 1712 and 1713, however, brought more enduring results than these American assaults. The delegates agreed first to establish equilibrium in America. They would then guarantee each other's possessions and pledge no future alienation of territory. They established in the treaties a kind of stability and order that seemed lasting and reasonable to them. France ceded to Britain title to many troubled areas in America like Newfoundland and the Hudson Bay, which had been already British for years, and Britain received the French territories of St. Christopher (St. Kitts) and Nova Scotia as well. Commissions in the future were to set definite boundaries for the contiguous territories. Britain also obtained the Assiento privilege of France for supplying the Spanish territories with black slaves: she could annually import 4,800 blacks into the Spanish colonies for the coming thirty years. In addition, she gained the privilege of sending a yearly ship of merchandise to the Spanish colonial port of Porto Bello. Britain gained possession from Spain of such strategic areas as Gibraltar and Minorca. The French, in general, lost much prestige, but retained most of Canada and received the right to place a member of their royal family on the Spanish throne. Though the countries were to be ever separated, the Bourbon family made a major acquisition of power and prestige. French merchants in particular were granted trading privileges in Cadiz and the end of a long and costly war.

The peace of Utrecht endured, if only precariously, for nearly a generation. In control of English policy during these years were the Whigs under the benevolent rule of Sir Robert Walpole, who balanced the hazards of war against the advantages of peace and carried sufficient numbers of his party with him to win votes of confidence for peace. For both England and America, these were years of prosperity, expansion, and development. Immigration of Scots-Irish, Germans, and English to the colonies doubled the population, and natural increases were likewise significant. Georgia was founded as a colony in 1732, and the back country of all the colonies with frontiers was penetrated with settlements, particularly Pennsylvania, which developed rapidly.

The population was well over a million people in 1739 when the War of Jenkins' Ear broke out. While the immediate cause of the war was the clipping of a smuggler's ear, rivalry between Spain and Britain had long irritated leaders of both nations who argued about British penetration of the border country of Florida and Georgia and trade relations in the Caribbean. Battles of the war were primarily in the Gulf of Mexico, with a major attack on Cartegena and assaults along the Georgia frontier. In 1744 France joined Spain and the war spread to Europe and concerned succession to the Austrian throne. Stalemates in Europe along with disasters in the Caribbean upset British imperialists. The only bright spot for them, and an embarrassing one at that, was a colonial-inspired attack on Louisbourg in 1745. The successful assault was organized by Governor William Shirley of Massachusetts and his merchant friends, who whipped up religious enthusiasm against papist domination of the West. New Englanders also hoped for the liquidation of French rule in Quebec and pressed hard for British assistance, but Britain withdrew the promised aid in 1746, 1747, and 1748 when it had crises in Scotland and on the continent, and gave Louisbourg back to France in the Peace of Aix-la-Chapelle. Its return was made, however, on the assumption that colonial rivalry could be ended by a peace commission and the American empires could be neutralized.

That assumption was totally unrealistic, but it represented also the thinking of the British cabinet which regarded Europe as more important in defense strategy than America. The royal family had its seat in Hanover; the Low Countries were a traditional part of the balance of power; and the peril of France and Spain was primarily in Europe. This assumption did not allow for French military activity in Quebec, with her forts along the frontier from Louisbourg to Crown Point and to Fort Duquesne in backwoods Pennsylvania. Nor did it allow for British colonial interests in the Ohio Valley, upper New York, and the St. Lawrence. Politicians like William Pitt, Lord Halifax, and William Shirley also used voice and pen to emphasize the importance of the colonies, often to the point of irritating the cabinet and king who could not understand their enthusiasm. Shirley, as governor of Massachusetts, urged repeatedly the liquidation of French Canada and claimed a boundary for the Bay Colony on the Mississippi

River. Like Lord Halifax, he wanted Britain to rule a great trading empire, and he grasped any plan that would bring this unity about. Pitt shared many of these same ideas, but not so consistently as Shirley and Halifax. In time his ability to orate and dramatize the value of the empire and his position as a member of the House of Commons gave him the prominence to spread his ideas to a large audience.

The Rising Crisis

The Peace of Aix-la-Chapelle in 1748 turned out to be more a truce than a peace for the great powers. Soon after the treaty, England tried to separate Spain from France by renegotiating the Assiento and succeeded in convincing Spain that a cash payment of £100,000 was equable. At the same time Britain let the Hudson's Bay Company spread its fur-trading activities into the northwestern plains of America; she decided to establish an English colony in Nova Scotia and made plans to remove the Acadians to other parts of the empire; and she moved unsuccessfully to occupy St. Lucia and other neutral islands in the West Indies. All this activity had a hostile impression upon the French in Quebec. They had already been worried about the moves of the land companies and the rising power of the British colonials. Their reaction could be anticipated: they built forts along the Bay of Fundy, increased the fire power of Louisbourg, Crown Point, and Ticonderoga, and ordered new forts along the Great Lakes and at present-day Pittsburgh (Duquesne). The French were concerned also about the vitality of their bases along the St. Lawrence, and plans were now being made to open colonies in the Ohio Valley. They sent Céloron de Blainville to scout the Ohio River and meet with the Indians. He buried leaden plates, as was the habit of conquerors, to establish French rights of sovereignty.

British Americans from Virginia countered these activities in the Ohio Valley with plans of their own to plant colonies. They sent William Trent in 1753 to the forks of the Ohio where he was ordered to build a fort, but he met a French expedition there, which forced him to withdraw. The next year George Washington of Virginia, who had previously surveyed some of this area, also was compelled to retire under threat of French arms.

These moves were admittedly small, but colonials on both sides of the frontier considered them serious incidents. Boundary negotiations in Paris as part of the Peace of Aix-la-Chapelle had broken down. Small issues had now enlarged. The British ministry, however, was not ready to wage war in America. Most ministers had little idea where the centers of dispute were and less knowledge about their importance. But they did feel that tensions should be reduced and their colonials should be protected. Some felt that the Americans should be controlled—that more guidance and a firm hand were needed.

There was much speculation in 1754 on what should be done about the crisis. The Board of Trade asked the governor of New York to call a meeting of colonial leaders, and he invited them to send delegates to Albany in July. The main reason for the conference, the governor said, was the formulation of a plan to defend themselves and win the help of the friendly Indians, primarily the Six Nations of Iroquois.

Reaction to the conference from a group of fiercely independent colonies was unexpectedly favorable. Seven governments sent delegates, and a few of the delegates brought plans for colonial union. Benjamin Franklin's Plan (or Albany Plan) is best known, but his plan and those of Thomas Hutchinson of Massachusetts and Thomas Pownall of London only pointed up the accepted need that people were troubled deeply by the crisis. The Franklin Plan, as it left the conference, provided for a governor-general, a grand council of representatives, and powers for an army and a civil service. The Plan was primarily concerned with Indian relations, trade, land policy, and immigration, but significantly the government was to have taxing power, military authority, and supervisory powers over the West.

The Plan's reception by the colonial legislatures was generally cool because suspicious people worried about the power of other colonies and of the British government. Only the Massachusetts legislature gave the plan full legislative debate, but on two successive votes the opposition registered decisive negative votes. The British ministry itself was not energetic either in backing the plan, and turned instead to a military solution. It decided to send over Major General Edward Braddock, who was fifty-nine years of age, plus two Irish regiments and some ships from the fleet, and to enlist Americans for two additional regiments. Its plan of action in theory was limited to the removal of French encroachments along the frontier. Its forces were pitifully inadequate to the task, if only because of their inexperience.

News of these British plans reached William Shirley at Boston in early December 1754, and in conferences with Charles Lawrence of Nova Scotia they developed a supporting plan of their own. They would raise volunteers and gather a small fleet for attacks on forts near the Bay of Fundy. In the meantime, Shirley also met with the New England governors or their representatives, who also included people from New York and New Jersey, and additional attacks were accepted in principle. Troops under a colonial leader would assault the French forts of Ticonderoga and Crown Point while Lawrence besieged forts on the Bay of Fundy. While forces numbering a few thousands were raised for this campaign, colonials awaited news of plans for the major attacks.

In the meantime, Edward Braddock had arrived in America. Brief consultations in Virginia with colonial officials convinced him that a general conference of governors should be called. The meeting in Alexandria, Virginia, in early April set the campaign objectives, which incorporated the two attacks already planned on the Bay of Fundy and the New York lake routes. Another one was planned into western New York along the Mohawk River to Oswego, with an attack on the French fort of Niagara. Braddock set the task of attacking Fort Duquesne for himself. He would go from Alexandria up the Potomac River and hence by forest trails to Fort Duquesne. After the conquest of Fort Duquesne, he expected to join Shirley in a victory at Niagara; then they would march to Albany and take possible action against the French on Lake Champlain. Finally, the season might close at Boston or on the Bay of Fundy. The spaciousness of the plan did not allow for distances, the hardship of frontier travel, the perils of Indian country, and the inexperience of everyone in these matters.

The campaign was fated to failure from the beginning. Braddock had difficulties moving his troops and matériel to the frontier, was delayed unnecessarily, and then fell into an ambush in July and was killed. At Braddock's death Shirley became the commander-in-chief, but he already had enough problems both in exercising his authority over William Johnson, who headed the march on the New York lake route, and in raising sufficient troops and supplies. Shirley was late in leaving for Oswego and was bogged down by the complexities of his march when Braddock was killed. He never reached Fort Niagara, but terminated his march at Oswego where he reinforced the fort. Johnson also was less than successful: wounded by Indians or French, he refused to give up his command and let the opportunity of an attack on Ticonderoga slip out of his hands. Only in the north were the British successful against the French forts.

The dismal results of the British campaign were reviewed in London, but no easy solution was found because the ministerial position was unstable and because there was uncertainty what military course to follow. In the meantime Shirley was permitted to hold the command without either much direction from home or money to finance new measures. Political quarrels among the colonies over contracting, direction of the war, and explanations for the 1755 disasters divided colonials and undercut Shirley's authority. Particularly serious was a quarrel with Wil-

liam Johnson, who claimed he was appointed an independent superintendent of Indian relations—a quarrel that involved New York and New
England as well as the direction of the war.

When the British ministers finally reached a consensus, they decided
to appoint another British general, John Campbell, the Earl of Loudoun:
to give him a military staff, troops, and naval support; and then to strike
out at French military power. War in the meantime was declared between
France and Britain, and the idea of limited war was abandoned. There was
still some debate among cabinet members concerning the direction of the
war and the importance of America.

In the early summer of 1756 when Loudoun arrived in New York
City, the French were already prepared to besiege Oswego which they
would capture in August. In turn, the loss of morale, confusion, and
bungling of operations brought a momentary standstill to plans for
attacking Canada. Because of this situation, the ministry regrouped in
November and December 1756 and admitted its major critic, William Pitt,
to the cabinet. Pitt became Secretary of State for the Southern
Department, which gave him directing authority of American affairs.

Pitt's rise to power brought an unusual person of great ability into
the government. Friend and foe alike praised Pitt as the greatest orator of
his age because of his eloquence, sarcasm, and wit. These were used to
dramatize his favorite policies, which were often a reflection of his egotism
and arrogance. But he was expert in his knowledge of military affairs,
interested in America, and contemptuous of ministerial bungling. Pitt was
an honest man whose standards of conduct were nearly unequalled in his
day. But he could rise to heights of emotion in which he denounced
colleagues, often with accusations that were grossly unfair. He was a
master of detail, completely dedicated to his responsibilities, and ready to
excite people about him to patriotic fervor.

Though Pitt was only forty-eight years of age when he took office,
he had poor health during much of his life. A tall, gaunt figure, he had few
close friends and many enemies. His popular following in London among
the common people gave him a base of power that was irresistible. He
entered into office, however, in partnership with the Whig party which
provided limits for some time on his initiative. Pitt was cautious both in
his opening speech to Parliament and in his policies but he asked for a
buildup of the navy and an effective militia. His modest promise reveals
much of the man, his spirit, and determination: "I know that I can save
England, and that nobody else can."

Pitt in Office

Once in office, Pitt set out to make the prosecution of the war more effective than it had been in 1756. He ordered a fleet for an attack on Fort Louisbourg, advised Loudoun to give military support to the navy, and got ready an expeditionary force of eight thousand troops for colonial defense. His plans, however, were strenuously opposed in Parliament and by the king, and for a few weeks Pitt lost control of military affairs and had to leave the ministry. A reorganization of the cabinet in early June brought in a coalition government in which he was given superior authority. But the loss of momentum in mid-1757 disrupted Pitt's plans and the campaign was generally a disaster. Fort William Henry on Lake George capitulated in August after a bloody siege and the navy missed later its target in a heavy fog at Louisbourg.

The year 1757 was gloomy for almost everyone. A newly appointed governor of Massachusetts, Thomas Pownall, replaced the experienced Shirley in August. By late fall Pownall and Loudoun were engaged in a serious dispute over the powers of the commander-in-chief to quarter soldiers in inns and to regulate their conduct in Massachusetts. The bitter argument brought a threat by Loudoun to use military force to provide quarters, and a declaration by the legislature in turn that it represented the will of the people and would not be intimidated.

The legislature became less vocal as Pownall worked out a compromise with Loudoun, but there remained a lasting impression that military power in a confrontation with civilian authority must give way. Loudoun's power to discipline the militiamen also raised arguments because these citizen-soldiers were not regulars and subject to military law. The heat of the argument, notwithstanding Loudoun's presence in the colonies, raised an issue in many minds about British military power and its relation to colonial charters and individual rights.

Less antagonism was raised about Indian affairs, but Loudoun confirmed William Johnson of New York in his position as Indian superintendent of the northern frontier. For the moment the frontier was ablaze and any measures to bring stability were welcomed. But Johnson had become a British official and was charged with the regulation of trade on the frontier. It could interfere with the rights of trade which colonials had claimed for themselves.

As Pitt assessed the results of the 1757 campaigns and colonial unrest, he decided to remove the Earl of Loudoun and elevate major general James Abercromby to the command. Abercromby was a fellow Scot, but less aggressive in personality and tactics than Loudoun. Pitt's appointment of Abercromby proved to be a poor one. However, Pitt put John Forbes in charge of an attack on Fort Duquesne and Jeffrey Amherst in command of the siege of Louisbourg, and he filled the ranks and staffs with many new, talented soldiers; these men were, on the whole, worthy of the trust Pitt lodged in them. Most importantly, Pitt decided to have Britain take over the entire cost of the war, which was hitherto partly financed by the colonies, and to use primarily regulars in the frontal operations. The war now had a professional direction, with Pitt giving the direction through his plans and leadership.

In 1758 only Abercromby failed in his mission. Without sufficient troops, regulars and militia, and staff support, he moved over the forest-lake route slowly toward Fort Ticonderoga. His tactics were poor in the siege that followed his late arrival, and the heavy losses from a frontal attack demoralized his forces. This reverse led to Abercromby's recall by Pitt late in 1758 and to the succession of Amherst as commander-in-chief. Otherwise, the results of Pitt's strategy were indeed successful, and colonial reaction everywhere was laudatory. Bonfires, fireworks, candles in the windows, and punchbowls of spirits were symbolic gestures of the happiness everyone felt for these British victories at Duquesne, Louisbourg, and at sea. Pitt became the "Darling of the Public"; and Parliament showed its regard by ordering great new expenditures so that French power in Canada could be liquidated.

The war would continue for another year or two as British forces stormed Quebec City and moved to force the surrender of other Canadian cities. In other operations the army or navy moved to take over posts in the Ohio Valley and on islands in the Caribbean. Their successes brought the collapse of French power and created a fear in Spain. In 1762 Spain and Britain formally declared war against each other. The fortunes of Spain, however, were against her from the beginning, with British seizures of Florida, Cuba, and the Philippines in rapid succession. Such victories gave Pitt visions of attacks on other Spanish territories, but members of his coalition, the new king George III, and the merchants questioned his wisdom in prolonging the war after the collapse of Canada and other parts of the French empire.

The Peace of 1763

Old King George II died in the fall of 1760 and his grandson succeeded him to the throne. The young man, often regarded as inexperienced by critics, brought with him to office his tutor and adviser Lord Bute, many friends, and a questioning attitude about the war. The debt had risen dramatically during the war; the tax burden was at the breaking point; and military levies were being resisted. Had England enough territory already, asked the king? What could she gain by taking more land from Spain? Pitt's reply was made in terms of the advantages of wealth, empire, trade, and the liquidation of Spanish power that Britain could obtain.

Almost needless to add, Pitt resigned when he was pressed by the king on the need to continue the war. Lord Bute took over, and negotiations for the peace proceeded quickly. However, some politicians were angry over Pitt's resignation and Bute's move into the center of power. The press occasionally ridiculed Bute, circulated scandal about Bute's affections with the king's mother, and applied pressure on the ministry to resign. They criticized the pending peace, but it was negotiated successfully, nonetheless, and Britain won more territory than most people wanted or dreamed necessary. France ceded Canada to Britain, including the Ohio Valley but not Louisiana. Spain exchanged Florida for Cuba and the Philippines. French possessions in India and Africa were also awarded to Britain. In a separate treaty France ceded Louisiana to Spain partly to compensate her for losses in the war. France was returned a few islands in the Caribbean and bases for trade in India, but these areas should be regarded as tastes of empire compared with what she lost.

The Seven Years War was thus ended. England became the greatest colonial power, the greatest sea power, and, in the hearts of colonials, the greatest of civilizations in culture, liberty, religion, and standard of living. The celebrations honoring George III's accession and coronation were a high point of patriotism for everyone in the empire.

The Impact of War

The decades of global war which ended with the Peace of Paris in 1763 had many consequences for the future. During those years of hostility Americans fought France both in the forests and on the sea lanes. The West for them had remained a bloody barrier for years when Indians and soldiers could turn back colonial traders and settlers. It was hazardous to live in exposed areas, and many colonials who wanted to migrate to Maine or backcountry New York or Pennsylvania hesitated as they heard stories of massacres and scalpings. The war had now removed the French menace, and gave colonials new hope that they could move to fertile lands and enjoy opportunities of a fresh start. Even during the war, New Englanders anticipated victory by moving up the Connecticut River into New Hampshire and Vermont, up the Merrimac River into New Hampshire, and by land and sea into backcountry Maine. The Mohawk River Valley of New York was also receiving adventurous settlers but even more daring people were moving through Maryland into the Shenandoah and Ohio valleys of Virginia. The war thus loosened up frontier barriers, and people grasped at opportunities to leave their social and economic problems in the tideland for an uncertain future.

Unfortunately, the frontier was not yet safe for settlement in the Ohio Valley. Even before war hostilities had ceased, a serious Indian uprising had imperiled thousands of settlers. The great Ottawa leader, Pontiac, had convinced his nation in 1762 that they should gather allies and fight the English. Almost everywhere in the valley they besieged forts, and settlers were either frightened into them or massacred in their homes. Amherst rushed troops into the area, and the show of strength, with a few pitched battles against the Delawares and Shawnee carried out by Colonel Henry Bouquet, eventually restored order. The peace remained tenuous, and the presence of troops was essential.

Britain was not at all happy by these extra expenditures to bring peace to the Ohio Valley. It plainly upset calculations to reduce costs and restore normalcy to imperial relations. Americans were less affected by the new campaign, though they provided some troops as auxiliaries. Most colonials had enjoyed the unusual advantages of having Britain wage war in America. Some served as contractors to supply food, masts, and services; others offered warehousing, docks, and longshoremen; still others provided ships and repair services. Almost all the colonies were paid for recruiting volunteers and providing services. The economies thus prospered, and exchange problems, which were hitherto difficult to solve in peacetime, were easily settled by the bills of credit drawn on the British government.

In spite of the prosperity, some smuggling with the enemy was suspected by Pitt's agents, and British authorities used search warrants to examine warehouses and stores for illegal goods. Reacting to the reports, Pitt issued an order in 1760 which was designed to stamp out illegal traffic, but the lessening war purchases after 1760 probably encouraged alternative ways to increase the flow of commerce. Units of the British navy were then stationed outside American ports, and sea captains were enticed to be on the alert for smugglers by sharing in the receipts from fines and confiscations. Reaction to seizures, however, was instantaneous in Boston. Tension there brought a challenge to the writs of assistance, and James Otis, Jr., a local attorney, denounced them as a violation of the natural rights of citizens. Governor Francis Bernard, who had succeeded Pownall in 1760, also faced a hostile opposition in the Massachusetts legislature which questioned his appointments, British trade policies, and colonial relations with England.

Difficult times in 1761 and 1762 became hard times in 1763 and 1764. Colonials had trouble returning to a lower level of economic activity, and a few firms actually went bankrupt. Some colonials looked to the West for trade in furs or to the sale of land to European and American immigrants. They revived the activities of the Ohio Company as well as those of the Indiana Company. Veterans also pushed for land grants as a reward for their services in the war.

These unsettled conditions took the edge off the peace celebrations of 1763. Most people were happy, however, that the war had been favorably concluded and praised King George and the ministry for their successful effort. Colonials were an independent lot, however, who had participated in the late war as their spirits had moved them. Their gratitude was measured, often restrained, and their conduct was frequently inglorious. During the war thousands refrained from offering their services, many deserted from the militia, thousands made profits, even fortunes, from contracting and provisioning. There was lukewarm cooperation from legislatures, with much debate over military levies and expenditures. Governors, British commanders, and colonial officials faced contentious, frequently obnoxious colonials who stood on rights, a colonial charter, or a law as they refused to bend for the common good. Contrariwise, thousands of persons accepted service, tramped into the wilderness, and suffered dysentery and the inconveniences of camp life. Their privations were frequently unrecognized by fellow colonials or by the British government. For many, therefore, the war's conclusion was a great event, but the peace brought problems that disturbed even the optimists.

9

An Empire in Crisis

Only weeks after the formal end of the Seven Years War in 1763, the British cabinet was reconstructed and the young king George III asked George Grenville to form a ministry. Grenville became its first Lord of the Treasury and Chancellor of the Exchequer. Long a member of the House of Commons and holder of offices in the cabinets, Grenville was a brother-in-law of William Pitt and an expert on finance. He was conscientious, hardworking, and moderate in his policies. Unlike Lord Bute, his predecessor as head of the government, he was an experienced officeholder who enjoyed the rough-and-tumble of politics for well over a generation. Grenville had no great vision concerning his role in history, but was determined to come to grips with the problems irritating the nation and to find solutions for them. His view of colonial policy was traditional, perhaps based upon suspicion of American smuggling and loyalty, and he sought practical solutions for pressing issues of government.

His ministry was confronted with many serious problems. Among them was the task of ruling vast territories in America, the Caribbean, and India, with their foreign populations and countless Indians in the frontier regions of North America. At home, he faced the problem of financing a national debt of nearly £139 million, which some people regarded as tantamount to bankruptcy. Trade was sluggish due to a post-war depression, and taxes were particularly burdensome. Unrest was evident in Cornwall and many port cities. A rabble-rouser in London, John Wilkes, was exciting the people and disciplinary action was stoutly resisted. Undoubtedly Grenville's greatest problem was finding working relations with the North American empire which had hitherto opposed any fundamental change in the government. Grenville had some appreciation of the popular conception that the assemblies possessed true legislative power, but he faced governmental issues everywhere that needed national solutions, and he chose to avoid consultations on a local level. He probably never dreamed, as did most Americans, that his legislative solutions to imperial problems would be explosive and tear the nation apart.

Grenville's Legislation

Many of Grenville's acts now fall naturally into place as self-evident, but he and his ministers never really thought in terms of a comprehensive program of reform. Others like Thomas Pownall and Francis Bernard had suggested policy development, and their ideas in time reached Grenville's desk. Pownall's *Administration of the Colonies* was first published in 1764 and then partly revised as new issues troubled the empire. This book was published sometime after Grenville initiated his reforms, and was read by the prime minister. The first of Grenville's acts was the Proclamation of October 4, 1763 which tightened customs controls. It was designed to suppress smuggling through the use of English naval vessels cruising American waters. Not an unusual order, American reaction was nevertheless almost immediately hostile in New York, Rhode Island, and Massachusetts. Governor Stephen Hopkins of Rhode Island wrote an essay on trade which protested British meddling, and the essay was sent to Grenville for his consideration.

Three days after the above proclamation was issued, another provided for law and order in settled territories. The settled area of Canada was defined as well as those of East and West Florida, and these regions, including the new colonies in the Caribbean, were then given English self-government. The unsettled area west of the high watershed of the Allegheny mountains was set aside for administration by the commanding general of British forces. Since many coastal colonies had claims to this region, their charters were thus technically violated and their trade with the Indians disrupted. To regulate the trade and land use, two Indian superintendencies were erected, and the army and superintendents were instructed to bring peace to the region. American speculators, traders, and legalists protested this invasion of colonial rights regardless of the danger of Indian attacks and feared the intrusion of British merchants into their territory. Whoever got the benefit of the regulation, the cost of this defense put an immediate strain upon British finances that were already burdened by debt. More than anything else the government needed new sources of revenue so that the army could be paid for occupying the Ohio Valley and Florida. Grenville first selected a small tax upon imports to meet his objective. Taxes were laid upon foreign wines, molasses, silks, indigo, coffee, and a few other items. His advisers also wanted to curb the flow of illegal goods in the empire and aid London merchants by directing trade into English ports. This Revenue Act, popularly called the Sugar Act, was thus both mercantilist as well as monetary. It favored the British West Indies and the English merchants and had an objective of redirecting trade into the British shipping lanes. Whether it would have produced much revenue is a serious point, because the duties upon foreign molasses probably would have seriously affected the flow of trade. In the meantime, opposition in America was immediate and determined.

Another Grenville act was the Stamp Act of 1765, which irritated colonials even more than the Revenue Act of 1764. Grenville had formulated the bill at the time of the Sugar Act, but held it cautiously for nearly a year, waiting, as it were, for advice and courage. News of the bill spread widely and evoked opposition among merchants who predicted dire consequences in America. The bill provided a slight tax upon legal documents, playing cards, newspapers, pamphlets, and other similar items. The tax was admittedly slight, but it required hard money to buy stamps, and the colonies were short of bullion. Depression conditions, trade controls, and a Currency Act in 1764 had restricted the flow of hard money, and the Stamp Act in this crisis put a premium on hard currency to pay the tax. Colonials were touched personally by the intended tax, predicted their coming hardships, and when the Grenville government went ahead with the tax, used drastic measures to dramatize their opposition. Seldom in British imperial history was a tax so despised as the Stamp Act. Within a few weeks of its passage every colony with varying degrees of opposition resisted its enforcement by parading, burning British property, and insulting stamp distributors. In Boston two nights of violence frightened the wits out of governmental officials and sobered citizens who saw Britain attacking their rights as Englishmen by levying the stamp tax. In Charleston a mob of 7,000 forced the stamp distributors to resign. In Virginia a young lawyer, Patrick Henry, secured the bold passage of some resolves which proclaimed rights of Englishmen to representation in matters of taxation. The Massachusetts legislature responded by calling for a congress of colonial leaders to consider matters of protest. Everywhere, one should repeat, opposition to the stamp tax and to Grenville was spontaneous. He had touched a vital cord.

Twenty-seven delegates from nine colonies met in New York from October 7 to 24, 1765. Three other colonies might have sent delegates had their governors convened the legislatures, but only New Hampshire rejected outright the invitation to be represented. A rather conservative group, these delegates, who included James Otis, Jr. and John Dickinson, were a bit bewildered by the emotion that had so quickly spread across the colonies, similar to a tidal wave, in an otherwise choppy period of relations. These taxes, like Grenville's other measures, took on the appearance of a plot, a program, to hurt the colonies. After much debate and reflection, the delegates voted a declaration of rights and grievances, but they expressed their "warmest sentiments and affection and duty to His Majesty's person and Government."

The Stamp Act Congress was undoubtedly the first act of Americans to register common feelings and grievances. They had felt no real unity in the Seven Years War, nor in other crises of defense. Here for a brief moment attention was focused on rights, liberties, and grievances. Congress had asserted that they were "entitled to all the inherent rights and privileges of. . .natural-born subjects within the kingdom of Britain."

Neither the king nor Grenville could long withstand this opposition and that of merchants from all over the empire. Grenville wanted to take a stand on the right to tax the colonies, but he and the king split on many issues large and small. The king looked for a successor to Grenville like William Pitt, but turned finally to the Marquis of Rockingham. Though the new leader did not like violence any more than Grenville did, and was really less wise than his predecessor, he had associated himself closely with the Whig tradition of 1689, whatever that meant in 1765, and repealed the controversial Stamp Act. The party then passed a Declaratory Act which reaffirmed that Parliament could still legislate for the colonies "in all cases whatsoever." This foolish sign of weakness overlooked the immediate need to tax and govern the colonies. Americans rejoiced at the repeal of the Stamp Act, and William Pitt gave a pathetic turn to the celebrations by announcing that he also rejoiced in seeing the American resistance.

During the rejoicing few reflected on the colonial problem that had brought the crisis. Money was still needed to pay the garrisons which were encamped in the West, and there were the army, British officials, and customs controls that still remained after the stamp tax was gone. Indeed, Parliament had passed a Quartering Act in 1765 which required the colonies to provide barracks or billeting in the inns or alehouses for soldiers on duty. This act grieved many people. The rejoicing was thus premature, and sober colonials soon realized that their troubles with London remained.

The crisis over the Stamp Act also heated colonial opinion regarding local issues. Some radical politicians used the opportunity to rid themselves of enemies or rivals. In Massachusetts they severely purged some leaders like Thomas Hutchinson from the council. In Pennsylvania, for a time, rivals of Joseph Galloway and Benjamin Franklin ousted them from the assembly. Tensions of a local nature took various forms: rivalry among politicians, rivalry between peoples living on the frontier and coastal regions, dissension over the amount of representation in the assemblies, and complaints about the burdens of taxes or appointees of the governor. The Stamp Act thus opened up issues or provided a wedge for politicians in Britain and America to vent their opinions.

In Britain politics continued to be unstable when Lord Rockingham lost his place to William Pitt, now Lord Chatham, in a cabinet shuffle that put an odd group of people into office. Less a party in power than a collection of politicians, the ministry had the young, inexperienced Duke of Grafton at its head, Lord Shelburne as Secretary of State for the Southern Department, and Charles Townshend as Chancellor of the Exchequer. Pitt's moderating influence and brilliance was lost before he could solve anything. Seriously ill, he left severe problems everywhere which seemed to get worse with time. In Massachusetts anti-British feeling was used to drive the governor's friends from office. The great pressure upon them eventually destroyed even the governor. Anti-British feeling in New York persisted over the Quartering Act and nearly brought an armed confrontation with the military. Elsewhere, doubt remained about British policy, particularly for the West where Indians were restless, traders abused their privileges, and speculators wanted to get their hands on land. Shelburne thought of creating new colonies there, and read with much sympathy plans of Phineas Lyman of Connecticut who would divide the Mississippi Valley into five or six colonies. Indian danger of attack, however, delayed the approval of the plan even though the cabinet gave Shelburne its consent.

The most urgent problem facing the Cabinet was financial support of colonial reforms, and in 1767 Charles Townshend gave his interpretation of the problem in the form of an act named after him. The Act provided excise duties instead of direct taxes because there was a prevailing idea that the colonists might accept the duties without much opposition. Over the years some duties had been imposed upon the colonies without more than the usual opposition, and Townshend now calculated that his duties on glass, painters' lead, tea, and paper would be acceptable. Besides paying defense expenses, the duties were intended to pay salaries for some crown appointees—a particularly sensitive issue in Massachusetts where the salary of the governor was frequently a legislative issue. The act provided for writs of assistance and a board of custom commissioners who would look after the enforcement of all British revenue laws. The Sugar Act of 1764 (modified in 1766) was still law, as were other earlier laws. The commissioners almost immediately got into trouble when their enforcement tactics touched important shippers. Customs laws had always been enforced in a relaxed manner, but the commissioners now took a hard line which seemed unreasonable. It looked, too, as if the commissioners and their associates were benefiting personally from the excessive rigidity of the enforcement.

Following hard upon the Townshend Duties were the reorganization of both the vice admiralty courts, with four new courts established, and the colonial administration in London. A secretary of state for colonies was appointed; the first appointee was the Earl of Hillsborough, who replaced Lord Shelburne in directing colonial affairs. Hillsborough, a well-meaning man, lacked the sensitivity of the liberal Shelburne and was rigid in his opinions and tactics.

These measures were received with contempt in most colonies, and another wave of opposition swept over them. Boston's merchants organized their resistance openly and forced the British government to quarter troops in the town. New Yorkers threatened its custom officials, who feared for their lives. In Pennsylvania John Dickinson published a powerful statement of his own on the illegality of custom duties, and in Virginia the legislature passed the so-called Virginia Resolves which denounced taxation without American representation. Everywhere merchants joined associations and refused to buy British goods. Nonimportation agreements, in turn, made their informal actions "legal" in many colonies. The legality of the agreements was enforced by the Associations which used tar and feathering and other forms of coercion to make their will effective. Government moved for a time to the associations of merchants, as governors became powerless in the face of civil disobedience. In Boston troops kept their presence, but custom officials took refuge at an island fort and were guarded by a naval vessel. The legislature reacted strongly to the military display and sent circular letters to other colonies urging common resistance to martial law and duties. When Hillsborough heard of this disobedience from Massachusetts, he aggravated the situation by threatening any legislature which cooperated with Massachusetts', and Governor Bernard dissolved the Massachusetts legislature when it refused to withdraw the circular letter. This drastic action, the first of its kind in twenty-five years, shocked those in all the other colonies who were sensitive about American liberty.

The reaction was bitter in Massachusetts, especially when the ministry ordered four regiments of regulars to Boston. There had already arisen in the town popular leaders who gained control of the press, exercised coercion against those who wavered in their resistance, and used pageantry, music, and sermons to dramatize the opposition. Elsewhere in America the degree of opposition was not so great, but Englishmen everywhere discussed the crisis and wondered about the future of the empire.

The Rising Tide of Opposition

Two events occurred on March 5, 1770 which contributed markedly to the increase of emotion. In England the Townshend Duties were abolished save for the duty on tea. Almost at the same time Frederick Lord North became prime minister. North was as able a man as King George could find for the job, but he had little knowledge of administration or American affairs, and he did not have the powerful men in his cabinet. He was determined to maintain the power of Parliament and treat the colonies at the same time fairly. A firm hand, he believed, was needed if the crisis in imperial affairs would pass successfully. North unfortunately had little imagination and was not willing to speculate about the future of the empire. The colonial secretary, Lord Dartmouth, his brother-in-law, was a weak but good man who did not have the decisive qualities of mind to advise him.

The other event on March 5 was the Boston Massacre, which was the result of a continuing, nagging contact between the British soldiers and the townspeople of Boston. At nine o'clock on that night of March 5 the weather was cold and wet, with snow on the ground; most people were at home preparing for bed. A few boys and workmen were still on the streets and were gathered around the sentry at the customs house. Some threw snowballs at the sentry, while others watched and laughed. Soldiers were called, insults were traded, and muskets were fired. When the firing stopped five people were dead, and a town quickly was shocked by what had happened. Tension lingered as town officials investigated; by the end of the year a public trial was held for the soldiers who were charged with murder. Two were convicted of manslaughter, but the others were released.

Every year for nearly a decade orators on March 5 rehearsed the bloody facts of the Massacre. Recounting the circumstances of the victims' deaths, their burials, and the solemn issue of liberty and justice, the orators thus gave the townspeople a yearly opportunity to relive in their minds the experiences of March 5. For a time in 1770 the acting governor, Thomas Hutchinson, felt so much the burdens of office that he offered his resignation. He regarded himself isolated from the people—"absolutely alone," he said—and wondered whether he could ever restore order. While Hutchinson awaited British action in London, he decided to keep the legislature meeting in Cambridge. Bernard had transferred it there in 1769, and Hutchinson continued the practice in spite of the anger that was aroused by his order. The country, he felt, was more loyal and quiet than Boston where town meetings were noisy and turbulent and sedition was in the air.

Though Hutchinson was soon appointed governor, the impact of the Massacre lingered to affect his policies. His decision to keep the legislature in Cambridge was challenged, and serious debates erupted that blocked ordinary business for nearly two years. In the meantime, the governor searched for ways to build up a political base, using offices to win friends, friends to intercede with strangers, and contracts to bind the greedy. The unfortunate problem for Hutchinson was his lack of rich rewards for loyalty and his inability to master events. His office was plainly too weak to command the kind of support that he needed, and events in London and elsewhere were beyond his power to influence.

The *Gaspee* Incident, Salary Matters, and Tea Dumping

In June 1772 a British revenue cutter ran aground near Providence, Rhode Island, while it was hunting for smugglers. The overzealous efforts of the commander had earned him enough hatred from citizens that his misfortune was used to avenge his deeds. On the night of the grounding a group of men, without much disguise or caution, boarded the vessel and set it afire. News of the burning shocked most officials in capitals all over America and in England, but worse, as Hutchinson had predicted, it awakened the British lion and brought retaliation. The ministry ordered a probe by a panel of chief justices, but the guilty parties, known to be prominent men of Rhode Island, were not indicated. The North ministry was, nonetheless, aroused and condemned the mischief. To make matters worse, the Rhode Island legislature challenged the right of the British government to conduct the inquiry. It asked its neighbors to form committees of correspondence which would apprise each other of such activities by the ministry. Thomas Cushing of the Massachusetts House of Representatives labeled the inquiry as an act of slavery.

The *Gaspee* incident thus brought out irrational outbursts on both sides, and obviously increased the tension. Soon after these outbursts the Massachusetts legislature contested a British plan to pay salaries of officials, particularly the salaries of the judges and governor. The house accused the ministry of a "dangerous innovation" and of threatening "despotism." The Boston town meeting, in a frenzied moment, appointed a committee to draw up a statement of colonial rights, and it was then circulated in the colony for support. Hutchinson took this occasion to argue the constitutional basis of the empire and to set his fellow subjects aright about their liberties. His speech in early January 1773 only served to draw a reply from the House of Representatives.

The pot was boiling in Boston, and more ingredients were put into it as the months passed. Ordinary folk became inflamed, and people were labeled as Tory or Whig in the newspapers and assaulted on the streets. Probably no colony was as angry as Massachusetts, but people everywhere argued about colonial rights, and a feeling that revolution was approaching frightened many colonials as they thought of the future.

The most serious episode of 1773 occurred first in London, where Parliament enacted a law to export tea directly to the colonies. Known as the Tea Act, the measure provided for low taxes on East India Company tea and in some cases direct sale of tea to American consumers, so that tea consumption could be stimulated. The company was facing bankruptcy because of financial outlays in fighting the French in the 1750s, but it had also been forced to put down a series of political clashes in its trading areas in the 1770s. Since the Townshend Duties of 1767 the company's tea market was seriously disturbed in America by resistance to the tax. For these and other reasons that related to company management, Parliament passed the Tea Act and provided a loan to bail the East India Company out of immediate difficulties.

Reaction to the act was at first mild, but then cries of monopoly and taxation aroused groups in most colonial towns. No one could say why people were so angry, and the response, except for Massachusetts, was similar. Ship captains were encouraged to return the tea, while merchants in Philadelphia and New York issued manifestos which branded the act harmful, insidious, and a threat to liberty. In Massachusetts merchants tried to get the consignees to resign their commissions and return the tea to England. Failing to convince them after bitter arguments, the merchants then took government into their own hands. Tea from the three anchored ships in Boston Harbor was ceremoniously dumped into the water during the night of December 16 by a large crowd of workers and others dressed as Indians.

This defiance of British authority, as in the *Gaspee* incident, again irritated the ministry. Only this time the episode was so outrageous, deliberate, and challenging that the ministers felt forced to meet contempt with coercion. News of the outrage excited London and, as one might expect, Lord North reacted in anger because of the irresponsible actions of the mob. But he was already prepared for this bad news by another episode, and his temper was more explosive than it needed to be. Early in 1773 some private letters from Hutchinson and others commenting on American loyalty were sent to Boston by Benjamin Franklin. Soon they were published and became the object of a bitter debate in the House of Representatives which demanded the governor's removal for what in their eyes amounted to treason. This exposure brought much excitement also in London, especially when it was learned that Franklin, a colonial agent for a few colonies, was in the thick of the business. He had secured the letters (maybe stolen them), and had also commented privately on British policy and advised the colonies to call another congress to protest the spirit of British policy. A published explanation by Franklin followed news of his involvement in the publication of the letters, but by this time tempers were breaking and the Privy Council held a formal hearing on the Massachusetts demand. Ministerial people rallied to Hutchinson's side, and Franklin was lashed openly for his part in the episode. Though Hutchinson was cleared, indeed praised for his loyalty, everybody concerned in the hearing was angry, tense, and bitter. At that moment of aggravation the dumping of the tea became known to Londoners.

The Coercion Acts

Lord North immediately put the matter of the tea before Parliament, but he probably did not realize the full implications of the American opposition. The tea was symbolic of a breakdown of authority and of a revolutionary situation. He did realize, however, that some form of coercion was necessary against Massachusetts, and moved to have legislation passed which would apply force. There followed in well-spaced order bill after bill which carried out the intent of the ministry to break the resistance. In March 1774 the Boston Port Bill was swiftly pressed through the parliamentary committees; it closed the Boston harbor and moved the custom house to Marblehead. In April and May another bill passed quickly, which transformed the colony's representative institutions into appointive ones and limited the power of town meetings and juries. A final bill in May, the Quebec Act, extended the territory of the province into the Ohio Valley. Otherwise, the act provided for necessary changes in Quebec institutions which permitted the French language, law, religion, and customs to exist legally in the province. The colonial attitude toward Catholicism was sufficient to blind people, and their intolerance made the Quebec Act seem to be an attack upon American liberty.

In Massachusetts the first of the Coercive Acts went into effect on June 1, and on that day the last of the civilian governors of colonial Massachusetts left the colony. Thomas Hutchinson, a native of the colony, graduate of Harvard College, wealthy merchant, and devoted civil servant of nearly forty-five years, went into exile. Hatred for him was intense, but he had long since lost power to the leaders of the House of Representatives. His successor, General Thomas Gage, had his troops to support the office but he, too, had little authority to combat merchant resistance.

As the paralyzed town faced the Port Act, the House of Representatives called for an inter-colonial meeting of the committees of correspondence. The response was generally favorable elsewhere. Virginia was less aggravated, but members of the House of Burgesses were also aroused by the Tea Act and had plotted privately to take "an unequal stand in the line with Massachusetts." They ordered a day of fast and prayer, which brought a dissolution of the assembly by Governor Lord Dunmore. The burgesses then met in the Raleigh Tavern nearby and voted to spread the seeds of resistance to the colony. One of their number, Thomas Jefferson, drafted his now-famous *A Summary View of the Rights of British America* in which he denounced the arbitrary acts of Parliament. By September 5 the other colonies, one by one, responded to the Coercive Acts by pledging to meet in Philadelphia. Only Georgia did not send delegates.

The Continental Congress

Those persons who assembled in the Quaker City were peaceful, conservative in their inclinations, and a bit shaken by the predicament in which the colonies found themselves. Revolution for them was a frightening thought to ponder. Most were admittedly aggravated at Britain and believed that something, even something drastic, was necessary. But war was a dreadful idea. Joseph Galloway, the famous lawmaker from Pennsylvania, argued for a union under the crown, with a president general, legislature, and a constitutional arrangement which would give the colonies much autonomy in their own affairs. His plan, though well debated and voted down by a single vote, touched the feelings of less than a majority who desired something not so drastic as a union. The delegates turned instead to a declaration of their rights and a condemnation of the coercive acts against Massachusetts. They also threatened nonimportation, nonconsumption, and nonexportation in order to underscore the peaceful intent of their petition to King George. Six days later, however, they actually formed an "Association" which would carry out the trade boycott:

We, His Majesty's most loyal subjects, the delegates of the several colonies...deputed to represent them in a Continental Congress...to obtain redress of these grievances, which threaten destruction of the lives, liberty, and property of His Majesty's subjects in North America, we are of the opinion that a non-importation, non-consumption, and non-exportation agreement...will prove the most speedy, effectual and peaceable measure.

The Congress adjourned on October 26. In those six weeks since September 5 much had happened. Patrick Henry pronounced in a vivid way what others had not dared to say—"I am not a Virginian, but an American." But the Congress, too, had assumed the right to speak for all Americans, and it had provided the means for resistance. Events now moved rapidly as the Association was formed.

Moving into Violence

While the colonies organized their resistance, in England elections were held on November 1 in order to meet the requirement of elections every seven years. The right to vote was extremely limited, but those who voted returned people pledged to the coercive policy of the government. Lord North was returned to office with firm backing and proposed additional coercive measures. The army was to be increased and trade restrictions to counter nonimportation were to be levied against New England. Restrictions against other colonies were also to be applied if they continued their hostility. Lord North's policies were not without opposition, however, and when debate on American policy was held in January 1775, it was frequently sharp. Lord Chatham, Edmund Burke, and the Earl of Shelburne urged conciliation. Thomas Pownall, the onetime governor of Massachusetts, was particularly forceful in his speeches for peace. The London community, moreover, had many influential people who regretted this drift toward belligerence by both sides and urged compromise.

Even though Chatham and Burke tried to appeal to the common feelings of British nationalism, they were only partly successful in convincing Lord North that he should tarry and await a return of rational feelings. North did, however, offer a plan of conciliation in February 1775. It provided for an exemption from taxation if any colony contributed sufficient money to pay governmental expenses. This eleventh-hour plan arrived in America when the colonies were particularly upset by North's new coercive measures, and thus did not receive the consideration that it probably deserved.

The people of Massachusetts were building up their stores of arms and preparing for the worst. In Boston, General Thomas Gage was increasing his forces and plotting how he might restore loyal rule to the colony. He hit upon a plan to send troops in the early morning of April 19 to Lexington and Concord, probably to seize military stores at Concord and to arrest patriots Samuel Adams and John Hancock in Lexington. The plan was foolishly developed and was fairly well known by the night of the 18th. To sharpen the information, Paul Revere, William Dawes, and others carried word of the march to the countryside and church bells rang the alarm. One thousand soldiers were part of this British force that left Boston, and though Revere awakened colonials to their presence, the troops met little real opposition on the road to Lexington and Concord. At a bridge north of Concord, however, some bloodshed occurred when colonials gathered in sufficient numbers to challenge the marching troops. The opposition was serious enough to convince the British commander that he should turn back to Boston. On the way the troops encountered musket fire from the rock walls, and the harassment persisted until they were met by reinforcements near Lexington. Of the total British troops engaged in the operation, 273 out of 2,500 were killed, wounded, or captured. The Americans lost less than a hundred.

News of this skirmish did not spread around the world, but the reports excited New Englanders in a way that now seems incomprehensible. Adults and youth from hamlets everywhere in New England rushed toward Boston to besiege the British troops in Boston; perhaps as many as forty thousand persons came forth. Stories of atrocities at Concord fed the emotion and gave the battle at the bridge heroic qualities that would not be forgotten. The first blood was indeed spilled there, but Concord was only a preview for other battles.

Soon after the fight at Lexington and Concord the Second Continental Congress convened at Philadelphia. Delegates from all the colonies were present, as one might expect in this crisis, and the talk of members was upon the deepening crisis in Massachusetts. Present were Benjamin Franklin, Thomas Jefferson, John and Samuel Adams, and many of the people who were present at the first congress. Lord North's plan for conciliation was first discussed, but the members then passed a series of resolutions which blamed the mounting crisis upon Britain, which called for a restoration of peace, and which urged George III to use his good offices. Even so, the delegates turned to the military crisis, and they soon chose George Washington of Virginia as commander-in-chief. They also declared their reasons for taking up arms—that famous "Declaration" was signed July 6, 1775, just short of a year before the more famous Declaration of Independence:

Lest this declaration should disquiet the minds of our friends and fellow-subjects in any part of the Empire, we assure them that we mean not to dissolve that union which has so long and so happily subsisted between us, and which we sincerely wish to see restored...we have not raised armies with ambitious designs of separating from Great Britain, and establishing independent States. We fight not for glory or for conquest.

Much more of this document could be quoted if space were not a problem. It emphasized the basic defensive nature of American resistance and pleaded to God "the impartial Judge and Rule of the Universe" for help in the period of trial. The Congress would continue its deliberations and create by the fall various administrative committees which would handle the growing number of problems associated with the movement toward open conflict.

In the meantime New Englanders gathered about Boston, almost surrounding the town and placing General Gage in the uncomfortable position of being in a besieged city. Most colonial business was transferred from Boston elsewhere. Newspapers were published in Watertown and the legislature eventually also met there. Trade in the port city was disrupted, but some was transacted from Salem and Gloucester or Providence and Newport in the south. The deadlock in Boston worried both sides, but Gage was unwilling to risk battle with uncertain gain. By June he had six thousand troops and an offensive was possible. He agreed then to some defensive moves—fortification of Dorchester Heights and Charlestown, particularly Breed and Bunker Hills. Whatever else he might have ordered is uncertain because of colonial countermeasures. The colonials had pondered the cost of battering Boston and of confronting regular troops. They had lacked available cannon, however, though some were now in colonial possession at Ticonderoga since the successful capture of the fortress in May. British moves to spread the area of occupation were known to them almost as soon as the troops knew about the plans, and countermoves were quickly made against the British.

The news of intended British operations against Charlestown brought forth an American counterplan to occupy the hills on the narrow peninsula. The militia moved in the darkness of night to Breed's Hill, which was not as high and defensible as Bunker's, but a bit closer to Boston. Their effort was directed toward digging entrenchments and a redoubt. It is now difficult to say what their real purpose was, because Bunker Hill was more defensible and both hills required cannon and powder for any lengthy maneuver.

The noise atop Breed's Hill was soon heard by the British in Boston where plans were immediately formed to handle the foolish colonials.

Strategy was leisurely debated, but the generals finally agreed that a conventional, frontal attack was preferred rather than a maneuver across the neck behind Bunker Hill. The troops were then moved in place sometime in the afternoon of June 17. British assaults were primarily frontal, and two or three times they were turned back by colonial musket fire. The 2,100 colonials gave a good account of themselves but they lacked powder, experience, and strategy. In the end the colonials retreated to Bunker Hill and to the mainland, leaving casualties of nearly four hundred. The British lost nearly half their attacking forces, perhaps as many as one thousand.

This bloody battle was sobering indeed for Gage and his generals, who now debated the defenses of Boston. The summer passed without incident, and in October William Howe succeeded Gage. Gage's recall was undoubtedly a result of the shock of American resistance, but in many ways Howe was no better than Gage in taking the offensive. He faced, too, the debilitating problems of morale in a besieged city.

The Battle of Boston occurred before Washington took charge of the American volunteers. Washington brought little with him except the recognition that his presence made the siege an American instead of a New England battle. He had no troops, no ammunition, no cannon, no artillery. His job was to organize an army and prepare to break the siege. He pondered a direct attack upon the British forces, but for a time at least his common sense ruled out another Breed Hill.

By the winter of 1775-76 Congress had given Washington permission to bring the fifty-nine cannon from Ticonderoga to Boston, a distance of a few hundred miles over snowy, frozen land. The promise of this fire power made it possible for Washington to plan an attack. In early March, during another night of great effort, New Englanders placed the cannon on Dorchester Heights. Noise revealed their presence to the British, but a low fog drifted in just in time to protect their positions. Better organization this time, plus fresh troops, made the presence of Americans at Dorchester critical for the British. Howe pondered the possibility of an attack, but decided instead to abandon Boston, "this cursed place," and ordered his troops and over a thousand refugees into waiting ships. The evacuation began about March 17.

The Revolution

John Adams of Massachusetts is frequently quoted on the progress of the Revolution. He affirmed that "the revolution was complete, in the minds of the people, and the Union of the colonies, before the war commenced in the skirmishes of Concord and Lexington on the 19th of April, 1775." Adams is also known for his opinion on the separation of people into revolutionary groups: he believed only a third were backing the revolution in 1776, a third were against, and a third were on the fence. Both positions cannot be right. Adams was a participant, nonetheless, while the historian looks back over two hundred years and more to the events from 1760 to 1775. Adams witnessed the changes in terminology: British Americans became Americans; Whig (American) and Tory (Briton) separated the political groups; and attitudes toward Parliament, the King, and England changed. Loyalty toward England was thus evaluated over the years in books and pamphlets, and in some cases the people saw differences in affection and institutions between the colonies and Britain. Adams himself also changed from a colonial and New Englander who was content to live within the empire, to an American aware for the first time of the larger geography of North America and of the greater political necessity of colonial association. Adams also thought of America as having a destiny separate from England's, a mission, he felt, that would bring greater realization of liberty and knowledge than was capable under Britain. Further, he joined those Americans who were suspicious of Britain, who questioned the motives of the politicians, who were insecure about the safety of their rights, and who pondered the future of Great Britain as a force in human affairs.

Historians may concede much that Adams cites as evidence of revolution, but they are reminded that on the surface at least Americans resisted thoughts of revolution. It was a nasty word. They were angry at Britain, most assuredly, because of the tax legislation, but opposition, even anger, was far different for them than revolution. They hated many of their officials—the armed forces, the governors, and the tax collectors—but they regarded union with Britain part of their heritage and identity.

One might ask, when is a revolution a revolution? How much of a shift of opinion, philosophy, social values, or religion occurs in the process? Is it possible that the revolution occurred during the actual war against Great Britain? As Americans fought England, they realized that they were becoming different peoples and that a return to pre-revolutionary conditions was no longer possible. Was that the time of revolution?

10

The American Revolution

The year 1776 was a revolutionary time for Americans. Early in that year Thomas Paine published his *Common Sense* which ridiculed the monarchy, aristocracy, and imperialism in words few people even now can forget. His verbal assault was too much for these institutions to withstand. There followed other pamphlets in March and April that reaffirmed what Paine had brilliantly written. In March, George Washington forced the withdrawal of British troops from Boston and, for a time, New England was free of any hostile forces. In June, Congress debated and in July proclaimed the Declaration of Independence, which gave heart to those battling the imperial connection. In June, too, Americans held the shores of South Carolina in their own declaration of independence and turned away the assault of the British navy at Charleston. Six or seven thousand troops under Charles Lee defended the city until the British commanders lost heart and sailed off to New York. In July, there began a time of trial at New York in which Americans battled the British army and navy. The fight went badly for George Washington, whose inexperience and inferior numbers compelled him to retreat out of the city into the state and then into New Jersey. He fled finally across the icy Delaware River into Pennsylvania. But at the close of the year, in late December, Washington successfully besieged Trenton and Princeton in New Jersey, easily captured those British garrisons, and finally established winter quarters in the brown hills of Morristown not far away. These surprise victories, though minor on the field, gave excitement to Americans who "are all liberty-mad again." No year of the war was as crucial for Americans as was 1776. It illustrated both the kind of struggle that would persist during the coming seven years of war and the inability of Great Britain to stamp out quickly the rebellion. When the British army abandoned New England in March 1776, General William Howe sailed for Halifax (and Henry Clinton for Charleston) where he regrouped his forces in the spring and prepared for the grand assault of the summer which would supposedly crush the rebellion. New York was Howe's target because it was one center of the colonies, probably the most strategic, and had in addition many people loyal to Britain. Joining Howe in New York was his brother, Admiral Richard Lord Howe, who was accompanied by a vast expeditionary force of 34,000 troops and hundreds of vessels.

With such resources at his disposal General Howe should have immediately challenged Washington's inferior numbers and untrained men. But Howe saw only the difficulties of winning a complete victory and crushing the resistance. Further, he prepared slowly for the attack. Not until August 22, about five weeks after his arrival in New York, did he order the full assaults. In the meantime Howe had offered to parlay on the causes of the war and to pardon those who would lay down their arms. No concessions, however, were to be offered by the Howes on the issues that brought on the rebellion. The reaction from colonials could have been predicted.

On August 22, General Howe ordered twenty thousand of his troops to land at Gravesend Bay, and four days later they attacked Israel Putnam's eight thousand men. Though the Americans had erected strong fortifications at Brooklyn Heights, they were unable to anticipate British strategy which pressed their weak left flank and made a frontal charge. In short order, Howe and his generals killed or captured three thousand men and seized two American generals.

Washington quickly ordered most of the remaining army across the East River onto Manhattan Island. The shift of these forces was very dangerous because of British naval might, but General Howe refused to use the navy to block their retreat, and they easily joined Washington's main forces. All the remaining troops were then evacuated under cover of night, rain, and a rear guard action that disguised the movement. On Manhattan Island, then, were most of Washington's forces and Long Island was left to Howe. Both he and Washington took weeks to assess what had happened; both were somewhat bewildered, and Howe actually tried to reopen negotiations to end the war.

The next phase of battle soon followed. Washington decided that New York City was indefensible but should not be harmed, and that he could find a better position in Harlem Heights. His movement of troops

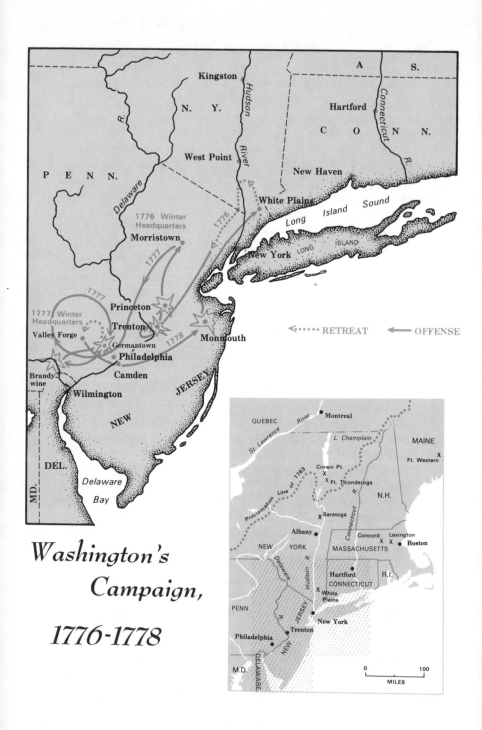

Washington's Campaign, 1776-1778

was disorderly, but a small skirmish with British forces near the Heights was successfully repulsed. Temporary fortifications were raised and much time was wasted by both sides as they again considered their strategy. Howe first removed the obstructions from the harbor and made plans to sail up the Hudson. But he also spent his time gathering forces to send up the East River to New Rochelle, where they were expected to cross White Plains and block Washington's route for a retreat. Since Howe did not know the geography of the region, he landed first at Throg's Neck, where he encountered resistance and gave Washington sufficient warning of his plans.

Fortunately for Washington the British moves were deliberate, and he was able each time to escape possible traps. However, Washington's luck often depended less upon his skill as a general than upon circumstances of weather and Howe's inertia. Unfortunately, Washington did not calculate the safety of forts Washington and Lee which were situated on both sides of the Hudson River, and as he evacuated Manhattan Island, Fort Washington became an enclave of American strength. Its vulnerable condition quickly became obvious to Howe who used a land and sea assault and conducted a successful siege against it, taking easily its three thousand troops and supplies. The loss of such numbers was a major disaster.

Stimulated by the victory, Howe sent Lord Cornwallis' army into New Jersey, and their presence was enough to frighten the garrison out of Fort Lee and to force its retreat without a battle. He dispatched a naval squadron to Newport, Rhode Island, and easily captured the port. Even so, Washington remained out of the reach of General Howe, and by successive marches succeeded in staying ahead of the British army as he made his way through New Jersey to the Delaware River, where he collected all the boats for miles along the river and thus kept Lord Cornwallis from pursuing him into Pennsylvania.

Though Washington took a severe loss of troops in these maneuvers, he was lucky to receive from time to time reinforcements that added substantial strength. In Pennsylvania he had more than six thousand troops available for action, and they were soon employed successfully against Trenton and Princeton.

The year 1776 undoubtedly held many lessons for both Washington and the Howes. But the most important was the obvious one that Washington had escaped serious battle, even though his losses at times were great.

Toward a Climax

Unlike any other year of the Revolution, the year 1777 seemed to be potentially decisive. The British were at first confident of final victory as they planned the grand offensive, and the Americans counted their blessings at Trenton and Princeton; but the Americans also fought well in 1777 and had won a major victory at that year's end.

As the year opened the British could not get together on their campaign plans. Sir William Howe was indecisive: his mind was probably perplexed by the military situation after Trenton and Princeton; and he was making far too great a demand upon the ministry when he asked for 35,000 troops. He pared the number to 19,000 even before the ministry rejected the larger number. At various times he sent three plans home, but the campaign generally took this form: Howe would early in the year capture Philadelphia, John Burgoyne would march south from Montreal to Albany, and Barry St. Leger would come to Albany by way of Fort Oswego and the Mohawk River. Finally, Howe would support Burgoyne by keeping additional military forces on the Hudson River where they might draw troops away from upper New York. Although the use of these forces was unclear, they probably were intended to be employed as a diversionary force. The objective of these several campaigns was obviously to separate New England from the other colonies and break morale.

The British military underestimated the difficulty of travel from Montreal to Albany, as well as the distances and time in travel, and they calculated on greater Tory help in Pennsylvania than was to materialize. Joseph Galloway, the famous Tory, believed at various times that upwards of half the people of Pennsylvania were loyal to Britain. Whatever their number, most sat upon their hands when called to the defense of the empire.

While Howe's plan of attack was being perfected, Washington waited for him to move his troops and resisted several overtures by Howe to engage in an open battle. Finally, Howe embarked for Philadelphia with an armada of over 265 ships (about fifteen thousand troops). They reached the Delaware River on July 29, but Washington had blocked the river and threatened any landing. Howe foolishly then changed his course and took the Chesapeake Bay route to Philadelphia. On August 25 the army disembarked and began the long march to the city. It took nearly a month to enter the city, as battles and skirmishes outside its limits continued for weeks. On September 11, major forces had faced each other at Brandywine, with some losses for and a disorderly retreat by the Americans; and on September 16 a lesser battle occurred at Warren Tavern. Once in Philadelphia, the British made much of their victories, but Washington's forces remained a threat at Germantown and White Marsh, and Howe

George Washington at Princeton (1943), by Charles
Peale Polk. *(National Gallery of Art, Washington; gift
of William C. Freeman.)*

finally concluded that he could not rely on the Tories for the city's
defense. For all practical purposes Philadelphia became a burden for Howe
because it tied up his forces, and he had expended too much valuable time
in its conquest. Howe at times lost sight of his military objective which
was the defeat or capture of Washington's forces. Washington was usually
wise enough to avoid battle and threaten attack as he lingered off
Philadelphia.

In the meantime General Burgoyne had been in London setting his
political house in order and had returned to America in early May.
Relations between him and the Governor of Canada, Sir Guy Carleton,
were tense because of political spoils, but cooperation between the men
did not materially interfere with campaign preparations. On June 14
Burgoyne took his 9000 troops southward to the wilderness area of Lake
Champlain. Some days later Barry St. Leger went up the St. Lawrence
River to Lake Ontario and Oswego, on his way also to Albany,
accompanied by a thousand Indians and a few thousand other troops.

Burgoyne moved slowly toward Fort Ticonderoga and on July 1
began his siege, which was readily accomplished because the defenders
were disorganized and the fort was undermanned. The victory brought

great joy to Burgoyne and much gloom to the Americans, but the fort's importance was undoubtedly overestimated. It did cause Burgoyne to carry heavy cannon with him and increased the time for preparations.

For some reason Burgoyne then selected a longer route to Albany and made plans to capture Fort Edward on the Hudson. He moved as a result fifty-two pieces of siege cannon, which delayed his passage by several weeks. The longer route also increased problems of carriage because excess baggage, provisions, and luxury items for his officers slowed down travel over paths that were blocked often by cut timber. The commander of the American forces, Philip Schuyler, with much forethought, had made the woods hazardous and difficult to pass through. As might be expected, Burgoyne only got to Skenesboro (now Whitehall) by July 24 and Fort Edward by July 29.

His slow passage gave Schuyler time to gather forces to oppose him. While Schuyler was undoubtedly preparing well for a victory, he was gloomy about the future. Congress was not certain of his ability and thus replaced him in early August with Horatio Gates, who was given almost dictatorial powers. Gates may not have been a better commander, but he was popular with New Englanders. In his command were Benjamin Lincoln, Benedict Arnold, and nearly five thousand continentals, with some New England militia and New York Indians as auxiliaries.

With the army preparing to engage Burgoyne, it was aided substantially by the resistance of Americans in the Mohawk Valley which was in the path of Barry St. Leger's march. Fort Stanwix (now called Schuyler) had been reinforced in the early summer and given the help of two hundred militiamen just as St. Leger was threatening the fort. Feeling strong, the forces withstood heavy assaults, even though they were outnumbered. When help from Nicholas Herkimer also arrived, they held the fort in the face of severe cannonading. Herkimer and his militiamen battled St. Leger in the forests and hills as they tried to relieve the fort, sometimes in direct hand-to-hand confrontation with St. Leger's men. Such bravery checked St. Leger's advance, but at a heavy price for both sides, and St. Leger still remained outside the fort waiting for its imminent surrender. To force St. Leger back, Schuyler sent Arnold with a few thousand troops in early August, and this additional strength finally convinced St. Leger to abandon the siege.

These setbacks for St. Leger denied Burgoyne some additional aid as he moved near Albany. Short now of supplies, Burgoyne could have used the help to round up horses and provisions which might have been available at Schenectady or Albany. Instead, he chose to move into hostile Vermont for these supplies, and he risked about seven hundred troops.

With General John Stark waiting for them at Bennington, the British faced three times their number, colonials who were defending home and hearth. The Americans pressed the attack and captured not only the original party but some others who had been rushed to their defense. The loss of these troops and, even worse, the loss of additional provisions put Burgoyne in a precarious position. His five thousand regulars and his Tory and Indian auxiliaries were inferior to Gates's seven thousand troops and auxiliaries.

Gates realized the weakness that threatened Burgoyne and decided to press an attack. He moved to Bemis Heights which was an excellent position, with the Hudson River on the right and bluffs and woods on the left. Fortifications were well laid out by Thaddeus Kosciuszko, and Burgoyne, camped just three miles north, had no good knowledge of the terrain. Burgoyne chose to test the enemy, and the woods proved his undoing. The Americans fought bravely, tested the strength of the British lines in hand-to-hand actions, and gave Burgoyne double their losses by their rifle and musket fire in the woods.

Pulling back, Burgoyne ordered his troops to dig in since he anticipated relief from New York. But three weeks passed, and instead of Burgoyne's receiving help to equalize the forces, the Americans grew in strength, with hundreds of New Englanders and New Yorkers joining the army. Schuyler at Albany also helped with supplies. In the meantime, Gates used his cannon to soften morale, his scouting parties to test positions, and his main forces to strengthen the fortifications. He put Burgoyne in a critical situation which mounted in seriousness. Only a retreat was possible, but Burgoyne's honor and his enormous egotism were both barriers, even when his advisers recommended retreat.

As Burgoyne's situation became precarious, his men lost heart, and a council of war was unenthusiastic when it recommended an assault on the American left. Even so, Burgoyne pressed an attack on October 7 and was hit head-on by the Americans. Casualties were thus heavy for Burgoyne, perhaps three for every one American; worse still, Burgoyne's army was now surrounded. Though Clinton was rushing aid from New York, Burgoyne faced certain defeat, which could be bloody and useless; so he bargained with Gates for the best possible surrender, pledging finally to leave America and to withdraw entirely from any future military activity. The terms, a bit too generous, were accepted quickly by Gates, but were later violated by American authorities who refused to give over the army to Britain. Burgoyne did, however, regain his freedom and returned to London where he told his version of the defeat to the court and press. The disaster had an immediate impact upon Clinton, who hastened back to New York. The surrender of the five thousand men, in Clinton's opinion, was a crushing blow which delayed still longer the inevitable victory over the Americans.

The French Alliance

The British disaster at Saratoga certainly was a turning point in the Revolution. The momentum that Britain had achieved in 1776 and 1777 was slowed considerably, and plans for a quick, decisive victory with Tory assistance were shelved or at least not given the prominence in ministerial thinking that they once had had. The most important result of the victory, however, was the decision by the French ministry to become a full partner in the war. Already a silent partner, the ministry, through a French agent, Caron de Beaumarchais, had provided money, arms, advice, and other kinds of encouragement since 1776, and had permitted American envoys, particularly Benjamin Franklin, to achieve standing as diplomats. Franklin had won sufficient popularity within a few months of his arrival that he moved easily in Paris society and was in demand in the company of scientists, philosophers, and fraternal societies. Through his activities the American cause achieved an excitement, a popularity, and a philosophical thrust that was nearly irresistible. The ministry was likewise affected, but mainly they saw the possibility of cutting Britain down to size and restoring the balance of power that had been lost in 1763. These considerations of power also had much influence upon Spain, which had followed the lead of France in its foreign policy. Both made substantial contributions to the support of American resistance in 1777.

The victory at Saratoga thus did not bring France into the war because she was already a partner, but brought open help and a treaty of friendship and assistance in 1778. The French foreign minister, the Comte de Vergennes, was an energetic, calculating statesman who moved quickly to involve his country, Spain, and America in the conflict, and a treaty was signed on February 6, 1778, between France and the United States. Months later Spain became an open participant. Vergennes also used his influence in the Netherlands, Denmark, Sweden, and Russia so that Britain found the Baltic closed to its vessels and trade severely restricted. The immediate result of Vergennes' diplomatic initiative turned the Revolution into a European war as well, and Britain was forced to defend the homeland from possible attack from the French and Spanish fleets. For Americans this recognition of nationhood was undoubtedly more important than the Declaration of Independence. It would shortly bring French troops to America, a navy into the Caribbean, and large military provisions.

In February when the French treaty was announced to the House of Commons by Lord North, it raised the serious issue of the war's prosecution and the dire need for a peace offensive. By April a commission headed by Lord Carlisle sailed for America, bringing tidings that the tea duties, the Coercive Acts, and other hated British measures were repealed! This commission actually had little power, but strong leadership might have explored the basis of a peace. Americans, however, had moved farther down the path of independence, and concessions by Britain became increasingly more difficult to make.

The Internal Revolution

Since 1775 every state had considered the possibility of drafting a new constitution, and most had enacted some legislation. Virginia and New Jersey were among the first, but in 1777 six others followed their lead. The process of change in Massachusetts and New Hampshire was more difficult because the people wanted a direct voice in shaping the new order. Their legislatures finally were forced to call constitutional conventions.

The new constitutions were frequently the object of much debate, but in general form they were not very different from the old colonial charters. In spirit, they reflected the experience of the last six decades of colonial self-rule and the political philosophy of Great Britain since the Revolution of 1689. That spirit had permeated colonial life increasingly in the eighteenth century. Perhaps the new spirit of revolution brought more change in language than in anything else. People talked of equality, of natural rights of life, liberty, and property, of religious toleration, and of slave emancipation, and the talk was given some reality in legislation. Even women benefited in the discussion of equality because they gained access to education, land ownership, and divorce. The spirit of the times is well described by a woman author in the *Lady's Magazine* when she wrote of marriage: "The obedience between man and wife, I conceive, is, or ought to be mutual. Marriage ought never to be considered as a contract between a superior and an inferior, but a reciprocal union of interests, an implied partnership of interests, where all are accommodated by conference; and where the decision admits of no retrospect."

The constitutions changed slightly the election base. More governors were chosen by the people, more officials were chosen by the legislature, and more people could vote than in colonial times. But whether people were actually participating more in government is an issue. Land still was used to qualify the voter and officeholder, and many people looked to their betters for guidance. Land ownership increased somewhat during the Revolution, but there remained many people who were landless and hence without the right to vote or hold office. Probably the significant change was the availability of the electoral right. As people became used to the idea of ruling themselves, the right became exercised.

In Pennsylvania and Virginia redistribution of political power was important. The overrepresentation of Philadelphia and eastern, rural Pennsylvania gave way to larger western representation. It replaced Quakers and their German allies with a Presbyterian and Scottish population. In Virginia the Chesapeake low country lost power to the Piedmont and Shenandoah Valley regions, which increased the power of small farmers and Presbyterians. These changes were followed by similar ones in South and North Carolina, and to some extent in Massachusetts. The result was significant in bringing governmental services such as courts and the registry to western areas. The redistribution of seats brought into the legislatures many new men who challenged coastal leadership and raised various issues of taxation, credit, and social control.

Religious freedom was certainly one of these issues. Before the Revolution toleration had spread everywhere, but there remained many restrictions and burdens. Actual freedom of religion in the twentieth-century sense existed nowhere, because taxes were collected for state churches, oaths were required to support Protestant institutions, office-holding was restricted to Protestants, and a variety of annoying other laws were enforced against minorities. The disestablishment of state churches during the Revolution was easier against the Anglican than against the Congregational churches because in no state did Anglicans enjoy a majority. The movement, nonetheless, took time and aroused much bitterness. In Virginia, the Anglican church was disestablished quickly, but in Massachusetts, New Hampshire, and Connecticut the Congregational churches held their privileged positions for nearly a half-century longer. Former laws requiring church attendance, a declaration of religious belief, and tax support were abolished in many states. Full toleration, however, would take decades because membership in a church would be associated with loyalty to the nation and the ability of persons to make independent judgments.

Freedom for blacks was another issue that excited some reformers. Since blacks accounted for nearly one-fifth of the population, their presence was obvious to everyone. Particularly obvious was their enslaved condition, because the Revolution fought for human rights and thousands of blacks served in the army. Color may have excused slavery, but slavery as an institution affected the consciences of many people, not only in the northern but in the southern states. Before the war, laws in a few colonies had prohibited the importation of slaves, but Britain generally discouraged legislation in the large colonies. With the break in relations other colonies passed restrictive legislation against the slave trade. An antislavery society was founded in Philadelphia with the hope of convincing people to outlaw servitude; some colonies responded to this campaign by providing for gradual emancipation; in this movement Pennsylvania and Massachusetts led the way. As the war continued, others joined their ranks, particularly the other states of New England.

The most prominent revolutionary leaders joined the movement for emancipation, but often in a peculiar way. They wanted the blacks "removed beyond the reach of mixture," to use Thomas Jefferson's words. He wanted blacks out of the new nation and felt that there was no social place for them. Like many other persons Jefferson was interested in purifying and liberalizing American institutions. Jefferson and his colleagues were republicans who wanted to rid the new country of aristocracy and class legislation, and some even felt the emergence of a new order in history. Their letters do not indicate with any certainty what they expected except that humanity had in its hands a chance to reconstruct society, and that justice and virtue would be important qualities in its laws and institutions.

A rising emotional movement spread over the former colonies as people sensed the beginning of a new order. They tried to capture their feelings in music, poetry, and pageantry. Their regard for George Washington as general and leader spread, and the cause of independence won more and more of the noncommitted. The people rid themselves of British relics and turned often upon the Tory whom they exiled, tarred and feathered, or kept under house arrest. Thousands of Americans, both white and black, volunteered for military service, though often for only a few days or weeks, and many subscribed to war bonds and paid war taxes. The Revolution was undoubtedly a deepening process which spread everywhere and convinced people that a successful war against Britain was possible. Gage's victory at Saratoga was thus warmly celebrated in many parts of America in spite of sectional suspicions, and Washington's battles often were regarded as personal confrontations with Britain. Few Americans abandoned the cause of revolution and more joined the cause. People searched for ways to help win the war. Women everywhere spun cloth, managed the home, collected funds for the soldiers, harassed Tories and, in general, took an active role with their male partners in fighting the war. Abigail Adams, the wonderful wife of John, described the Ladies' Association which had raised money for the troops as a sign that "virtue exists, and public spirit lives—lives in the Bosoms of the Fair Daughters of America, who, blushing for the languid spirit, and halting step, unite their efforts to reward the patriotic, to stimulate the brave, to alleviate the burdens of war, and to show that they are not dismayed by defeats or misfortunes."

Continental Congress

For people to look to the Congress for help was a new experience that was quickly accepted, if reluctantly, as necessary to winning the war. Philadelphia became the permanent headquarters, except when Sir William Howe occupied the city, and then Baltimore served as the refuge. Congress early assumed the right to handle revolutionary problems and did so with a spirit of enthusiasm, zeal, and loyalty that now seems amazing. It became a body that debated and deliberated, mostly through committees, and handed down both good and bad decisions that kept the conflict going until peace was finally achieved in 1783. Most of the revolutionary leaders at one time or another served in the Congress and then went off to other duties. Over the years Congress had thus a large number of people participating in its functions, which created much instability but had the effect, too, of associating leaders with the national cause.

The Second Congress until 1781 was the national government of the United States. It created a committee system which did the work of coordinating revolutionary activities. As laws were passed the committees searched for matériel, money, and men, and they worked with Washington as commander-in-chief, with the diplomats abroad, and with the various employees in the offices of government to promote the cause of revolution. They even advised the states on the conduct of the war. The committees had to counteract local jealousy, however, as states held to their rights, and many times the committee's will was frustrated by local officials. Proper relations between the central government and the states took time to develop. Suspicion, jealousy, and inexperience often troubled relations.

Even before the Declaration of Independence, Benjamin Franklin had circulated a plan of union. For many delegates it raised such radical issues of independence and union that they had turned it down without much discussion. But once independence had been accepted as a principle of the Revolution, Congress appointed a committee of thirteen to draft a constitution, and in mid-July 1776 the Franklin document, sharpened and polished in language by the committee and John Dickinson of Pennsylvania, was ready for congressional debate. Discussed in late July and most of August, the plan encountered much hostile criticism, centered mainly upon the equality of representation and the ownership of western lands.

Dickinson had given Congress power to set the western boundaries of the states, but his plan plainly interfered with the ambitions of states like New York and Virginia which had charter rights to vast western lands. Some states had no definite western lands, and they pressed for equal opportunity to explore the west. Maryland, in particular, gathered the support of Delaware and New Jersey and refused to ratify the constitution until the states with land gave up their claims. For more than four years debate continued as various leaders sought compromises. A union without Maryland was suggested at one point, but finally Virginia offered to cede its lands in exchange for some controls over land speculators, primarily those involved in the Illinois-Wabash Company. Its compromise brought a softening of position by the other states, and in 1781 the Articles of Confederation were ratified as the constitution of the United States.

The Articles of Confederation were the basis of government from 1781 to 1789; before their ratification Congress acted as if it had full constitutional authority. The significance of ratification is that it was a formal act of union and association; probably it brought no more power than Congress had already exercised since 1774, and Congress had as much power as the states were willing to give it. The Articles of Confederation set up a single-house legislature, with the states equally represented, voting by states, and their delegates annually elected. Congress in theory possessed great power, but in actuality its lack of power to tax weakened its overall authority.

The focus should not be on the powers of the Articles, but on the revolutionary act in 1776 which set in motion the creation of a national government. Few people were willing at first to give distant government authority over their lives, but later necessity, the success of the Revolution, and experience made the idea seem practical. The Articles might have developed into a sophisticated form of government had there been time to experiment. But the primary need of 1776 and later was different. Americans tested their willingness to unite and experience the dangers of disorganization, and they had a war to fight which often seemed to overwhelm them.

After Saratoga

Events in the winter of 1777-78 did not reflect the glory of Saratoga. Washington and his men endured a needless ordeal of suffering at Valley Forge, while some Americans made money selling food to the

British in Philadelphia. At Valley Forge both food and clothing were scarce, and meat was not available for nearly a week at one point. In the Congress, much criticism of Washington was drummed up by a group of men who surrounded Thomas Conway, an Irish colonel, and a few members of the army. They challenged Washington's management of the army and engaged in some intrigue that was less dangerous to his authority than aggravating to him personally. The intrigue had its effect upon camp morale, and the army lost men by the hundreds. Less than 2,800 men were in the army by January 1778.

The British in Philadelphia seemed to be the winners of Saratoga, but their forces were less in number by four thousand men. General Howe lived well in the city; his forces were suitably housed and provisioned; and he ate meat and fish regularly and his staff raised tankards of ale frequently to toast the distant king. Howe had nearly twenty thousand men in his command, but curiously remained in the warmth of the city rather than being willing to travel out to the icy waste of Valley Forge and challenge Washington's ragged, half-fed army. Why? Even Britons wondered about Howe's decision, and Howe later replied to queries by reminding his British critics that there was little to gain in tramping through the snow when Washington would still be there in the spring. The logic was inescapably bad because in the spring Howe was superseded in his command by Henry Clinton, who faced a reinforced American army and a French navy.

Even before Clinton took over the command, the ministry had decided to anticipate the harmful effects of the French alliance with America by dispersing forces in Clinton's army. Five thousand men were dispatched to the West Indies to help capture St. Lucia and three thousand were sent to St. Augustine and Pensacola where they would await battle plans. Clinton was expected to abandon Philadelphia and depart by sea to New York. The ministry also planned another peace offensive and sent Lord Carlisle to offer the olive branch. If he failed in his peace maneuvers, then Clinton was to take the troops to Canada. Apparently New York was to be abandoned while Newport, Rhode Island, would be held as a base.

Philadelphia was evacuated in early June. The navy took nearly three thousand loyalists aboard the transports, while Howe marched the troops overland to New York. Their passage was slowed by rain, humidity, and mischief from American militia who destroyed bridges and felled trees. These tactics caused Howe's troops to be overextended and thus vulnerable to attack. Unfortunately, Washington's staff divided on the best strategy, and at first only harassing actions took place. Then Washington decided to attack Howe near Monmouth Courthouse and sent Charles Lee to test the soft spots in Howe's defenses. Lee was dilatory—perhaps disobedient and gave confusing orders to his subordinates so that there was little or no coordination of effort.

Apparently these tactics were speedily reported to Washington who took hold of the situation. With lectures for Lee, some regrouping of militia forces, and support from the regular army, Washington was able to present a strong line of fire against Howe. He blunted a bayonet attack with musket fire, turned back attacks on their flanks, and finally forced Clinton to withdraw. Washington wanted to push his advantage but darkness set in, and the British left the battlefield in the night. Howe saved both his baggage and his men, and Washington lost a chance for a decisive battle. Casualties on each side were about three hundred. Charles Lee was eventually court-martialed and found guilty of disobedience, misbehavior, and disrespect for his commander. Lee was removed from his command and not given any other posts.

Following the night march, Clinton continued to New York where he found the warships and transports safe in the harbor. All were awaiting the arrival of the French fleet under the command of Count d'Estaing, who was expected to engage them and take the British post in Rhode Island. The French were slow in their passage across the Atlantic and then unable to enter New York harbor. The eventual challenge occurred in Rhode Island, but was a standoff when a heavy storm disrupted the battle. Easily discouraged, Estaing left for Boston to make repairs on his ships, and various militia units, angry because Estaing did not put ashore the French army he was transporting, pulled out of the battle. In the end some hard fighting occurred between British regulars and militia, with losses about the same for both sides.

Americans were generally irritated by the conduct of Estaing, whom they regarded as irresponsible. Some riots in Boston also embittered feelings. When the fleet left for the West Indies in November, leaders were pleased for the opportunity to repair relations. But an opportunity was lost to remove the British from both New York and Rhode Island, and the war dragged into 1779.

In the north, Clinton was confined primarily to New York and its surrounding area and Rhode Island. Washington remained in the area and tested British defenses from time to time, but he was sufficiently clever not to be drawn into any engagement. Exchanges of territory were made at Stony Point, Verplanck's Point, and Paulus Hook, sometimes with much heroism and effort. Otherwise, Clinton and Washington were facing a stalemate. Elsewhere in the north there were isolated attacks on British posts in Maine, New York, and on the western frontier. These moves against forts may have reduced the peril of Indian massacre and checked some atrocities, but they were not decisive in combating British forces.

In the south the British quickly recovered Georgia in 1778 and returned royal governor Sir James Wright to office. They also withstood a siege of Savannah by Admiral Estaing in September and October 1779, when the French fleet cooperated with American militia in trying to take the town. The allied casualties were unbelievably heavy because of poor timing and tactics and Wright was, as a result, assured of firm control over the colony. American resistance melted away when the French fleet sailed for the West Indies.

The collapse of resistance in Georgia gave Britain an opportunity to concentrate major forces against Charleston, South Carolina; Clinton shifted his operations for a time to the south and directed personally British forces against the city. The American defense was in the charge of Benjamin Lincoln, a tenacious fighter who depended upon strong water batteries, trenches, and redoubts and the help of five thousand men to hold off the British. Lincoln, however, was a realist who sized up the military situation and weighed the odds.

Before the city, Clinton placed the threat of fourteen thousand men and a powerful fleet, and the danger of his presence was immediately evident to Lincoln who calculated that surrender of the city was only a matter of time. By May 12, 1780, not only did the city fall to Clinton, but the army also was captured, because Clinton skillfully blocked the escape route. The loss of men and matériel was one of those few severe disasters of the war. After Charleston's capture Clinton hastened back to New York, where he met the threat to Newport of a French army and navy. In charge of completing operations in Charleston was Lord Cornwallis, an experienced and talented veteran of American fighting. Cornwallis immediately sent forces into the interior to pursue other American forces, and at Waxhaws British forces under Banastre Tarleton caught up with the Americans. With sabers and shot the British all but destroyed the enemy in this bloody encounter. Resistance in both Georgia and South Carolina seemed crushed, and Clinton in great joy urged the return of William Bull as royal governor of South Carolina.

Soon after these British victories the Americans turned to hit-and-run fighting, attacking the enemy in surprise raids at almost any time of day or night, and these daring assaults confused and demoralized Tory forces often charged with keeping the peace. The Continental Congress, too, sent northern militia into South Carolina and, in July 1780, put Horatio Gates in charge of a small army. Without any loss of time Gates selected Camden as a place to make his stand against the British, although his army was hungry and suffering from dysentery. Both armies traveled toward each other during the night of August 15 and met in the morning at Saunder's Creek, where Gates had the superior site and numbers. Unfortunately, Gates's men were less experienced and broke lines quickly when confronted by the bayonets of the regulars. The hard fighting that followed cost the Americans dearly and they retreated and scattered to the winds. Other centers of American resistance also were hit which left them with casualties and losses of supplies. But the Battle of Camden itself was a most severe loss for the Americans because it left the British an open route to North Carolina.

The pacification of the country thus was succeeding very well for the British, and in January 1781 Clinton sent 2,500 reinforcements to South Carolina and 1,200 to Virginia. Cornwallis probably had four thousand men in his fighting forces, and the only organized force in South Carolina and Georgia. Still Cornwallis admitted that the country was hostile to Britain and peace was uncertain.

The Shadows of Yorktown

American disasters had followed one upon another, and Congress especially reacted to the loss of Camden by naming Nathaniel Greene to head the resistance. This courageous and brilliant tactician, who had little previous battle experience, had enough knowledge of war just the same to make good judgments. Besides the 1500 men he had in his army, Greene had Daniel Morgan and Light-Horse Harry Lee, two unusual men of great energy and bravery. Their immediate job was to harass Cornwallis without ever meeting the general in face-to-face combat. Morgan's and Lee's planned retreats gave them unusual flexibility and threw the British off-balance.

An early success of their tactics was at Cowpens in January 1781: Tarleton challenged Morgan who retreated by a prearranged route, drawing Tarleton into unfamiliar grounds and then counterattacking unexpectedly. Tarleton was routed with heavy casualties. There followed similar maneuvers by Greene. One with Cornwallis at Guildford Court House in March was a victory for the British, but Greene inflicted many casualties on the enemy. Greene and his commanders kept up the pressure during the summer of 1781 so that the countryside was all but wrested from the British, who found themselves confined to garrison posts like Savannah, Charleston, and St. Augustine.

The lesson for the British was obvious to the commanders. Even though they had eight thousand men and minor detachments of Tories in the South, the British were not able to cope with local, hit-and-run resistance, even when it challenged them face-to-face on a battle line. Victories did not amount to much as casualties increased and new enemy forces seemed to spring forth like the arms of a hydra.

Cornwallis became convinced that his problems in the South stemmed from a fluid frontier in Virginia, and he thus decided to attack these seedbeds of resistance. His march into this hostile country was in direct opposition to the will of the commander-in-chief, Henry Clinton, who thought that Cornwallis should strike at local opposition in the Carolinas from British bases rather than take the risks of fighting in Virginia. Clinton was himself bedeviled by Washington's forces and by a French army under the Count de Rochambeau. Both British commanders thus debated the best use of British forces and the perils of action from a French fleet upon British bases, and both worried about security of the southern area. Cornwallis, nonetheless, decided to enlarge the war in Virginia even though he fought without the consent of his chief and was far from supply lines. He created much turmoil in Virginia, destroyed large quantities of tobacco and munitions, and frightened the governor and legislature into taking refuge. Unfortunately for Cornwallis, he captured few Americans, convinced few Tories, and became confused himself about his objectives. Clinton in New York urged him to fortify Yorktown and Old Point Comfort and send the remaining troops to the north. Cornwallis decided instead to fortify Yorktown and count upon the control of the sea to give the base security.

The vulnerability of Cornwallis' position became obvious to the Americans who gathered troops to besiege his position. At the same time, Washington and Rochambeau were meeting in Connecticut to make plans that could be used in cooperation with a French fleet under Admiral de Grasse. The fleet was expected to be in American waters in July and August. Washington wanted a campaign against New York, while the French urged an attack in the Chesapeake—something swift and decisive. Yorktown became an attractive objective in Rochambeau's thinking, and he finally convinced Washington of its practicality. Both armies then hastened to Virginia and a meeting with de Grasse who, in the meantime, decided to take his entire fleet into American waters.

Fortunately, the allies confused the British long enough on land and sea to build up superior forces in the Chesapeake area. With superior forces on land and the French navy surrounding Yorktown peninsula by sea, Cornwallis faced almost certain disaster unless Clinton could rescue him. His seven thousand troops encountered an equal number of French troops and an equal number of Americans, not to mention large militia forces from Virginia, Maryland, and Pennsylvania. The siege began September 30,

Surrender of Lord Cornwallis' army. *(Library of Congress)*

but the great cannon that were dragged in place a week later only softened the defenses slowly. By October 17, however, Cornwallis' forces were nearing exhaustion. He counted ultimately upon assistance from New York, where the navy had just received reinforcements and was preparing to sail southward. Dock facilities and provisions were limited, and so the navy lingered in port longer than was planned. By the time the ships entered the Atlantic, Cornwallis capitulated at Yorktown.

The loss of seven thousand men was a major blow to the British, but it was a major victory for the French and Americans in getting their tactics together for a single assault upon British power. The alliance had finally achieved the benefits the allied planners had envisioned in 1778. The band on that 19th day of October 1781 played "The World Turned Upside Down," and it was soon to be true, as Lord North threw up his arms in disgust and Parliament questioned the practicality of continuing the war. Bitter war was not over by any means; men would fight and die on the battlefields into 1782; but the British had long since stopped thinking of the Americans as "their colonials." Some Britons still hoped, nonetheless, for a British-American empire, living under a single king and law and trading in a custom union that would be mutually beneficial.

The Military War Ends

The end of formal fighting in America raises many questions, but one is most important. Why did the British pull back and sue for peace? They were certainly not defeated—Yorktown was a great battle, but it did not destroy the British army or the navy. Probably the answer to the question is simply that the British were wise enough to realize that a continuation of the war was foolish and that negotiation now was likely to win them more than another campaign or two. Lord North himself realized that the colonies had grown in power. Many within and outside Parliament underscored through their opposition the futility of additional sacrifice. Taxes had risen, the national debt was burdensome, and discontent was apparent in the press. Lord North and his colleagues were heroic in their decision to begin negotiation; they concluded that backing away from combat was not defeat—that there was much to be won by dealing with an independent United States.

11

Seeking Peace and Stability

The great bells of Notre Dame Cathedral rang out as the priests prepared to celebrate a *Te Deum*. Parisians hailed the battle of Yorktown as a great victory for the Franco-American alliance, and now talk of peace filled the cathedral and streets. In London Lord North thought of resigning, but out of loyalty to George III he lingered a few weeks longer in office. His enemies persisted in their criticism of him and the war, and "his capacity for passive obedience" to the king's wishes was nearly exhausted: "I hope," Lord North said, "whoever those ministers might be, they would take such measures as should tend effectually to extricate the country from its present difficulties, and to render it happy and prosperous at home, successful and secure abroad." Finally, when the Commons voted on March 4 to abandon the war, Lord North resigned on March 20.

Though the king pondered his own abdication, he recovered his sense of duty to the nation and tried to gather a friendly coalition, but then asked the aging Lord Rockingham to form a government. The new cabinet was almost entirely drawn from the former opposition to Lord North, with Charles James Fox and the Earl of Shelburne as the new Secretaries of State. The cabinet immediately replaced Henry Clinton in America with Sir Guy Carleton and instructed the new commander to refrain from any major engagement. It sent an envoy to Paris to begin negotiations for peace with Benjamin Franklin. Both initiatives were taken with the hope of splitting the allied alliance and persuading the states to accept some kind of union with Great Britain.

The British calculated that America and her allies were not of one mind either on the purposes of the war or the objectives of the peace. Spain in 1778 had refused to join France in the alliance with the United States, partly because it feared future American expansion into Florida and Louisiana. Spain persisted in desiring limits to American territory and independence, but reluctantly granted loans to the American envoy, John Jay—loans which permitted him to live modestly in Madrid during the war. France in 1781 sympathized with her European ally and favored giving Spain both the territory east of the Mississippi River and the old province of Florida. But France also wanted peace because of the burdens of military expenditures upon her weakened, debt-ridden economy, and sometimes grabbed at straws in hope of ending the dispute. For a time France considered arranging a truce between Britain and America, and the Count de Vergennes even sounded out John Adams, the American peace envoy, about a peace conference sponsored by Austria and Russia which had suggested a truce. However, Adams made the American position clear: it would accept no negotiated peace without a recognition of independence and the departure of British troops from American coastal cities.

Congress was less firm (and certainly less suspicious of France) than Adams was. Most members accepted the Alliance of 1778 as a capstone of policy and regarded French advice and leadership essential to the success of the Revolution. Their instructions in 1781 to the peace commissioners revealed great confidence in French good will and wisdom: "to undertake nothing. . .without. . .[her] knowledge and convenience; and ultimately to govern yourselves by. . .[her] advice and opinion."

First only Benjamin Franklin conducted negotiations with Richard Oswald because the other American envoys were either out of the city or ill. Oswald was a special commissioner without formal diplomatic status who was expected to examine the problems of arranging terms of peace. In their discussions Franklin insisted upon independence as the primary objective of any negotiation, but he realized that Lord Shelburne was deeply interested in some future alliance or union. The discussions were informal and without the apparent knowledge of the French government, but Franklin was generally committed like Vergennes to a peace settlement which involved all the participants. These conversations shifted slightly when Rockingham died on July 1, 1782, and Shelburne became prime minister. Oswald remained as an informal envoy, while another became the representative of the ministry to the French government. Franklin now gave a full statement of the American position to Oswald. This included the granting of independence, good boundaries, fishing rights in the Newfoundland banks, and a trade treaty. These outlines of a possible treaty met with some favor by Shelburne, but Franklin—and now

John Jay, who joined him—discovered that Oswald had no power to deal with an independent United States, only with the American colonies. The symbolism of the commission, they felt, was important in the negotiations with France and Spain.

Already Jay had discovered that France, in her own negotiations with Spain and England, was supporting Spanish claims to territory west of the Appalachian Mountains and south of the Great Lakes. His protests had brought a modified plan which he did not like because it gave Britain the Ohio Valley and the Indians a large reservation reaching from Florida to the Ohio River. The tribal area would be protected by Spain! In short, Spain and France were trying to erect a barrier to American expansion over the protests of the American commissioners.

Jay was rightly suspicious of France, and he convinced Franklin that they should urge Lord Shelburne to recognize United States independence. The cabinet partly responded to their request by giving Oswald new credentials which referred obliquely to the status of the colonies now as the "Thirteen United States." The credentials had the effect, however, of putting Britain formally behind the move for separate negotiations. These occurred quickly and produced in early October a draft treaty which was favorable to America. Boundaries followed lines, except for Ontario, that the Americans desired and included provisions for access to northern fisheries, free trade in the dominions of each country, and British navigation of the Mississippi.

Such speed and agreement was almost too much to expect in these technical and emotional matters. When the proposed treaty reached London, Shelburne was less generous than he had been earlier, which reflected politics in his party and the military situation. He refused to accept free trade for both countries in each other's territories and insisted upon a British right to navigate the Mississippi River. He also raised questions of merchant debts and Tory losses because of the war. Even more significant than Shelburne's hardened position was the inclusion of another envoy in the negotiations, Sir Henry Strachey, who joined Oswald.

When they resumed negotiations with the Americans on October 26, John Adams had reached Paris. Likewise suspicious of France and Spain, Adams welcomed these private negotiations with Britain and favored minor concessions to Britain when necessary, if the major objective of the peace could be easily won. He wanted a boundary for the district of Maine on the St. Croix River, and with his colleagues he stoutly argued against any real concessions for those hated Tories. Other issues in these discussions included setting the boundaries of Florida and Vermont. Later, in London, the ministry made some modifications in these agreements, but in general it accepted the proposed treaty. The next problem the American negotiators faced was the reaction of France to their underhanded activities. French attitude was, moreover, important because the Americans needed another loan to help pay for the expenses of the American government. On being told of the negotiations, Vergennes was outwardly miffed, and he vented his feelings in a letter to the Congress and in a personal exchange with Franklin. But he permitted a loan of six million livres to be approved for the American government.

When the preliminary treaty of peace was finally initialed on January 20, 1783, hostilities ended soon afterward, and a final draft of the treaty was then to be written for a later signing. In the meantime, the Shelburne ministry was turned out of office in late February, and a coalition formed by Charles James Fox and Lord North agreed to accept the responsibility of a ministry. Fox then opened a discussion with the American envoys regarding some issues of trade and union. But too many party members were sensitive about privileges of trade for them to weaken the navigation laws, and Fox did not dare test his majority. The final treaty was signed in September amid restrained expressions of joy. George III expressed well how he and his friends felt about the signing: "I am glad it is [to be done] on a day I am not in Town, as I think this completes the Downfall of the lustre of the Empire; but when Religion and Public Spirit are quite absorbed by Vice and Dissipation, what has now occurred is but the natural consequence; one comfort [for me is] that I have alone tried to support the Dignity of the Crown and feel I am innocent of the Evils that have occurred, though [I am] deeply wounded that it should have happened during my Reign."

In brief, the treaty of peace for the United States recognized its full independence and provided for the evacuation of British troops from the coastal cities and anywhere else in the now independent states. The treaty also provided boundaries from Florida to Canada that seemed clear and precise, and it permitted private debts of Americans to British citizens (amounting to approximately £5 million) to be collected with the help of government. Tories were given a vague promise of help in getting compensation for their confiscated estates.

Fruits of Independence

As sweet as were the fruits of European peace, there remained for Britain bitter fruits of past hostilities that needed to be digested. Britain had plainly never recognized the fact that she had lost the war and was thus unwilling either to accord full diplomatic relations or to negotiate a

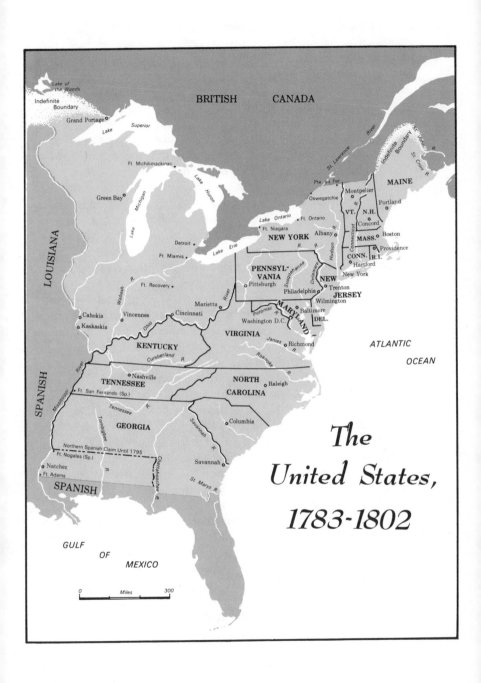

Lake of
the Woods

Indefinite
Boundary

BRITISH   CANADA

Grand Portage

Lake   Superior

St. Lawrence   River

Ft. Michilimackinac

Lake Michigan

Lake Huron

Pte. au Fer

Oswegatchie

Montpelier

MAINE

Portland

Green Bay

Lake Ontario   Ft. Ontario

VT.   N.H.

Concord

St. Croix R.

St. John R.

Indefinite Boundary

Ft. Niagara

NEW YORK

Albany

Detroit

Lake Erie

Ft. Miamis

R.

R.

Hudson R.

MASS.   Boston

Providence

CONN.   R.I.

Hartford

Connecticut R.

LOUISIANA

PENNSYL-
VANIA

Pittsburgh

Susquehanna

Delaware R.

New York

Ft. Recovery

Wabash R.

Marietta

River

Cincinnati

Ohio R.

Philadelphia

NEW
JERSEY

Trenton

Wilmington

DEL.

Cahokia

Vincennes

MARYLAND

Potomac R.

Baltimore

Kaskaskia

Washington D.C.

KENTUCKY

Cumberland   R.

VIRGINIA

James R.   Richmond

Roanoke R.

ATLANTIC

OCEAN

SPANISH

Mississippi River

Nashville

TENNESSEE

Ft. San Fernando (Sp.)

Tennessee R.

NORTH
CAROLINA   Raleigh

Tombigbee R.

GEORGIA

Savannah R.

Columbia

Northern Spanish Claim Until 1795

Ft. Nogales (Sp.)

Natchez

Ft. Adams

Chattahoochee R.

Savannah

St. Marys R.

SPANISH

The

United States,

1783-1802

GULF

OF

MEXICO

0   Miles   300

commercial treaty. In fact, she violated the peace treaty by ordering her garrisons, without any provocation from the Americans, to remain at certain western posts. John Adams, as the first American minister, was treated just at the tolerance level, with a large measure of cold civility and stuffy ceremony. Even though trade flourished and would pass pre-Revolutionary levels by 1789, the government maintained its bittersweet policy. The famous English pamphleteer of the day, Lord Sheffield, argued against this dog-in-the-manger attitude, and pleaded that self-interest alone would dictate concessions. But his arguments and those of other friends of moderation had little impact upon the ministries.

Relations with Spain were no less tense because her court never was reconciled to American independence and never was happy about American claims to the trans-Appalachian region. Now that the states were awarded this vast area, Spain took countermeasures. She refused to abide by the 31st parallel as the boundary between West Florida and the United States, and claimed a major piece of land from the Yazoo River northward beyond the 32nd parallel. These claims were primarily based upon the results of Spanish military operations during the war. She intrigued with the Creek and Cherokee Indians by providing them firearms and also tried to convince some American settlers to throw in their lot with her. Pressure on settlers was applied by closing the Mississippi River to trade.

Both England and Spain had agents traveling through this back country. They sowed seeds of discontent among settlers and Indians, offering bribes, merchandise, and security. The British trading posts such as Oswego, Detroit, and Michilimackinac stabilized relations with the Indians, but at the price of monopolizing their trade. British success reflected both the inability of the United States to maintain peace in the West and the activities of some eastern politicians to sacrifice the West for eastern interests. As Secretary of Foreign Affairs, John Jay at one point proposed giving up the right of navigation on the Mississippi for twenty-five years in exchange for a commercial treaty with Spain.

The weakness of the United States certainly influenced its western policy with Spain and England. But its relations with France were little better than those with the other powers. France granted some trade concessions in the West Indies, but restrictions were applied to the size of the ships and the ports to be used. In France Thomas Jefferson was sufficiently popular as United States minister, though he admitted that his position "was an excellent school of humility."

In general, the United States also suffered because it was a republic. The stability of such governments in the past was notoriously short and left a poor record. Most European powers thus expected a breakup of the states into warring nations, and they waited not too patiently to pick up the pieces. Also America was regarded as a dangerous experiment which might pass from sight in a relatively short time, but in the meanwhile it provided an example for oppressed peoples everywhere. America could easily be a seedbed for other revolutions.

The New Republic

Americans anticipated the peace by improving life in many ways, but they found that the reality of independence was not what they had imagined it to be. The Revolution released many new forces, provided much disruption of life, and raised many issues that troubled some people. One is not certain how many favored the Revolution, but by its end at least 85,000 Tories left the United States; perhaps twice as many migrated into western areas to find a new life by separating themselves from seaboard radicals; and others may have quietly accepted the inevitable. Certain is the fact, nonetheless, that in 1783 a large majority of Americans welcomed the promise of peace and the opportunity to better their lives. There was a restlessness that pervaded almost everything that occurred.

Most people wanted some changes in education. In less than a decade they formed new colleges almost everywhere, and older schools secularized or diversified their offerings. Presbyterians established four colleges: Hampden-Sydney, Liberty Hall, Dickinson College, and Transylvania Seminary. Episcopalians founded Washington College, St. John's, and the Citadel, and in 1789 the Roman Catholics, still small in numbers, started their first college, Georgetown. Some southern legislators even voted funds for state universities. In both Philadelphia and Boston students were offered improved medical education, and in some of the older colleges professorships of law and modern languages replaced those of divinity and the ancient languages. In 1784 Judge Topping Reeve of Connecticut opened the first law school at Litchfield, which used moot courts and case studies as part of its curriculum.

This amazing multiplication of educational opportunities does not reveal the successful attempts at creating academies, day schools, and various kinds of public schools. The Phillips Academies, at Andover and Exeter, were the most famous. Less known were the accomplishments of Timothy Dwight and Caleb Bingham who opened schools for boys and girls. Noah Webster of Connecticut responded to the need for books by publishing first a speller, then a school reader, and sometime later a dictionary. Joel Barlow, his classmate at Yale College, provided the famous epic poem, *Vision of Columbus*, as a piece of American literature and inspiration for the new nation. Other persons were also writing poems and histories, and a few would find publishers for their works by the end of the decade.

To catch the spirit of the age John Trumbull of Connecticut painted the epic canvases, "The Battle of Bunker's Hill Near Boston" and "The Death of General Montgomery," which departed greatly from the traditional painting in America. Portraiture was more common and continued to be for another decade or two. Trumbull would perfect his style, moreover, and accept a commission in later life to do eight pictures for the rotunda of the capitol in Washington.

This new spirit of republicanism was also felt in religion. Most obvious was greater toleration of beliefs and practices of worship among Protestants, who now thought of each other as fellow human beings. Emphasis, too, upon freedom to worship without regard for state laws was spreading so that Catholics and Jews, also brethren of a sort, were tolerated as members of society. For many holding these ideas God was no less held in reverence, but the practices of worship were challenged; the exact influence of God in the lives of men was questioned; and old-time doctrines were frequently repudiated. Reason was substituted for revealed religion, and the Old Testament view of creation was rigorously criticized. The importance of reason as an instrument cannot be overemphasized, as Americans everywhere stressed the role of conscience as authority, the right of inquiry, and the divinity of human nature. Some of these people were Deists, more were Unitarians, and the majority were Christians who rejected authoritarianism and intolerance.

Organized churches in these years probably suffered a drop in membership, but for them there were also some changes in structure. The Methodists split from the Church of England (Episcopal Church) and in 1784 formed a separate communion called the Methodist Episcopal Church. Its zealous leader, Bishop Francis Ashbury, rode horseback from congregation to congregation bringing his flocks together. The Protestant Episcopal Church, too, underwent changes, but most significantly it secured bishops, denied to it until the Revolution, and some revisions in the Book of Common Prayer. Samuel Seabury, a Tory of the Revolution, returned to Connecticut in the new dignity of a bishop of the church. As a newspaper writer in Boston exclaimed: Would wonders ever cease—"a Bishop in Connecticut!"

Neither Congregational nor Presbyterian churches experienced many changes. The Presbyterians did clarify their discipline, adopting a confession of faith and catechisms. The Roman Catholics, however, struggled for direct relations with Pope Pius VI instead of going through an

English vicar apostolic or some French cleric. In 1784 the pope chose John Carroll of Maryland to be apostolic prefect; a few years later Carroll became the first Bishop of Baltimore, and his diocese encompassed the entire United States until 1804.

Government of the Republic

Until 1789 the government of the republic was exercised under the Articles of Confederation, which was finally ratified on March 2, 1781. In this constitution federal power was not well distributed and the states remained in a position to challenge the Congress at any time. The focus of authority thus was as much on the Congress as on the government of the states. Congress, in general, was organized to do what the states could not do themselves and to do what the king and Parliament did before the Revolution. It thus had powers to wage war and maintain the peace, to establish a post office, to set standards of weights and measures, and to coin money. It also had power to regulate Indian affairs and govern the territories. Unfortunately, Congress did not have power to levy and collect taxes or to regulate commerce or ratify treaties, except with the consent of nine of the thirteen states. To amend the Articles, furthermore, required unanimous consent of the states, an impossible measure as experience was to prove.

Since Congress could not collect taxes or change the constitution to secure a tax levy, the government depended upon grants from the states and loans. The states, however, provided very little money in relation to costs and Congress regularly had to negotiate foreign loans to defray ordinary operating expenses. Foreign money was borrowed regularly over the years until the debt mounted to $12 million by 1790, an increase of $5 million since 1783.

If it were not for the Dutch loans, the nation would have been bankrupted. As it was, the debt rose, interest payments were not made, and more money was borrowed. Continental securities fell yearly, and Congress used public lands to satisfy debts to soldiers. Added to this crisis was the credit condition of the states. Paper money had eroded credit, and large purchases in Britain had drained the hard money from circulation. Trade elsewhere did not restore the balance of payments so that there was little relief for the economy. Further, most states increased their debt because of their inability to raise sufficient taxes or to regulate commerce.

Congress also did not have power to regulate commerce or credit. Merchants traded to their advantage, but bought more than the economy could absorb. Government thus looked helplessly on without authority to bargain, regulate, or set prices in the handling of foreign trade. Everyone became saddled with debts, and debtors looked to their legislatures for relief, whatever that might be.

Still there was some profitable commerce. Renewed smuggling with the West Indies brought profits to a few merchants; trade with the French Indies was valuable; and trade voyages into the Mediterranean area, though hazardous, were lucrative. Some merchants joined in voyages to the Pacific Ocean, to Hawaii and China. This trade was limited, but encouraging in its high profit margins. The economy was improving yearly; good profits inspired speculation of dock facilities and warehouses; and new enterprises met the challenge. Still people worried about instability of the government, credit, and foreign markets. An odd mixture of optimism and depression pervaded the land.

For many the solution to their economic problems lay in the West, in its land and trade with the Indians, and Americans sought these opportunities. Over fifty thousand people moved into the trans-Appalachian area by 1783, and sixty thousand additional people moved there by 1790. New forts for their protection were built, the army made its presence felt, and Indian treaties were negotiated. Unfortunately, the government was not strong enough to guarantee the settlers continued protection.

The Congress responded to this migration by passing two major laws. First, it passed the Land Ordinance of 1785, which provided for surveys of public lands; divided land into townships, each consisting of 36 sections of 640 acres; and sold land at a price of not less than one dollar per acre. Some land was set aside for the maintenance of schools. Second, Congress passed the Northwest Ordinance of 1787. This great piece of legislation provided for the evolution of territories into states in the Northwest and the equality of the new with older states in the Union.

Both statutes, in their unique ways, were cornerstones of the nation, which the builders laid well, but Congress for the moment was unable to provide protection for the inhabitants. Also both Britain and Spain, as was mentioned earlier, encouraged settlers and Indians to be disloyal to the United States. With their taking of bribes, some settlers imperiled the security of the area and made control of the Indians almost impossible. Incredible barbarities were committed along the southern frontier in 1787 and 1788, and few settlements anywhere in the trans-Appalachian region were safe from assaults.

The mounting crisis, therefore, reflected weakness of the Congress to raise money, to regulate credit, and to maintain governmental services. Leaders everywhere recognized this crisis for what it was and wondered about the future. They began in time to exchange thoughts about the crisis, to speculate on plans for its solution, and to mobilize support. While they were nervous about the future, they moved slowly because their contacts with each other were primarily by correspondence.

Two episodes occurred in 1786 that heightened public awareness of what was happening to the United States. In the back country of Massachusetts hundreds of farmers, led by Daniel Shays, prevented the courts from sitting and handing down decisions that would take their lands to satisfy debts. The farmers hoped to keep the courts closed until they won an election and could challenge their creditors in the legislature. Open violence instead brought repressive measures by the governor, and militia and farmers met in pitched battles. Bested by the militia, the farmers retreated into the forests and mountains, where some were pursued through the snowdrifts and taken prisoners. Convicted in court and sentenced to death, they were later either pardoned or given light sentences. The outbreak, however, frightened good people everywhere who felt America was drifting into revolution.

About the time that the embattled frontier farmers resisted authority in Massachusetts, delegates from five states gathered at Annapolis, Maryland, to consider trade disputes among the states. They met at the behest of the Virginia legislature which was irritated by its relations with Maryland over navigation of the Potomac River. Other states had equally aggravated problems with their neighbors and searched for solutions. In the discussion at the convention Alexander Hamilton of New York and James Madison of Virginia, two of the younger members of the group, urged their colleagues to use the occasion for a petition to Congress. They asked for a larger meeting of the states in which the Articles of Confederation could be considered for amendment. Most were worried about the Union, the violence in Massachusetts, the weakness of the Articles, and the lack of a public spirit. In good time Congress received the petition and in February 1787 invited the states to send representatives to a convention at Philadelphia in late spring, "for the sole and express purpose of revising the Articles of Confederation."

The gloom spreading across the United States was serious in 1786 and may be felt through the words of George Washington to Henry Lee: "I am lost in amazement when I behold what intrigue, the interested views of desperate characters, ignorance, and jealousy of the minor part, are capable of effecting, as a scourge on the major part of our fellow citizens of the Union... Let the reins of government then be braced and held with a steady hand, and every violation of the Constitution be reprehended. If defective, let it be amended, but not be trampled upon whilst it has an existence."

The Constitution Convention

The fifty-five delegates to the Federal Convention met in a tense atmosphere of mounting crisis. The republic seemed to be disintegrating under the Articles, and some major changes in the government were necessary for its survival. Most of these delegates had had legislative service during the Revolution; a few were lawyers; two were college presidents; and almost all had a college education or its equivalent. Most, too, were relatively young men; five were under thirty years old; four had reached sixty or older. Franklin was 81, Washington, 55, and James Madison 34. Only Rhode Island was unrepresented, and conspicuous by their absence were such controversial figures as Samuel Adams, Patrick Henry, and George Clinton. Busy with other important matters were John Jay, John Adams, and Thomas Jefferson.

Most of these delegates were even-tempered at the sessions and looked upon the proceedings as a serious and urgent matter. Only a few were suspicious of their colleagues, believed the convention was an attack upon states rights and human liberties, and refused eventually to sign the new constitution.

The sessions opened on May 25, 1787, in the old State House where the independence of the United States had been proclaimed in 1776. Some preliminary business was then transacted and an agreement to keep the proceedings secret was passed. On the fourth day Edmund Randolph of Virginia presented what has become known as the Virginia or large-state plan. It laid before the membership a three-part government—legislative, executive, and judiciary—with the legislature composed of two houses and the number of delegates apportioned according to the population. Legislative power, significantly, was extensive—to make laws in areas where the states were "incompetent" and to negate state laws contravening the constitution. The executive was chosen by the legislature and was ineligible for reelection. His powers were not defined, but he and some members of the judiciary would be part of a council of state which would pass upon proposed laws and act as a temporary negative. Repassage of any law would guarantee its final approval. The judiciary consisted of one or more tribunals and inferior courts, as determined by the legislature. They possessed the power to rule on tax cases, admiralty matters, and citizenship questions, and also they had jurisdiction in impeachment cases. Judges served for life or good behavior. Randolph concluded his presentation "with exhortation, not to suffer the present opportunity of establishing general peace, harmony, happiness and liberty in the United States to pass away unimproved."

Randolph's plan then was debated for two weeks by the delegates, who met in a committee of the whole (for more flexibility of discussion than floor debate) and considered various amendments. On June 10 William Patterson of New Jersey tried to resolve some problems of the continuing debate by presenting the New Jersey or small-state plan, which reflected the current practices of the Articles of Confederation. It provided thus for a single-house legislature in which the states were equally represented. This Congress, he observed, "would act with more energy and wisdom" than Randolph's legislature and would be manageable in size and able to keep secrets. Patterson's plan grasped, nonetheless, the current problem of national sovereignty by declaring boldly that all Acts of Congress and all treaties made and ratified "under the authority of the United States shall be the supreme law of the respective States. . .and the Judiciary of the several States shall be bound thereby to their decisions." The enforcement authority, unfortunately, he placed in the armed forces.

Both plans were defective in creating a federal republic, but the delegates aligned themselves behind these plans. Hamilton, in a moment of great insight, observed that this division of the delegates was artificial—"It is a contest for power, not for liberty." He believed both plans fell short of the goal of a truly representative government that would be federal in its distribution of powers. He recommended instead a centralized government that had full power, wiping away for most purposes the government of the states.

Hamilton's observations did not resolve matters. In fact, a deadlock occurred between advocates of the two plans, and debate in early July was at times tense and bad-natured. But the delegates continued to search for a compromise, which was eventually found in the Connecticut Plan. This plan provided for equal votes of the states in the upper house and representation by population in the lower house. The lower house was given the power to originate money bills.

Soon after the Connecticut Compromise was accepted, other issues rose in importance. Problems of democracy and mob rule loomed large, especially in discussions of voting qualifications for members of the House of Representatives. The admission of new western states also caused some expression of feeling because it would disturb balances of sections and interests. Perhaps the wrong kinds of people would gain power. Other members, particularly southerners, worried about sectional votes in the Congress. They urged the use of a two-thirds majority to pass commercial legislation.

By September 17, 1787, the Constitution was finished, polished, and presented for signature. The members provided that it would be then placed before special conventions in the states for approval, thus bypassing the Articles of Confederation Congress. The delegations, in adjourning to a tavern for toasts and dinner, realized that the hard battle for ratification now had begun but that the special conventions gave them a fighting chance of success.

The Ratification of the Constitution

Only 39 of the 55 delegates signed the Constitution for presentation to the nation. This significant minority of Anti-Federalists included prestigious leaders such as George Mason, Luther Martin, and Elbridge Gerry who became active in its opposition. In general, the older, wealthier men and the old radicals of the Revolution were the critics, while the younger, poorer men and the rising new leaders were the supporters. Exceptions could be made in any grouping, but undoubtedly a majority of the people were Anti-Federalists in 1787 if a national vote could have been taken.

The Constitution's supporters, however, had powerful people on their side. Statements by Washington and Franklin went far to convince wavering and uncommitted people. Also a series of newspaper articles entitled "Publius," later known as *The Federalist*, was influential in providing the essential arguments in favor of ratification. The opposition was unable to find anyone who could write as well as Madison, Hamilton, and Jay. They were realists, against disorder, and willing to move to another stage of American development in which a federal government would provide integration of political society and power to handle problems of commerce, foreign affairs, and civil disturbance.

Fortunately for the cause of the Constitution the first ratifications in Delaware and Pennsylvania were relatively easy. Most of the people in Pennsylvania did not even go to the polls to vote and the issues were not well debated. The convention for ratification of the Constitution was convened almost before the opposition could organize, and the vote in convention was taken nearly as fast. Even before the 46 to 23 vote in favor of the Constitution was publicized, Delaware gave its unanimous consent. New Jersey soon followed Delaware's example with a unanimous vote.

The big test of ratification, in the opinion of most Federalists, was to be in Massachusetts. The situation there was tense because of Shays' Rebellion and opposition from John Hancock and Samuel Adams. Many of the delegates in early January 1788 were opposed to the Constitution, and Hancock would not honor the convention by presiding over it. But the friends of ratification were unusually active, and they reached Hancock by promising him support for the vice presidency if he joined the cause, and reached Adams by giving contracts to his merchant supporters. Probably their most telling strategy, however, was a promise of amendments to the Constitution which would add a bill of rights. The Constitution had no bill of rights because the federal government was one of limited and enumerated powers, and such rights would normally be matters of state legislation. As a tactic Hancock was asked to present the future amendments to the convention, to the great surprise of the Anti-Federalists, and the maneuver threw them into disarray. Argument ceased as Adams joined his rival. Massachusetts voted in favor of the Constitution 187 to 168, and the mood of the convention at adjournment was conciliatory in spite of a hard-fought battle—"All appeared willing to bury the hatchet of animosity, and to smoke the calumet of union and love."

Between February and July conventions were held in Maryland, South Carolina, and New Hampshire, when nine states had given their approval of the Constitution, and it was now put in force. The agreement of Federalists to future amendments undoubtedly paved the way for these successes, but it was probably also true that the Constitution was now better known.

Even so, the battles in Virginia and New York would determine the success of the new government, because they and North Carolina and Rhode Island were essential blocks to a strong edifice. Virginia's convention opened in early June, and the initial argument was made by Patrick Henry who emphasized the need for caution and the drastic nature of the change proposed. He plainly did not like the creation of a federal government—"a great consolidated government, instead of a confederation"—and thought the republic to be in great danger as a result. George Mason followed Henry in denouncing the Constitution as a consolidated government: "It was totally subversive of every principle which has hitherto governed us. This power is calculated to annihilate totally the State governments." Friends of the Constitution replied; particularly powerful were James Madison and Edmund Pendleton as they answered arguments on whether the proposed government was too powerful. Madison pointed out that Henry and his followers misunderstood the way the federal government would work: "the powers of the Federal Government are enumerated, it can only operate in certain cases. It has legislative powers on defined and limited objects, beyond which it cannot extend its jurisdiction."

While Henry was not convinced by any arguments in favor of the Constitution, enough members eventually tired of the oratory and bickering to move for its adoption. It was ratified by the close vote of 89 to 79, and the vote surprised even the victors who counted at one point only three or four votes. Why did the Federalists eventually win? The Anti-Federalists also asked this question, and one put his finger, he thought, on the ultimate answer. The promise of having Washington as first President had weakened their opposition: "Be assured his influence carried this government."

The Richmond convention adjourned on June 23, while the New York delegates were debating the merits of the Convention. The Federalists, led by Hamilton, Livingston and Jay, challenged their opposition as agents of disunion and as petty politicians, and reminded them that if New York remained outside the national union, its isolation would be disastrous for the state. And worse—possibly New York City might break away from the state and join the Union as a separate state. In the heat of debate Governor Clinton lost control of his following long enough for his majority to melt away. Though the convention recommended a bill of rights and other amendments, ratification won by a vote of 30 to 27, with the governor so disaffected that he cast no vote.

Though Rhode Island had called no convention, North Carolina's was scheduled to meet in July 1788 when the news from Virginia and New York would certainly be available. Anti-Federalists were in a controlling position when the convention met in July and their leader, Willie Jones, was able and dedicated. However, Jones's power depended upon assumptions that North Carolina could remain out of the Union until it had bargained for concessions. The basic concession he wanted was a bill of rights now assured by the action of other states, which made its passage a condition of ratification. The convention, nonetheless, voted 183 to 84 to adjourn without a decision and meet again in November.

For the Federalists there were some anxious moments in the summer and fall as Anti-Federalists gathered in a kind of afterglow of opposition. A convention at Harrisburg, Pennsylvania, had a disappointing number of delegates and accomplished nothing in promoting Anti-Federalism. Most of the opposition, however, decided to work for amendments in the new Congress, and Elbridge Gerry and men of his brilliance agreed to be congressmen.

In the meantime, the Articles of Confederation Congress called for elections for the first congress under the Constitution, arranged for the selection of electors for President and Vice President, and set March 4, 1789 as the beginning of the first presidency. The House of Representatives, however, did not meet until April 1 and did not count the electoral ballots until April 6. But George Washington and John Adams were notified soon afterwards of their choice as President and Vice President of the United States of America. Congress had already decided on New York as the first capital, and Washington hastened to the northern city for his inauguration on April 30.

That moment of oath-taking for Washington ended the revolutionary era that had begun in the 1760s. The nation found both a leader and a Constitution. Fisher Ames of Massachusetts thought the President looked "grave, almost to sadness." The French minister believed the President had "the soul, look and figure of a hero united in him." The Constitution gave him and Congress the opportunity to organize government and mold institutions so that the experiences of the Revolution would become a reality.

12

Suggestions for Further Reading

The vitality and excitement of American history has drawn a particularly energetic group of scholars into the early American period. Their research over the past fifty years has challenged assumptions repeatedly, and a new appreciation of America's origins has arisen. The result has been an unusually rich number of studies, biographical and topical, which gives depth to almost every conceivable aspect of early American life. Along with this writing has come the gathering of manuscripts and the development of libraries so that vast new collections are available to scholars. In some cases the use of new kinds of research—genealogical, computer, and family reconstitution—has expanded horizons, put old materials into new perspective, and broadened the base of research.

In the 1930s the bicentennial of George Washington's birth brought as great an interest in his papers and life as it did in the entire period of early American history. John C. Fitzpatrick edited the 39 volumes of *The Writings* (Washington, D.C.: Government Printing Office, 1931-1944), and the success of that project encouraged in the 1950s and 1960s the beginning of even better-edited and more comprehensive editions of the writings of Washington's contemporaries. Among the edited papers are Julian P. Boyd *et al*, eds., *The Papers of Thomas Jefferson* (Princeton, N.J.: Princeton University Press, 1950–); Leonard W. Labaree, ed., *Papers of Benjamin Franklin* (New Haven, Conn.: Yale University Press, 1958–); Harold C. Syrett and Jacob E. Cook, eds., *The Papers of Alexander Hamilton* (New York: Columbia University Press, 1961–); and Lyman H. Butterfield, ed., *Diary and Autobiography of John Adams* (Cambridge,

Mass.: Harvard University Press, 1961). Other editions of Adams' works and those of Samuel Adams, John Dickinson, and John Jay add to this richness of biographical material. Similar publications for the early period of American history have also brought forth excellent editions of papers. The most important of these has been *The Complete Writings of Roger Williams* (New York: Russell and Russell, 1963).

Stimulated by this expansion of printed materials, historians have reinterpreted the lives of the great men of the period so that there is a good biographical selection on almost every important figure. **Exploration**. The most important biography of Columbus is still Samuel E. Morison, *Admiral of the Ocean Sea* (Boston: Little, Brown and Company, 1942). Morison's *The European Discovery Of America: The Northern Voyages, A.D. 500-1600* (New York: Oxford University Press, 1971) is likewise a fine account of explorers and their exploits. Less so is his *Samuel de Champlain: Father of New France* (Boston: Little Brown and Company, 1972). Other good studies of explorers are Bailey W. Diffie and George D. Winius, *Foundations of the Portuguese Empire, 1415 to 1580* (Minneapolis: University of Minnesota, 1977); Charles M. Parr, *Ferdinand Magellan, Circumnavigator* (New York: Thomas Y. Crowell, 1964); and J.H. Parry, *The Age of Reconnaissance* (Cleveland: The World Publishing Company, 1963). Since navigation was so important to the success of the first explorers the following books emphasizing geographical influences should be consulted: John N.L. Baker, *A History of Geographical Discovery and Exploration* (London: G.G. Harris and Company, 1937) and R.A. Skelton, *Explorer's Maps: Chapters in the Cartographic Record of Geographical Discovery* (New York: Frederick A. Praeger, 1958).

English Colonizers. Recent biographical studies of Sir Walter Raleigh's activities are numerous and excellent. The best short accounts are David Quinn, *Raleigh and the British Empire* (London: Hodder and Stoughton, 1947) and A.L. Rowse, *Sir Walter Raleigh* (New York: Harper and Row, Publishers, 1959). Also valuable is James A. Williamson, *The Age of Drake*, 4th ed. (London: A. and C. Black, 1960). The best work on Richard Hakluyt is still George B. Parks, *Richard Hakluyt and the English Voyages* (New York: The American Geographical Society, 1928), and on Drake is undoubtedly Julian C. Corbett, *Sir Francis Drake* (London: Macmillan and Company, 1901). For perspective one should consult Theodore K. Rabb, *Enterprise and Empire: Merchants and Gentry Investment in the Expansion of England, 1575-1630* (Cambridge, Mass.: Harvard University Press, 1967).

The Planters of Colonies. Not much biographical material is available on early Virginia, but Philip Barbour's *The Three Worlds of Captain John*

Smith (Boston: Houghton Mifflin Company, 1964) is excellent. The best, long account of Virginia history to 1763 is Richard L. Morton, *Colonial Virginia* (Chapel Hill, North Carolina: The University of North Carolina, 1960) and Wesley Frank Craven, *Southern Colonies in the Seventeenth Century* (Baton Rouge, Louisiana: Louisiana State University Press, 1949). For the Plymouth colony George D. Langdon's *Pilgrim Colony: A History of New Plymouth* (New Haven: Yale University Press, 1966) and John Demos, *A Little Commonwealth: Family Life in Plymouth Colony* (New York: Oxford University Press, 1970) should be read as supplements of each other. Massachusetts has many more biographical works: Edmund S. Morgan, *The Puritan Dilemma: The Story of John Winthrop* (Boston: Little, Brown and Company, 1958); Samuel E. Morison, *Builders of the Bay Colony* (Boston: Houghton Mifflin Company, 1930); and Robert Middlekauff, *The Mathers: Three Generations of Puritan Intellectuals, 1596-1728* (New York: Oxford University Press, 1971). Rhode Island's Roger Williams has had many good biographers, but interpretations vary widely. See Edmund S. Morgan, *Roger Williams: The Church and the State* (New York: Harcourt Brace Jovanovich, 1967); Cyclone Covy, *The Gentle Radical: A Biography of Roger Williams* (New York: Crowell-Collier and Macmillan, 1966); and Samuel H. Brockunier, *The Irresponsible Democrat, Roger Williams* (New York: The Ronald Press Company, 1940). In Connecticut the lives of Winthrop and Hooker are important in its history: see Robert C. Black, *The Younger John Winthrop* (New York: Columbia University Press, 1966) and Warren S. Archibald, *Thomas Hooker* (New Haven, Conn.: Yale University Press, 1933). The works on William Penn are generally very good, but scholars disagree on whether any current biography is definitive. See Catherine Owens Peare, *William Penn* (Philadelphia: J.B. Lippincott Company, 1957); Joseph E. Illick, *William Penn the Politician* (Ithaca, New York: Cornell University Press, 1965); and Mary Staples Dunn, *William Penn: Politics and Conscience* (Princeton, New Jersey: Princeton University Press, 1967). The founders of Georgia are well treated in William W.W. Abbot, *The Royal Governors of Georgia, 1754-1775* (Chapel Hill, North Carolina: The University of North Carolina Press, 1959).

England's Neighbors. For New France the most charming of biographical accounts is Samuel E. Morison's *Samuel de Champlain: Father of New France* (Boston: Little, Brown and Company, 1972), but more important for the colony's development is William J. Eccles' *Frontenac, the Courtier Governor* (Toronto, Canada: McClelland and Stewart, 1959). An older but interesting study is Julian Winsor's *Cartier to Frontenac* (Boston: Houghton Mifflin Company, 1894). On New York the best in a narrow selection is Henry H. Kessler and Eugene Rochlis, *Peter Stuyvesant and His New York* (New York: Columbia University Press, 1937), and Thomas J. Condon, *The Commercial Origins of New Netherland* (New York: New York University Press, 1968). **The Glorious Revolution.** The best English account is G.M. Trevelyan, *The English Revolution, 1688-1689* (New York: Oxford University Press, 1938), but a good supplement is David Ogg's *England in the Reigns of James II and William III* (New York: Oxford University Press, 1963). For the colonies David S. Lovejoy's *The Glorious Revolution in America* (New York: Harper and Row, Publishers, 1972) is excellent. The best biographies are Kenneth B. Murdock's *Increase Mather* (Cambridge, Mass.: Harvard University Press, 1925) and Jerome R. Reich's *Leisler's Rebellion* (Chicago: University of Chicago Press, 1953).

The Eighteenth Century. Virginia's history can be studied best through the biographies of her future great men, especially through the six volumes of Irving Brant's *James Madison* (Indianapolis, Indiana: The Bobbs-Merrill Company, 1941-1961); the seven volumes of Douglas S. Freeman, *George Washington* (New York: Charles Scribner's Sons, 1948-1957); and the five volumes of Dumas Malone, *Thomas Jefferson* (Boston: Little, Brown and Company, 1948–). Good modern biographies of the William Byrds and Patrick Henry are also available. Less extensive are the biographies of New England leaders: Page Smith's *John Adams* (Garden City, New York: Doubleday and Company, 1962); Edmund S. Morgan's *Gentle Puritan: A Life of Ezra Stiles* (New Haven, Conn.: Yale University Press, 1962); and Ola E. Winslow's *Jonathan Edwards* (New York: Crowell-Collier and Macmillan, 1940). Single-volume studies of the following political leaders give insight into colonial life: John J. Waters, Jr., *The Otis Family in Provincial and Revolutionary Massachusetts* (Chapel Hill, North Carolina: The University of North Carolina Press, 1968); John A. Schutz, *William Shirley* (Chapel Hill, North Carolina: University of North Carolina Press, 1961); and Bernard Bailyn, *Thomas Hutchinson* (Cambridge, Mass.: Harvard University Press, 1974). Pennsylvania has even less extensive studies than New England, but the biographies of Benjamin Franklin are excellent. See Verner W. Crane, *Benjamin Franklin and a Rising People* (Boston: Little, Brown and Company, 1954); Carl Van Doren, *Benjamin Franklin* (New York: The Viking Press, 1938); and William S. Hanna, *Benjamin Franklin and Pennsylvania Politics* (Stanford, California: Stanford University Press, 1964). For more general biographical materials, see Carl Bridenbaugh's brilliant studies of the colonial cities and Frederick B. Tolles' *Meeting House and Counting House: The Quaker Merchants of Colonial Philadel-*

phia, 1682-1763 (Chapel Hill, North Carolina: The University of North Carolina Press, 1948). New York has a few good biographical studies by Arthur Pound, *Johnson of the Mohawks* (New York: Crowell-Collier and Macmillan, 1930), and Lawrence H. Leder, *Robert Livingston, 1654-1728* (Chapel Hill, North Carolina: The University of North Carolina Press, 1961). For the role of women see Mary Beth Norton, *Liberty's Daughters: The Revolutionary Experience of American Women, 1750-1800* (Boston-Toronto: Little, Brown and Company, 1980). Compare interpretations of Norton with Joan Hoff Wilson, "The Illusion of Change: Women and the American Revolution," in Alfred H. Young, ed., *The American Revolution...* (DeKalb, Illinois: Northern Illinois University Press, 1976).

Revolutionary Biography. Perhaps the richest source of information is contained in studies of Washington, John Adams, and Jefferson, but there are biographies too numerous to mention of the other leaders. Representative are William M. Fowler, Jr., *The Baron of Beacon Hill: John Hancock* (Boston: Houghton Mifflin Company, 1980); John C. Miller, *Sam Adams* (Boston: Little, Brown and Company, 1936); Oliver P. Chitwood, *Richard Henry Lee* (Morgantown, West Virginia: West Virginia University Library, 1968); and the works of George A. Billias, particularly his *George Washington's Generals* (New York: William Morrow and Company, 1964).

The British Side of the Revolution. The best general histories of men and events are the outstanding studies of Lawrence H. Gipson, *The Coming of the American Revolution, 1763-1775* (New York: Harper and Row, Publishers, 1954) and Charles R. Ritcheson, *British Politics and the American Revolution* (Norman, Oklahoma: University of Oklahoma Press, 1954). Among the good biographies of military leaders are Troyer S. Anderson, *The Command of the Howe Brothers in the American Revolution* (New York: Oxford University Press, 1936); Franklin and Mary Wickwire, *Cornwallis...* (Boston: Houghton Mifflin Company, 1970). There are also many good biographies of George III, but no definitive one. The pioneering work of Lewis B. Namier should be consulted, especially his *England in the Age of the American Revolution* (London: Macmillan and Company, 1930).

The Post-War Period, 1783-1789. Cited earlier are the great, multi-volume biographies of Washington, Adams, and Madison, but also one should consult Clinton Rossiter, *Alexander Hamilton and the Constitution* (New York: Harcourt Brace Jovanovich, 1964); Gerald Stourzh, *Alexander Hamilton and the Idea of Republican Government* (Stanford, California: Stanford University Press, 1970); and Adrienne Koch, *Jefferson and Madison: The Great Collaboration* (New York: Oxford University Press, 1950, 1964). Much information, too, is available on the founding fathers as a group. See Charles Beard, *An Economic*

Interpretation of the Constitution (New York: Crowell-Collier and Macmillan, 1935); Robert E. Brown, *Charles Beard and the Constitution* (Princeton, New Jersey: Princeton University Press, 1956); and Stanley M. Elkins and Erick McKitrick, "The Founding Fathers: Young Men of the Constitution," *Political Science Quarterly,* Volume 76 (1961), pp. 181-216.

Important Literature on Selected Topics

England on the Eve of Colonization. Much has been written on English conditions as motivations for colonization. See particularly Carl Bridenbaugh's *Vexed and Troubled Englishmen, 1590-1642* (New York: Oxford University Press, 1968); Wallace Notestein's *The English People on the Eve of Colonization* (New York: Harper and Row, Publishers, 1951); and A.L. Rowse's *The Elizabethans and America* (New York: Harper and Row, Publishers, 1956).

English and American Puritanism. No topic has been developed more extensively or better than Puritanism. The basic work, however, was done by Perry Miller, particularly in *The New England Mind: The Seventeenth Century* (New York: The Macmillan Company, 1939) and *From Colony to Province* (Cambridge, Mass.: Harvard University Press, 1953). Other important works are William Haller's *The Rise of Puritanism* (New York: Harper and Brothers, Publishers, 1957) and Alan Simpson's *Puritanism in Old and New England* (Chicago, Illinois: University of Chicago Press, 1955). A delightfully written book that makes Puritanism understandable is Emery Battis' *Saints and Sectaries: Anne Hutchinson and the Antinomian Controversy* (Chapel Hill, North Carolina: The University of North Carolina, 1962).

The Caribbean Isles. Interest in the area has been stimulated by recent excellent scholarship. The best studies are Carl and Roberta Bridenbaugh, *No Peace Beyond the Line: The British in the Caribbean, 1624-1690* (New York: Oxford University Press, 1972) and Richard S. Dunn, *Sugar and Slaves: The Rise of the Planter Class in the English West Indies, 1624-1713* (Chapel Hill, North Carolina: The University of North Carolina Press, 1972). For greater detail on English colonization, consult the works of Vincent T. Harlow, Arthur P. Newton and James A. Williamson. An essential work for the other European nations is Newton's *The European Nations in the West Indies, 1493-1688* (London: A. and C. Black, 1933).

Town and Community Studies. Microstudies of New England townships represent a relatively new phase of scholarship. The most successful have been Sumner Chilton Powell's *Puritan Village* (Middletown, Conn.: Wesleyan University Press, 1963); Philip J. Greven, Jr.'s *Four Generations: Population, Land, and Family in Colonial Andover, Massachusetts* (Ithaca, New York: Cornell University Press, 1970), and Kenneth A. Lockridge's *A New England Town, the First Hundred Years: Dedham, Massachusetts* (New York: W.W. Norton and Company, 1970). For the New England colonies as a whole, Edward M. Cooke, Jr., *The Fathers of the Towns* (Baltimore, Maryland: Johns Hopkins University Press, 1976) has studied patterns of community leadership. In the pages of the *William and Mary Quarterly* are published many articles on the New England township, many represented by heavy reliance on computer techniques of research.

Frontier and Western Studies. During colonial times the frontier was ever present, and there are studies that emphasize the rim of civilization. For the early years both Alden T. Vaughan's *New England Frontier: Puritans and Indians, 1620-1675* (Boston: Little, Brown and Company, 1965) and Wesley F. Craven, *The Southern Colonies in the Seventeenth Century* (Baton Rouge, Louisiana: Louisiana State University Press, 1949) are excellent studies. The French frontier in North America is an equally important area, and John F. McDermott describes its perils very well in his *The French in the Mississippi Valley* (Urbana, Illinois: University of Illinois Press, 1965). For the later period Jack M. Sosin has two major works, *Whitehall and the Wilderness* (Lincoln, Nebraska: University of Nebraska, 1961) and *The Revolutionary Frontier, 1763-1783* (New York: Holt, Rinehart and Winston, 1967). Also important is Thomas P. Abernethy's *Western Lands and the American Revolution* (New York: Appleton-Century Crofts, 1937) and John R. Alden's *John Stuart and the Southern Colonial Frontier* (Ann Arbor, Michigan: University of Michigan Press, 1944).

The American Revolution. The bicentennial of the Revolution encouraged many reinterpretations. The best single volumes on the revolutionary causes and war are Lawrence H. Gipson, *The Coming of the American Revolution, 1763-1775* (New York: Harper and Row, Publishers, 1954) and John R. Alden, *A History of the American Revolution* (New York: Alfred A. Knopf, 1969). An interpretive essay by Jack P. Greene in his edited volume, *The Reinterpretations of the American Revolution, 1763-1789* (New York: Harper and Row, Publishers, 1968) puts the current literature in focus. A well-cited volume also is Bernard Bailyn's *The Ideological Origins of the American Revolution* (Cambridge, Mass.: Harvard University Press, 1967). It should be read with Edmund S. and Helen M. Morgan, *The Stamp Act Crisis* (Chapel Hill, North Carolina: The University of North Carolina Press, 1959) and Charles R. Ritcheson,

British Politics and the American Revolution (Norman, Oklahoma: University of Oklahoma Press, 1954). For perspective one should consult the brilliant two volumes of Robert R. Palmer, *The Age of the Democratic Revolution* (Princeton, New Jersey: Princeton University Press, 1959-1964).

Military Aspects of the Revolution. The best single volume is Willard M. Wallace, *Appeal to Arms* (New York: Harper and Row, Publishers, 1951). One should also consult Don Higginbotham's *The War for American Independence: Military Attitudes, Policies, and Practices, 1763-1789* (New York: Crowell-Collier and Macmillan, 1971) and Charles Royster, *A Revolutionary People at War. . .* (Chapel Hill, North Carolina: The University of North Carolina Press, 1980).

The Internal Revolution. The classic account is Merrill Jensen's *The Articles of Confederation* (Madison, Wisconsin: University of Wisconsin, 1940 and many printings). Newer accounts are Robert E. Brown, *Middle-Class Democracy and the Revolution in Massachusetts, 1691-1780* (Ithaca, New York: Cornell University Press, 1955) and Gordon S. Wood, *The Creation of the American Republic, 1776-1787* (Chapel Hill, North Carolina: The University of North Carolina Press, 1964). More exciting are Jesse Lemisch's "The American Revolution Seen from the Bottom Up," in Barton J. Bernstein, editor, *Towards a New Past* (New York: Random House, 1967) and Staughton Lynd's *Intellectual Origins of American Radicalism* (New York: Pantheon Books, 1968).

The Loyalists and Tories. The story of these unpopular people has been better told in recent years, with William Nelson's *The American Tory* (New York: Oxford University Press, 1961); Wallace Brown's *The King's Friends* (Providence, Rhode Island: Brown University Press, 1965); and Douglass Adair and John A. Schutz, editors, *Peter Oliver's Origin and Progress of the American Rebellion* (Stanford, California: Stanford University Press, 1967).

The Blacks in Early America. Although there were 700,000 blacks, there are few accounts of their activities. John Hope Franklin's *From Slavery to Freedom,* 3rd edition (New York: Alfred A. Knopf, 1967) is still the best general account. See also Benjamin Quarreles, *The Negro in the American Revolution* (Chapel Hill, North Carolina: The University of North Carolina Press, 1961) and Philip D. Curtin, *The Atlantic Slave Trade* (Madison, Wisconsin: University of Wisconsin Press, 1969).

The United States Constitution. Many good studies are available on the making of the Constitution, but Max Farrand's *The Framing of the Constitution of the United States* (New Haven, Conn.: Yale University Press, 1913) is still the best. Carl Van Doren's *The Great Rehearsal* (New

190   The Dawning of America, 1492-1789

York: The Viking Press, 1948) is more readable. One should consult
Robert A. Rutland's *The Ordeal of the Constitution* (Norman, Oklahoma:
The University of Oklahoma Press, 1966) and *The Birth of the Bill of
Rights 1776-1791* (Chapel Hill, North Carolina: The University of North
Carolina Press, 1955).

Historians of Early American History

Modern Pioneers. Charles M. Andrews, the great professor of history
at Yale University, published in four volumes *The Colonial Period of
American History* (New Haven, Conn.: Yale University Press, 1934-1938)
and emphasized in the first three volumes the interaction of England and
the colonies during the first years of settlement. The fourth volume
discussed British colonial policy. Andrews was a prolific author and also
wrote books about the Connecticut and New Haven colonies. His graduate
students carried on the tradition of fine scholarship by publishing books
on nearly every aspect of colonial life. See Isabel M. Calder, *The New
Haven Colony* (New Haven, Conn.: Yale University Press, 1934) and
Dorothy Deming, *The Settlement of the Connecticut Towns* (New Haven,
Conn.: Yale University Press, 1933).

Samuel E. Morison died only recently after an extraordinarily long
life devoted to scholarship and teaching. His professorship at Harvard
University reflected his interest in most aspects of Massachusetts history.
His *Builders of the Bay Colony* (Boston: Houghton Mifflin Company,
1930) uses biographies to tell the story of early Massachusetts. His
Founding of Harvard College (Cambridge, Mass.: Harvard University Press,
1935) is a beautiful account of the nation's oldest college. Morison also
wrote biographies of Christopher Columbus, Samuel de Champlain, and
Matthew C. Perry.

Francis Parkman, like Samuel E. Morison, wrote narrative history,
but Parkman for his years of the nineteenth century had no equal as a
writer on early American history. His *Montcalm and Wolfe: France and
England in North America,* in two volumes (Boston: Little, Brown and
Company, 1884) possesses great power in storytelling. His *Conspiracy of
Pontiac and the Indian War after the Conquest of Canada,* in two volumes
(Boston: Little, Brown and Company, 1896), has been superceded by
Howard Peckham's *Pontiac and the Indian Uprising* (Princeton, New
Jersey: Princeton University Press, 1947), but it still contains much
descriptive material that will absorb one's time and interests.

Perry Miller, who wrote primarily about Puritanism, has left a major
impression on the interpretation of early American civilization. His three

great books cover the history of New England from its founding until the eighteenth century: *The New England Mind: The Seventeenth Century* (New York: The Macmillan Company, 1939), *Orthodoxy in Massachusetts, 1630-1650* (Cambridge, Mass.: Harvard University Press, 1933), and *From Colony to Province* (Cambridge, Mass.: Harvard University Press, 1953). For clarity and appreciation, Miller's works should be read with Darrett B. Rutman, *Winthrop's Boston* (Chapel Hill, North Carolina: University of North Carolina, 1965); Bernard Bailyn, *The New England Merchants in the Seventeenth Century* (Cambridge, Mass.: Harvard University Press, 1955); and Ola Elizabeth Winslow, *Meetinghouse Hill: 1630-1783* (New York: The Macmillan Company, 1952). A good collection of Miller's essays, published after his death in 1963, is *Nature's Nation* (Cambridge, Mass.: Harvard University Press, 1967).

Philip A. Bruce, the great historian of Virginia, authored major works on the colony. Though now a bit dated, these books are still valuable because of sound manuscript research and balanced judgments. See his *Institutional History of Virginia in the Seventeenth Century* (New York: G.P. Putnam's Sons, 1910) and *Economic History of Virginia in the Seventeenth Century*, 2nd Edition (Lynchburg, Virginia: J.P. Bell, 1927).

Thomas J. Wertenbaker, of Princeton University, did much pioneering research on Virginia. His *Virginia Under the Stuarts, 1607-1688* (Princeton, New Jersey: Princeton University Press, 1922) and *Patrician and Plebeian in Virginia* (New York: Russell and Russell, 1959) are his major works. Also of importance is his *Norfolk: Historic Southern Port* (Durham, North Carolina: Duke University Press, 1937).

Other modern pioneers include Clarence W. Alvord, who did major research on the Ohio Valley, and published *The Mississippi Valley in British Politics,* 2 volumes (Cleveland, Ohio: The Arthur H. Clark Company, 1916). Thomas P. Abernethy's *Western Lands and the American Revolution* (New York: Appleton-Century-Crofts, 1937) was a major interpretation of the Revolution and is still well regarded. Carl Becker did interpretive work on the Revolution, the Declaration of Independence, and Revolutionary New York. His *The History of Political Parties in the Province of New York, 1760-1776* (Madison, Wisconsin: University of Wisconsin Press, 1909) is undoubtedly his most original book. George L. Beer, who published earlier than Alvord and Abernethy, is best known for his *British Colonial Policy* (New York: Crowell-Collier and Macmillan, 1907) which is useful for an understanding of British policy and the Seven Years War. Evarts B. Greene, known for his bibliography of New York historical materials, published also *The Revolutionary Generation, 1763-1790* (New York: The Macmillan Company, 1943), which is regarded still as a major interpretation of the social consequences of this Revolution. Curtis P. Nettels, known as an economic historian because of his work on paper money and trade, was the author of *The Roots of American Civilization* (New York: Appleton-Century-Crofts, 1963), which has good interpretive materials. Lowell J. Ragatz, long a professor at Ohio State University, was known for his bibliography on the West Indies and for *The Old Plantation System in the British West Indies* (London: B. Edwards Press, 1935). Claude H. Van Tyne wrote an early study of the Tories in which they are sympathetically treated. See *The Loyalists in the American Revolution* (New York: Crowell-Collier and Macmillan, 1902).

Selected Modern Historians and Their Histories

John Alden has published books on the South, the frontier, and the American Revolution. See his very readable *The American Revolution, 1775-1783* (New York: Harper and Row, Publishers, 1954).

Bernard Bailyn has written many well-researched, interpretive studies of the Revolutionary period. His best-known study is the *Ideological Origins of the American Revolution* (Cambridge, Mass.: Harvard University Press, 1967). He has written about the Loyalist Thomas Hutchinson, as well as about colonial education and the political order.

George Billias looks at the military politics and policies of the American Revolution in several important books. His *George Washington's Generals* (New York: William Morrow and Company, 1964) and *George Washington's Opponents* (New York: William Morrow and Company, 1969) give short, excellent biographies of the military leaders.

John B. Brebner describes the rim of the New England frontier Nova Scotia, its commerce, resources, and people. His *Nova Scotia in New England's Outpost: Acadia Before the Conquest of Canada* (New York: Columbia University Press, 1927) was his most attractive work.

Carl Bridenbaugh is the most prolific of present historians, with books on the founding of the colonies, the cities, architecture, religion, the Revolution, and the West Indies. His *Mitre and Sceptre: Transatlantic Faiths, Ideas, Personalities, and Politics, 1689-1775* (New York: Oxford University Press, 1962) is illustrative of his work. See also *Cities in Revolt: Urban Life in America, 1743-1776* (New York: Alfred A. Knopf, 1955).

Robert E. Brown raised serious questions about the political structure of Massachusetts and much controversy has raged about wealth and politics ever since the publication of his *Middle-Class Democracy and the Revolution, 1691-1780* (Ithaca, New York: Cornell University Press, 1955).

Trevor Colburn traces the origins of American Revolutionary thought in *The Lamp of Experience: Whig History and the Intellectual Origins of the American Revolution* (Chapel Hill, North Carolina: The University of North Carolina Press, 1965).

Elisha P. Douglas has an unusual book on the revolutionary struggle in America—*Rebels and Democrats: The Struggle for Equal Political Rights and Majority Rule During the American Revolution* (Chapel Hill, North Carolina: The University of North Carolina Press, 1955).

E. James Ferguson analyzes credit, paper money, and inflation in the revolutionary era. See *The Power of the Purse: A History of American Public Finance, 1776-1790* (Chapel Hill, North Carolina Press, 1961).

Lawrence H. Gipson lived long enough to complete his famous *The British Empire Before the American Revolution,* in 15 volumes (New York: Alfred A. Knopf, 1936-1970) and do a one-volume survey of the Revolutionary causes, *The Coming of the American Revolution, 1763-1775* (New York: Harper and Row, Publishers, 1954). His work surveys extensively the military, political, and international developments in the British empire from 1750 to 1776.

Jack P. Greene has done excellent interpretive work on the American Revolution, but particularly on the role of the southern legislatures. See *The Quest for Power: The Lower Houses of Assembly in the Southern Royal Colonies, 1689-1776* (Chapel Hill, North Carolina: The University of North Carolina Press, 1963).

Oscar Handlin has done interesting research on Boston, immigration, and the Revolution. Particularly important is his (with Mary F. Handlin) *Commonwealth: A Study of the Role of Government in the American Economy; Massachusetts, 1774-1861* (New York: New York University Press, 1947).

Wilbur Jacobs writes about the frontier and environment, but important for early America is his *Wilderness Politics and Indian Gifts: The Northern Colonial Frontier, 1748-1763* (Lincoln, Nebraska: University of Nebraska Press, 1966).

Merrill Jensen is the author of a comprehensive study of the Revolution which emphasizes the political breakup of the empire. See *The Founding of a Nation: A History of the American Revolution, 1763-1776* (New York: Oxford University Press, 1968). Even better known, however, is his classic *The Articles of Confederation* (Madison, Wisconsin: The University of Wisconsin Press, 1940).

Michael G. Kammen has interpreted the operation of the British empire in several good books, but his most useful is *A Rope of Sand: The Colonial Agents, British Politics and the American Revolution* (Ithaca, New York: Cornell University Press, 1968).

Frank J. Klingberg, the author of more than a dozen books on British-American relations, was interested in missionary activity of the S.P.G. The most unique of his works is the *Codrington Chronicle: An Experiment in Anglican Altruism on a Barbados Plantation, 1710-1834* (Berkeley, California: University of California Press, 1949).

Leonard W. Labaree is the editor of the Benjamin Franklin Papers, and author of works on colonial conservatism and on government. His *Royal Government in America* (New Haven, Conn.: Yale University Press, 1930) is an important work.

David S. Lovejoy has a major assessment of the 1689 revolution in America. See *The Glorious Revolution in America* (New York: Harper and Row, Publishers, 1972). Also he has written a good study of *Rhode Island Politics and the American Revolution, 1760-1776* (Providence, Rhode Island: Brown University Press, 1958).

Jackson Turner Main has described the Revolutionary society of 1763 to 1788 by citing hard data on wealth and social position. Among his best interpretations is *The Social Structure of Revolutionary America* (Princeton, New Jersey: Princeton University Press, 1965). It should be compared with Robert Brown's *Middle-Class Democracy. . .* cited above.

Robert Middlekauff, who researches in intellectual history and Puritanism, is the author of an excellent volume entitled *The Mathers: Three Generations of Puritan Intellectuals, 1596-1728* (New York: Oxford University Press, 1971).

John C. Miller, the biographer of Samuel Adams, has authored several major works on the Revolution. Perhaps the most readable and useful is *Triumph of Freedom, 1775-1783* (Boston: Little, Brown and Company, 1948).

Edmund S. Morgan, the foremost expert on Puritanism, is the author of many books on the first Americans. The most widely read is *The Puritan Dilemma: The Story of John Winthrop* (Boston: Little, Brown and Company, 1958), but equally instructive is his *Roger Williams: The Church and the State* (New York: Harcourt Brace Jovanovich, 1967).

Richard B. Morris has updated Samuel Flagg Bemis' work on the Revolution in *The Peacemakers: The Great Powers and American Independence* (New York: Harper and Row, Publishers, 1965).

Gary Nash's *Quakers and Politics: Pennsylvania, 1681-1726* (Princeton, New Jersey: Princeton University Press, 1968) is the most successful book on the relationship of England and America for this period of Pennsylvania history.

Richard Pares has published essential works on the West Indies, their trade, plantation economy, and peoples. See his *War and Trade in the West Indies, 1739-1763* (New York: Oxford University Press, 1936) and *Yankees and Creoles: The Trade Between North America and the West Indies Before the American Revolution* (Cambridge, Mass.: Harvard University Press, 1956).

Robert A. Rutland has published the best single book on the origin of the Bill of Rights. See *The Birth of the Bill of Rights, 1776-1791* (Chapel Hill, North Carolina: The University of North Carolina Press, 1955).

Max Savelle, an intellectual historian who has written a major volume on early America, *The Seeds of Liberty* (Seattle, Washington: University of Washington Press, 1967), also has published extensively on diplomacy. The most useful of those studies is *The Origins of American Diplomacy: The International History of Anglo-America, 1492-1763* (New York: Crowell-Collier and Macmillan, 1967).

Arthur Meyer Schlesinger, throughout a long life of research and teaching, interpreted early America in many books. His best-known volume is *Colonial Merchants and the American Revolution* (New York: Columbia University Press, 1918). Of great importance, too, are his *Prelude to Independence: The Newspaper War on Britain, 1764-1776* (New York: Alfred A. Knopf, 1957) and *The Birth of the Nation: A Portrait of the American People on the Eve of Independence* (New York: Alfred A. Knopf, 1968).

John A. Schutz, the biographer of several Massachusetts governors, is best known for his *Peter Oliver's Origins and Progress of the American Rebellion* (Stanford, California: Stanford University Press, 1967), edited with Douglass Adair. His *William Shirley: King's Governor of Massachusetts* (Chapel Hill, North Carolina: The University of North Carolina Press, 1961) is a modern account of the problems of a colonial governor.

Clifford Shipton spent most of his life tracing the careers of Harvard graduates and writing up his findings in short biographies. The best short collection of these biographies is *New England Life in the Eighteenth Century: Representative Biographies from Sibley's Harvard Graduates* (Cambridge, Mass.: Harvard University Press, 1963).

Richard H. Shryock explored the origins of science in early America and with Otho T. Beall published *Cotton Mather: First Significant Figure in American Medicine* (Baltimore, Maryland: The Johns Hopkins Press, 1954).

John Shy writes brilliant military history. His *Toward Lexington: The Role of the British Army in the Coming of the American Revolution* (Princeton, New Jersey: Princeton University Press, 1965) is the best one-volume account in print.

Page Smith has published many innovative historical studies, but is best known for his two-volume life of *John Adams* (Garden City, New York: Doubleday and Company, 1962).

Jack M. Sosin, in his reanalysis of Clarence Alvord's famous work, has himself developed two major volumes on the Mississippi Valley in British politics. See his *Whitehall and the Wilderness...1760-1773* (Lincoln, Nebraska: University of Nebraska Press, 1961) and *The Revolutionary Frontier, 1763-1783* (New York: Holt, Rinehart and Winston, 1967).

William Warren Sweet's classic remains a major interpretation of religion for the Revolution, *Religion in the Development of American Culture, 1765-1840* (New York: Charles Scribner's Sons, 1952). One should compare Sweet's book to Edwin S. Gaustad's newer interpretation, *A Religious History of America* (New York: Harper and Row, Publishers, 1966).

Thad W. Tate, Jr., has written many articles on Virginia politics— debts, religion, and trade. His *The Negro in Eighteenth-Century Williamsburg* (Charlottesville, Virginia: The University Press of Virginia, 1965) is an excellent study of considerable breadth.

Frederick B. Tolles, who served for years as librarian of the Quaker Collections at Swarthmore College, has written several books on Quaker religion and politics. See his fine study of merchant politics, *Meetinghouse and Counting House: The Quaker Merchants of Colonial Philadelphia, 1682-1763* (Chapel Hill, North Carolina: The University of North Carolina Press, 1948).

Richard W. Van Alstyne has challenged traditional interpretations of the Revolution in *The International History of The American Revolution* (New York: John Wiley and Sons, 1965). One should compare his with the older interpretations of Samuel F. Bemis, *The Diplomacy of the American Revolution* (New York: Appleton-Century-Crofts, 1935).

Clarence L. Ver Steeg has many good volumes on colonial politics, but his *Robert Morris: Revolutionary Financier* (Philadelphia, Pennsylvania: University of Pennsylvania Press, 1954) remains the best study of this major figure of the Confederation.

Wilcomb E. Washburn, who is interested in the frontier and Indians, traces brilliantly the events of 1675 and 1676 in Virginia, in *The Governor and the Rebel: A History of Bacon's Rebellion in Virginia* (Chapel Hill, North Carolina: The University of North Carolina Press, 1957).

John J. Waters, who has written many articles on the family in New England, pioneered research on the Otises. See *The Otis Family in*

Provincial and Revolutionary Massachusetts (Chapel Hill, North Carolina: The University of North Carolina Press, 1968).

Gordon Wood of Brown University has interpreted events that led to the founding of the new nation. Though difficult reading, *The Creation of the American Republic* (Chapel Hill, North Carolina: The University of North Carolina Press, 1969) will repay any effort. One should compare the works of Forrest McDonald, particularly *We the People: The Economic Origins of the Constitution* (Chicago, Illinois: University of Chicago Press, 1958), with Wood's study.

Louis B. Wright, editor and author, is well known for his editions of William Byrd's diaries. More useful is *The Cultural Life of the American Colonies, 1607-1763* (New York: Harper and Row, Publishers, 1957) and *The First Gentlemen of Virginia* (San Marino, California: The Huntington Library, 1940).

Selected Contemporary Historians, 1607-1789

New England. William Bradford's own history, *Of Plymouth Plantation 1620-1647,* edited by Samuel E. Morison (New York: Alfred A. Knopf, 1952), is a good source of information on Plymouth. Important, too, is Edward Johnson's *Wonder-Working Providence, 1628-1651,* edited by J. Franklin Jameson (New York: Charles Scribner's Sons, 1910), and *Winthrop's Journal, "History of New England," 1630-1649,* edited by James K. Hosmer (New York: Charles Scribner's Sons, 1908).

Virginia and Maryland. Captain John Smith's writings offer some information on the founding of the colony: *Travels and Works of Captain John Smith, President of Virginia, and Admiral of New England 1580-1631,* edited by Edward Archer and A.G. Bradley (Edinburgh, Scotland: John Grant, 1910). Also important is Robert Beverly's *The History and Present State of Virginia,* edited by Louis B. Wright (Chapel Hill, North Carolina: The University of North Carolina Press, 1947). *The Narratives of Early Virginia, 1606-1625,* edited by Lyon G. Tyler (New York: Charles Scribner's Sons, 1907) have interesting contemporary materials. For Maryland see *Narratives of Early Maryland,* edited by Clayton C. Hall (New York: Charles Scribner's Sons, 1910).

The Eighteenth Century. Cadwallader Colden, the important politician of New York, wrote *The History of the Five Indian Nations of Canada* (London: T. Osborne, 1747). Cotton Mather's history of the New England churches, *Magnalia Christi Americana* (New York: Russell and Russell, 1967), was published originally in 1702. It could be read with the autobiography of John Woolman, whose Quaker writings provide a contrast in religious spirit. See *The Journal and Essays of John Woolman* (New York: Crowell-Collier and Macmillan, 1922).

The Revolution, Its Causes and Aftermath. Thomas Hutchinson's famous *The History of the Colony and Province of Massachusetts Bay,* edited by Lawrence S. Mayo, in three volumes (Cambridge, Mass.: Harvard University Press, 1936), is a sober but honest account of the colony's history. Its tone should be compared with *Peter Oliver's Origin and Progress of the American Rebellion,* edited by Douglass Adair and John A. Schutz (Stanford, California: Stanford University Press, 1967) whose style is lively and content is controversial. David Ramsay, the author of a few important volumes, is best known for *The History of the American Revolution,* in two volumes (Philadelphia, Pennsylvania: 1789).

The Constitution
of the
United States of America

WE THE PEOPLE of the United States, in Order to form a more perfect Union, establish Justice, insure domestic Tranquility, provide for the common defence, promote the general Welfare, and secure the Blessings of Liberty to ourselves and our Posterity, do ordain and establish this CONSTITUTION for the United States of America.

Article I

Section 1. All legislative Powers herein granted shall be vested in a Congress of the United States, which shall consist of a Senate and House of Representatives.

Section 2. The House of Representatives shall be composed of Members chosen every second Year by the People of the several States, and the Electors in each State shall have the Qualifications requisite for Electors of the most numerous Branch of of the State Legislature.

No Person shall be a Representative who shall not have attained to the Age of twenty-five Years, and been seven Years a Citizen of the United States, and who shall not, when elected, be an Inhabitant of that State in which he shall be chosen.

[Representatives and direct Taxes[1] shall be apportioned among the several States which may be included within this Union, according to their respective Numbers, which shall be determined by adding to the whole Number of free Persons, including those bound to Service for a Term of Years, and excluding Indians not taxed, three fifths of all other Persons.][2] The actual Enumeration shall be made within three Years after the first Meeting of the Congress of the United States, and within every subsequent Term of ten Years, in such Manner as they shall by Law direct. The Number of Representatives shall not exceed one for every thirty Thousand, but each State shall have at Least one Representative; and until such enumeration shall be made, the State of New Hampshire shall be entitled to chuse three, Massachusetts eight, Rhode-Island and Providence Plantations one,

[1]   Altered by the Sixteenth Amendment.
[2]   Negated by the Fourteenth Amendment.

Connecticut five, New York six, New Jersey four, Pennsylvania eight, Delaware one, Maryland six, Virginia ten, North Carolina five, South Carolina five, and Georgia three.

When vacancies happen in the Representation from any State, the Executive Authority thereof shall issue Writs of Election to fill such Vacancies.

The House of Representatives shall chuse their Speaker and other Officers; and shall have the sole Power of Impeachment.

Section 3. The Senate of the United States shall be composed of two Senators from each State, chosen by the Legislature thereof, for six Years; and each Senator shall have one Vote.

Immediately after they shall be assembled in Consequence of the first Election, they shall be divided as equally as may be into three Classes. The Seats of the Senators of the first Class shall be vacated at the Expiration of the second Year, of the second Class at the Expiration of the fourth Year, and of the third Class at the Expiration of the sixth Year, so that one-third may be chosen every second Year; and if Vacancies happen by Resignation, or otherwise, during the Recess of the Legislature of any State, the Executive thereof may make temporary Appointments until the next Meeting of the Legislature, which shall then fill such vacancies.

No Person shall be a Senator who shall not have attained to the Age of thirty Years, and been nine Years a Citizen of the United States, and who shall not, when elected, be an Inhabitant of that State for which he shall be chosen.

The Vice President of the United States shall be President of the Senate, but shall have no vote, unless they be equally divided.

The Senate shall chuse their other Officers, and also a President pro tempore, in the absence of the Vice President, or when he shall exercise the Office of President of the United States.

The Senate shall have the sole Power to try all Impeachments. When sitting for that purpose, they shall be on Oath or Affirmation. When the President of the United States is tried, the Chief Justice shall preside: And no person shall be convicted without the Concurrence of two thirds of the Members present.

Judgment in Cases of Impeachment shall not extend further than to removal from Office, and disqualification to hold and enjoy any Office of honor, Trust, or Profit under the United States: but the Party convicted shall nevertheless be liable and subject to Indictment, Trial, Judgment, and Punishment, according to Law.

Section 4. The Times, Places and Manner of holding Elections for Senators and Representatives, shall be prescribed in each State by the Legislature thereof; but the Congress may at any time by Law make or alter such regulations, except as to the Places of Chusing Senators.

The Congress shall assemble at least once in every Year, and such Meeting shall be on the first Monday in December, unless they shall by Law appoint a different Day.

Section 5. Each House shall be the Judge of the Elections, Returns and Qualifications of its own Members, and a Majority of each shall constitute a Quorum to do Business; but a smaller number may adjourn from day to day, and may be authorized to compel the Attendance of absent Members, in such Manner, and under such Penalties, as each House may provide.

Each House may determine the Rules of its Proceedings, punish its Members for disorderly Behavior, and, with the Concurrence of two thirds, expel a Member.

Each House shall keep a Journal of its Proceedings, and from time to time publish the same, excepting such Parts as may in their Judgment require Secrecy; and the Yeas and Nays of the Members of either House on any question shall, at the Desire of one fifth of those Present, be entered on the Journal.

Neither House, during the Session of Congress, shall, without the Consent of the other, adjourn for more than three days, nor to any other Place than that in which the two Houses shall be sitting.

Section 6. The Senators and Representatives shall receive a Compensation for their Services, to be ascertained by Law, and paid out of the Treasury of the United States. They shall in all Cases, except Treason, Felony, and Breach of the Peace, be privileged from Arrest during their Attendance at the Session of their respective Houses, and in going to and returning from the same; and for any Speech or Debate in either House, they shall not be questioned in any other Place.

No Senator or Representative shall, during the Time for which he was elected, be appointed to any civil Office under the Authority of the United States, which shall have been created, or the Emoluments whereof shall have been increased, during such time; and no Person holding any Office under the United States shall be a Member of either House during his continuance in Office.

Section 7. All Bills for raising Revenue shall originate in the House of Representatives; but the Senate may propose or concur with Amendments as on other bills.

Every Bill which shall have passed the House of Representatives and the Senate, shall, before it become a Law, be presented to the President of the United States; If he approve he shall sign it, but if not he shall return it, with his Objections, to that House in which it shall have originated, who shall enter the Objections at large on their Journal, and proceed to reconsider it. If after such Reconsideration two thirds of that House shall agree to pass the bill, it shall be sent, together with the objections, to the other House, by which it shall likewise be reconsidered, and if approved by two thirds of that House, it shall become a Law. But in all such Cases the Votes of both Houses shall be determined by Yeas and Nays, and the Names of the Persons voting for and against the Bill shall be entered on the Journal of each House respectively. If any Bill shall not be returned by the President within ten Days (Sundays excepted) after it shall have been presented to him, the Same shall be a Law, in like Manner as if he had signed it, unless the Congress by their Adjournment prevent its Return, in which Case it shall not be a Law.

Every Order, Resolution, or Vote to which the Concurrence of the Senate and House of Representatives may be necessary (except on a question of Adjournment) shall be presented to the President of the United States; and before the Same shall take Effect, shall be approved by him, or being disapproved by him, shall be repassed by two thirds of the Senate and House of Representatives, according to the Rules and Limitations prescribed in the Case of a Bill.

Section 8. The Congress shall have Power To lay and collect Taxes, Duties, Imposts and Excises, to pay the Debts and provide for the common Defence and general Welfare of the United States; but all Duties Imposts and Excises shall be uniform throughout the United States;

To borrow money on the credit of the United States;

To regulate Commerce with foreign Nations, and among the several States, and with the Indian Tribes;

To establish an uniform Rule of Naturalization, and uniform Laws on the subject of Bankruptcies throughout the United States;

To coin Money, regulate the Value thereof, and of foreign Coin, and fix the Standard of Weights and Measures;

To provide for the Punishment of counterfeiting the Securities and current Coin of the United States;

To establish Post Offices and post Roads;

To promote the Progress of Science and useful Arts, by securing for limited Times to Authors and Inventors the exclusive Right to their respective Writings and Discoveries;

To constitute Tribunals inferior to the Supreme Court; To define and punish Piracies and Felonies committed on the high Seas, and Offenses against the Law of Nations;

To declare War, grant letters of Marque and Reprisal, and make Rules concerning Captures on Land and Water;

To raise and support Armies, but no Appropriation of Money to that Use shall be for a longer Term than two Years;

To provide and maintain a Navy;

To make Rules for the Government and Regulation of the land and naval forces;

To provide for calling forth the Militia to execute the Laws of the Union, suppress Insurrections and repel Invasions;

To provide for organizing, arming, and disciplining the Militia, and for governing such Part of them as may be employed in the

Service of the United States, reserving to the States respectively, the Appointment of the Officers, and the Authority of training the Militia according to the discipline prescribed by Congress;

To exercise exclusive Legislation in all Cases whatsoever, over such District (not exceeding ten Miles square) as may, by Cession of particular States, and the acceptance of Congress, become the Seat of Government of the United States, and to exercise like Authority over all Places purchased by the Consent of the Legislature of the State in which the Same shall be, for the Erection of Forts, Magazines, Arsenals, dock-Yards, and other needful Buildings; – And

To make all Laws which shall be necessary and proper for carrying into Execution the foregoing Powers, and all other Powers vested by this Constitution in the Government of the United States, or in any Department or Officer thereof.

Section 9. The Migration or importation of such Persons as any of the States now existing shall think proper to admit, shall not be prohibited by the Congress prior to the Year one thousand eight hundred and eight, but a tax or duty may be imposed on such Importation, not exceeding ten dollars for each Person.

The privilege of the Writ of Habeas Corpus shall not be suspended, unless when in Cases of Rebellion or Invasion the public Safety may require it.

No bill of Attainder or ex post facto Law shall be passed.

No capitation, or other direct, Tax shall be laid unless in Proportion to the Census or Enumeration herein before directed to be taken. No Tax or Duty shall be laid on Articles exported from any State.

No Tax or Duty shall be laid on Articles exported from any State.

No Preference shall be given by any Regulation of Commerce or Revenue to the Ports of one State over those of another: nor shall Vessels bound to, or from, one State, be obliged to enter, clear, or pay Duties in another.

No Money shall be drawn from the Treasury, but in Consequence of Appropriations made by Law; and a regular Statement and Account of the Receipts and Expenditures of all public Money shall be published from time to time.

No Title of Nobility shall be granted by the United States: And no Person holding any Office of Profit or Trust under them, shall, without the Consent of the Congress, accept of any present, Emolument, Office, or Title, of any kind whatever, from any King, Prince, or foreign State.

Section 10. No State shall enter into any Treaty, Alliance, or Confederation; grant Letters of Marque and Reprisal; coin Money; emit Bills of Credit; make any Thing but gold and silver Coin a Tender in Payment of Debts; pass any Bill of Attainder, ex post facto Law, or Law impairing the Obligation of Contracts, or grant any Title of Nobility.

No State shall, without the Consent of the Congress, lay any Imposts or Duties on Imports or Exports, except what may be absolutely necessary for executing its inspection Laws: and the net Produce of all Duties and Imposts, laid by any State on Imports or Exports, shall be for the Use of the Treasury of the United States; and all such Laws shall be subject to the Revision and Control of the Congress.

No state shall, without the Consent of Congress, lay any duty of Tonnage, keep Troops, or Ships of War in time of Peace, enter into any Agreement or Compact with another State, or with a foreign Power, or engage in Way, unless actually invaded, or in such imminent Danger as will not admit of delay.

Article II

Section 1. The executive Power shall be vested in a President of the United States of America. He shall hold his Office during the Term of four years, and, together with the Vice-President, chosen for the same Term, be elected, as follows:

Each State shall appoint, in such Manner as the Legislature thereof may direct, a Number of Electors, equal to the whole Number of Senators and Representatives to which the State may be entitled in the Congress: but no Senator or Representative, or Person holding an Office of Trust or Profit under the United States, shall be appointed an Elector.

[The Electors shall meet in their respective States, and vote by Ballot for two persons, of whom one at least shall not be an Inhabitant of the same State with themselves. And they shall make a List of all the Persons voted for, and of the Number of Votes for each; which List they shall sign and certify, and transmit sealed to the Seat of the Government of the United States, directed to the President of the Senate. The President of the Senate shall, in the Presence of the Senate and House of Representatives, open all the Certificates, and the Votes shall then be counted. The Person having the greatest Number of Votes shall be the President, if such Number be a Majority of the whole Number of Electors appointed; and if there be more than one who have such Majority, and have an equal Number of Votes, then the House of Representatives shall immediately chuse by Ballot one of them for President; and if no Person have a Majority, then from the five highest on the List the said House shall in the Manner chuse the President. But in chusing the President, the Votes shall be taken by States, the Representation from each State having one Vote; a quorum for this Purpose shall consist of a Member or Members from two-thirds of the States, and a Majority of all the States shall be necessary to a Choice. In every Case, after the Choice of the President, the Person having the greatest Number of Votes of the Electors shall be the Vice President. But if there should remain two or more who have equal votes, the Senate shall chuse from them by Ballot the Vice-President.] [3]

The Congress may determine the Time of chusing the Electors, and the Day on which they shall give their Votes; which Day shall be the same throughout the United States.

No person except a natural-born Citizen, or a Citizen of the United States, at the time of the Adoption of this Constitution, shall be eligible to the Office of President; neither shall any Person be eligible to that Office who shall not have attained to the Age of thirty-five years, and been fourteen Years a Resident within the United States.

In Case of the Removal of the President from Office, or of his Death, Resignation, or Inability to discharge the powers and Duties of the said Office, the same shall devolve on the Vice President, and the Congress may by Law provide for the Case of Removal, Death, Resignation, or Inability, both of the President and Vice President, declaring what Officer shall then act as President, and such Officer shall act accordingly, until the disability be removed, or a President shall be elected.

The President shall, at stated Times, receive for his Services a Compensation, which shall neither be increased nor diminished during the Period for which he shall have been elected, and he shall not receive within that Period any other Emolument from the United States, or any of them.

Before he enter on the execution of his office, he shall take the following Oath or Affirmation: — "I do solemnly swear (or affirm) that I will faithfully execute the Office of President of the United States, and will, to the best of my Ability, preserve, protect, and defend the Constitution of the United States."

Section 2. The President shall be Commander in Chief of the Army and Navy of the United States and of the Militia of the several States, when called into the actual Service of the United States; he may require the Opinion, in writing, of the principal Officer in each of the executive Departments, upon any subject relating to the Duties of their respective Offices, and he shall have Power to Grant Reprieves and Pardons for Offenses against the United States, except in Cases of Impeachment.

He shall have Power, by and with the Advice and Consent of the Senate, to make Treaties, provided two thirds of the Senators present concur; and he shall nominate, and by and with the Advice and Consent of the Senate, shall appoint Ambassadors, other public Ministers and Consuls, Judges of the Supreme Court, and all other Officers of the United States, whose Appointments are not herein otherwise provided for, and which shall be established by Law: but the Congress may by Law vest the Appointment of such inferior

[3]   Revised by the Twelfth Amendment.

Officers, as they think proper, in the President alone, in the Courts of Law, or in the Heads of Departments.

The President shall have Power to fill up all Vacancies that may happen during the Recess of the Senate, by granting Commissions which shall expire at the End of their next Session.

Section 3. He shall from time to time give to the Congress Information of the State of the Union, and recommend to their Consideration such Measures as he shall judge necessary and expedient; he may, on extraordinary occasions, convene both Houses, or either of them, and in Case of Disagreement between them, with respect to the Time of Adjournment, he may adjourn them to such Time as he shall think proper; he shall receive Ambassadors and other public Ministers; he shall take care that the Laws be faithfully executed, and shall Commission all the Officers of the United States.

Section 4. The President, Vice President and all civil Officers of the United States, shall be removed from Office on Impeachment for, and Conviction of, Treason, Bribery, or other high Crimes and Misdemeanors.

Article III

Section 1. The judicial Power of the United States, shall be vested in one supreme Court, and in such inferior Courts as the Congress may from time to time ordain and establish. The Judges, both of the supreme and inferior Courts, shall hold their Offices during good Behaviour, and shall, at stated Times, receive for their Services, a Compensation, which shall not be diminished during their Continuance in Office.

Section 2. The judicial Power shall extend to all Cases, in Law and Equity, arising under this Constitution, the Laws of the United States, and Treaties made, or which shall be made, under their Authority; — to all Cases affecting ambassadors, other public ministers and consuls; — to all cases of admiralty and maritime Jurisdiction; — to Controversies to which the United States shall be a Party; — to Controversies between two or more States; — between a State and Citizens of another State;[5] — between Citizens of different States, — between Citizens of the same State claiming Lands under Grants of different States, and Between a State, or the Citizens thereof, and foreign States, Citizens or Subjects.

In all Cases affecting Ambassadors, other public Ministers and Consuls, and those in which a State shall be Party, the supreme Court shall have original Jurisdiction. In all the other Cases before mentioned, the supreme Court shall have appellate Jurisdiction, both as to Law and Fact, with such Exceptions, and under such Regulations as the Congress shall make.

[4]   Qualified by the Eleventh Amendment.

The trial of all Crimes, except in Cases of Impeachment, shall be by Jury; and such Trial shall be held in the State where the said Crimes shall have been committed; but when not committed within any State, the Trial shall be at such Place or Places as the Congress may by Law have directed.

Section 3. Treason against the United States, shall consist only in levying War against them, or in adhering to their Enemies, giving them Aid and Comfort. No Person shall be convicted of Treason unless on the Testimony of two Witnesses to the same overt Act, or on Confession in open Court.

The Congress shall have power to declare the Punishment of Treason, but no Attainder of Treason shall work Corruption of Blood, or Forfeiture except during the Life of the Person attainted.

Article IV

Section 1. Full Faith and Credit shall be given in each State to the Public Acts, Records, and judicial Proceedings of every other State. And the Congress may by general Laws prescribe the Manner in which such Acts, Records and Proceedings shall be proved, and the Effect thereof.

Section 2. The Citizens of each State shall be entitled to all Privileges and Immunities of Citizens in the several States.

A Person charged in any State with Treason, Felony, or other Crime, who shall flee from Justice, and be found in another State, shall on demand of the executive Authority of the State from which he fled, be delivered up, to be removed to the State having Jurisdiction of the crime.

No Person held to Service or Labour in one State, under the Laws thereof, escaping into another, shall, in Consequence of any Law or Regulation therein, be discharged from such Service or Labour, but shall be delivered up on Claim of the Party to whom such Service or Labour may be due.

Section 3. New States may be admitted by the Congress into this Union; but no new State shall be formed or erected within the Jurisdiction of any other State; nor any State be formed by the Junction of two or more States, or parts of States, without the Consent of the Legislature of the States concerned as well as of the Congress.

The Congress shall have Power to dispose of and make all needful Rules and Regulations respecting the Territory or other Property belonging to the United States; and nothing in this Constitution shall be so construed as to Prejudice any Claims of the United States, or of any particular State.

Section 4. The United States shall guarantee to every State in this Union a Republican Form of Government, and shall protect each of them against Invasion; and on Application of the Legislature, or of the Executive (when the Legislature cannot be convened) against domestic Violence.

Article V

The Congress, whenever two-thirds of both Houses shall deem it necessary, shall propose Amendments to this Constitution, or, on the Application of the Legislatures of two-thirds of the several States, shall call a Convention for proposing Amendments, which, in either Case, shall be valid to all Intents and Purposes, as part of this Constitution, when ratified by the Legislatures of three-fourths of the several States, or by Conventions in three-fourths thereof, as the one or the other Mode of Ratification may be proposed by the Congress; Provided that no Amendment which may be made prior to the Year One thousand eight hundred and eight shall in any Manner affect the first and fourth Clauses in the Ninth Section of the first Article; and that no State, without its Consent, shall be deprived of its equal Suffrage in the Senate.

Article VI

All Debts contracted and Engagements entered into, before the Adoption of this Constitution, shall be as valid against the United States under this Constitution, as under the Confederation.

This Constitution, and the Laws of the United States which shall be made in Pursuance thereof; and all Treaties made, or which shall be made, under the Authority of the United States, shall be the supreme Law of the Land; and the Judges in every State shall be bound thereby, any Thing in the Constitution or Laws of any State to the Contrary notwithstanding.

The Senators and Representatives before mentioned, and the Members of the several State Legislatures, and all executive and judicial Officers, both of the United States and of the several States, shall be bound by Oath or Affirmation to support this Constitution; but no religious Test shall ever be required as a qualification to any Office or public Trust under the United States.

Article VII

The Ratification of the Conventions of nine states shall be sufficient for the Establishment of this Constitution between the States so ratifying the same.

Done in Convention by the Unanimous Consent of the States present the Seventeenth Day of September in the Year of our Lord one thousand seven hundred and Eighty seven, and of the Independence of the United States of America the Twelfth. In Witness whereof We have hereunto subscribed our Names.,

George Washington
President and deputy from Virginia

*Articles in Addition to, and Amendment of the Constitution of the
United States of America, Proposed by Congress, and Ratified by the
Legislatures of the Several States, Pursuant to the Fifth Article of the
Original Constitution.*

The Bill of Rights

Amendment I

Congress shall make no law respecting an establishment of religion, or prohibiting the free exercise thereof; or abridging the freedom of speech, or of the press; or the right of the people peaceably to assemble, and to petition the Government for a redress of grievances.

Amendment II

A well regulated Militia, being necessary to the security of a free State, the right of the people to keep and bear Arms shall not be infringed.

Amendment III

No Soldier shall, in time of peace, be quartered in any house, without the consent of the Owner, nor in time of war, but in a manner to be prescribed by law.

Amendment IV

The right of the people to be secure in their persons, houses, papers, and effects, against unreasonable searches and seizures, shall not be violated, and no Warrants shall issue, but upon probable cause, supported by Oath or affirmation, and particularly describing the place to be searched, and the persons or things to be seized.

Amendment V

No person shall be held to answer for a capital or otherwise infamous crime, unless on a presentment or indictment of a Grand Jury, except in cases arising in the land or naval forces, or in the Militia, when in actual service in time of War or public danger; nor shall any person be subject for the same offence to be twice put in jeopardy of life or limb; nor shall be compelled in any criminal case to be a witness against himself, nor be deprived of life, liberty, or property, without due process of law, nor shall private property be taken for public use, without just compensation.

Amendment VI

In all criminal prosecutions, the accused shall enjoy the right to a speedy and public trial, by an impartial jury of the State and district wherein the crime shall have been previously ascertained by law, and to be informed of the nature and cause of the accusation; to be confronted with the witnesses against him; to have compulsory process for obtaining witnesses in his favour, and to have the Assistance of Counsel for his defence.

Amendment VII

In suits at common law, where the value in controversy shall exceed twenty dollars, the right of trial by jury shall be preserved, and no fact tried by a jury, shall be otherwise reexamined in any Court of the United States, than according to the rules of the common law.

Amendment VIII

Excessive bail shall not be required, nor excessive fines imposed, nor cruel and unusual punishments inflicted.

Amendment IX

The enumeration in the Constitution, of certain rights, shall not be construed to deny or disparage others retained by the people.

Amendment X

The powers not delegated to the United States by the Constitution, nor prohibited by it to the States, are reserved to the States respectively, or to the people.

[Amendments I–X, in force 1791.]

Index